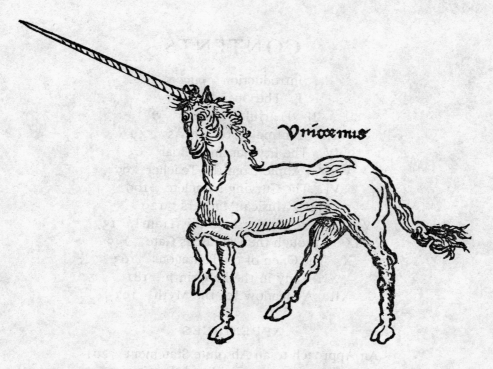

Vnicornis

THE BRAZEN HORN

A NON-BOOK FOR THOSE WHO,
IN REVOLT TODAY,
COULD BE IN COMMAND TOMORROW

BY DENIS JOHNSTON

CONTENTS

ISBN 0 85105 259 2
© Denis Johnston, 1976
Printed in the Republic of Ireland

INTRODUCTION

DIONYSIA — the predecessor to this book — was first published in 1953 under the more obvious title of *Nine Rivers from Jordan*, and is ostensibly a war autobiography. When it appeared, I was a little hipped to discover that the symbolic hand that had been placed by a thoughtful designer in the centre of the dust cover, was a left hand.

In the opinion of the Middle East, where the story opens, this particular paw has an unsavoury reputation, due to the fact that it is not so much associated with pointing the way or with delivering directives as with the wiping of the fundament. No good Arab will eat with the left hand for reasons that are as sanitary as they are ritualistic.

Why, therefore, must my book be offered to the public under the aegis of so sinister a sign, when there was a respectable alternative on the dexter side of the body that could have been used equally well? For a time I was suspicious of the artist's intentions. Maybe he didn't like my book. If he had been a companion of desert days I would probably have written him a *letter*.

It has since occurred to me, however, that he may have been thinking of Dawn's left hand which Omar Khayyam places in the sky for some purpose that must have been carefully considered. Perhaps it was intended to convey that it is the left hand that inaugurates the opening duties of the morning, leaving the more socially acceptable requirements of the day to the opposite member, and to a later hour when the light has turned to green. But such speculations are a waste of time and can be carried too far.

If we are going to pursue any fanciful analogies, the truth of the matter is that Gospel is golden, and is very properly dispensed from the right horn of the altar, while whatever has to be said about it is of brassier material, and may appropriately be relegated to the left.

It is a brazen act to blow one's own trumpet. But if nobody else will consent to come forward with the necessary Epistle in the course of twenty years, the only thing left for a man with something on his mind is to play Paul to his own Jesus, however much the operation may be over and above the ordinary call of duty.

This sequel is of necessity a work of the evening, and not of the dawn, and if it appears to be even more a product of the left hand than is its forerunner, I can only say that a lifetime spent in some Institute for Advanced Studies would be required to give it the precision and the correct interdepartmental vocabulary that the subject demands.

For this I have no longer the time nor the invitation; but the fact that one sometimes may be in error in one's rapportage of the current verbiage of Science does not necessarily mean that one's general conclusions are nonsensical.

If I only manage to damage myself by trying to push open a door into which I have already placed a modest foot, it is in the hope that others with much better equipment than mine, will follow the matter up by taking a look inside. I believe that there is something there. But even if I am deluding myself in this surmise, I have at any rate kept my appointment. And it is surely better to do this than to wait indefinitely for all the ammunition to arrive.

My people, throughout their long but somewhat undistinguished history, have been noted for stepping unwisely into No-man's-land while it is still too early for comfort; which may explain why *Plerumque Praecox* has now come to be regarded as the most appropriate family slogan.

IOWA, 1967

Rouze up, O Young Men of the New Age!
Set your foreheads against the ignorant Hirelings!
For we have Hirelings in the Camp, the Court and the University,
who would, if they could, for ever
depress Mental and prolong Corporeal War.

> . . . their God
I will not worship in their Churches,
Nor King in their Theatres.
There is a place where Contrarieties are equally True.

To Justify the Ways of God to Men.
Blake's MILTON.

It is your folly that you have no common or general interest in your view, not even the wisest among you; neither do you know, or inquire, or care, who are your friends, or who are your enemies.

The Drapier's Letters, No. 1.

Loud, heap miseries upon us yet entwine our arts with laughters low!

Finnegans Wake.

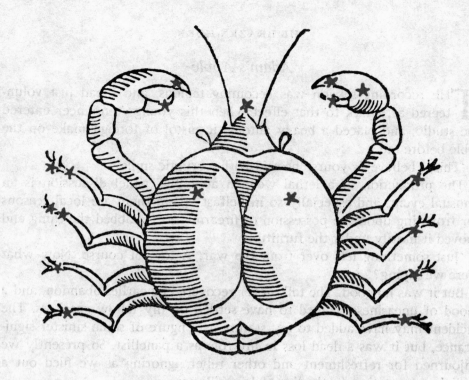

I THE OPEN PAST

Hoc agnosco
infinitatem unicam
nominis expertem
vatem ultimum
noctis creatorum dieique
boni auctorem malique
frigoris patrem florumque.

Adam's Apple

THE recording session was becoming tedious, and I had just volunteered a remark to that effect when this young Announcer entered the studio, and placed a heavy automatic pistol of foreign make on the table before me.

'This, I believe, is yours,' he said with a cryptic smile.

The production of a lethal weapon at a BBC panel discussion is an unusual event, and especially so in Belfast where there are local reasons for frowning upon the possession of firearms. So I grabbed the thing and shoved it hastily under the furniture.

'Just something left over from the war. A toy, of course. Now what were we saying?'

But it was no good. The talk never recovered its earlier abandon, and a mood of uneasiness seemed to have settled on my fellow speakers. The incident may have added to my stature as a figure of some sinister significance, but it was a dead loss in my rôle as a panellist. So presently we adjourned for refreshment and other relief, ignoring as we filed out a malicious quotation on the lips of James Boyce:

> . . . keep him hungry till his work is done.
> Will the wild ass bray while he has grass?

Have You Anything to Declare?

This was during the cold January of 1956. The original source of our embarrassment, however, went back to a date almost eleven years earlier when I passed through Belfast on my way home from the War. Why I had followed so circuitous a route in order to get from Paris to Dublin is itself a mystery, but it had probably got something to do with Travel Permits and the passport problems that were very obstructive at the time. Or maybe it was cheaper to go that way for some administrative reason. Whatever the cause, I had grown tired of my variegated baggage by the time I had reached Ulster, and I felt that I had got enough to explain to the southern customs without having to account for a pistol. So I had handed the thing to a friend in Broadcasting House with an invitation to dispose of it in any way he thought fit.

Even as it was, I had a little trouble with the officials at Dundalk over a plated soup tureen that I had picked up on the battlefield of Alamein, in an abandoned enemy Mess. This handsome piece of equipment had served as the focal point of many a pleasant evening in the desert when, filled with oily black *vino*, and to the strains of Lili Marlene, it had played host to late night visitors who had a way of appearing out of the murk to listen to the eleven o'clock news on our receiver. It had later occupied a table for a couple of years in one of the London newsrooms, where the fact that it was now black with dirt had probably saved it from being pinched. As it turned out, I managed to get it through the Irish customs by arguing that it came within the list of exemptions under the heading of a 'cup or other trophy won in a sporting contest' — the contest, I suppose, being World War 2. But it was touch and go, and I doubt if I could have got away with a Luger as well.

So I had left my weapon in Belfast, expecting that this would be the last I would see of it. But an automatic pistol can no more be disposed of in this casual sort of way than can a bad conscience. Or perhaps my old friend, Maurice Shillington, had too acute a sense of property to take my instructions seriously. It had been kept in a cupboard for eleven years, and although the suggestion that I might remove it had been made from time to time whenever I reappeared in Belfast, it had never actually been placed in my hands until now — when a new and more resolute cupboard-owner had brought the matter to a head. So here it was — back in my possession.

My first thought was to drop it quietly into the Blackstaff River on my way to Great Victoria Street Station; but I soon realised that to produce such an object in a populous Belfast thoroughfare, even for the purpose of throwing it into a stream, was an act that might be misunderstood, and might even result in a hue-and-cry, followed by tiresome explanations to the Constabulary. So I brought it with me to the non-stop train, thinking perhaps that I could pitch it out of the window when crossing the historic waters of the River Boyne. But, again, a coachful of happy families with little children romping in the aisles convinced me that this, too, would be an inappropriate moment to produce a pistol. So eventually I found myself bowling into Amiens Street terminus with the fruit of the Tree of Knowledge still protruding from my overcoat pocket.

The final denouement is something that I have no intention of recording publicly. It is enough to say that, symbolically speaking, a gun can be as hard to get rid of, legally or illegally, as Original Sin. One may try to throw it out or leave it behind, but it has a way of turning up again. Or else one goes back to look for it. Which parable may possibly indicate one of two things: either that man is incorrigible, or that his Fall is as essential a feature of the good life as is the coming of Grace.

Dionysia

In a book about some of my experiences as a War Correspondent, I have already described how I came into possession of this pistol in April, 1945, during the liberation of one of the great Concentration Camps. The English edition of this work (which in the bookshops had the alternative title) terminates in a kind of morality play with a double ending, and in one of these conclusions, I allege and describe how I was killed in the Brenner Pass with this gun by a Nazi called Otto Suder. When the book was re-issued in the United States, exception was taken by my American publishers to this piece of apparent whimsy. They considered that such an ending might have the effect of throwing some doubt on the rest of the volume, as a sober and accurate description of a very serious War.

This was quite understandable, although I still fail to see how the objection was met by the course that was actually taken. They deleted the more probable alternative ending and retained the objectionable one — leaving me dead.

However, I made no protests about this decision, since — apart from the English edition that was already in print — my original manuscript had been mimeographed, and deposited in some libraries, where the pristine version, in its earliest form, still remains out of reach of editorial hands, including my own. (Or so I hope.)

Actually the double ending is not a piece of whimsy so far as I am concerned, but refers to a phenomenon that I propose to mention again in more persistent tones in the course of the present book. This I also intend to deposit in a similar manner and for similar reasons.

The War ends in Europe

Any investigation of what actually occurred in my vicinity on the evening and the following morning of 3/4 May 1945 will confirm that there is not too little information, but too much. In addition to the two inconsistent stories reported in my previous book, there are the contents of my contemporary Field Notebooks, which also have been Xeroxed. There is as well a more elaborate reconstruction of both versions, written in 1956, shortly after the debacle in Belfast had brought the subject back to mind.

In this, the two accounts are labelled Take One and Take Two, following the verbiage of the Film Studios where those expressions are used to distinguish between retakes of the same shot that contain significant variations. All these documents can be seen by anyone with the time and the inclination to pursue the matter further. Meanwhile, for our immediate purposes, such of the copy as seems to be the most relevant to our present concerns is to be found below, in Appendix A.

Another Part of the Forest

What emerges from this brief is that I went into Innsbruck on the evening of the 3rd with the leading elements of the American mixed tank and infantry column that took the city, and I was present at the formal capitulation. Indeed, it was to me, absurdly enough, that the initial surrender of Innsbruck was mistakenly tendered.

On the following morning I went up the Brenner Pass to the summit. Whether I went up by myself as an armed hitchhiker in an American truck, or whether I made the journey unarmed with Abe Goldberg of the Associated Press and an officer/guide in a small convoy of two jeeps, depends upon the version of the story that is selected. In Take One I had a conversation with a picket of Austrian regulars whom I met on the way up; and subsequently I encountered this Nazi, Otto Suder, to whom I lent my Luger, with fatal results. In Take Two — in which I never met Suder — our small party passed through the Austrian picket, on the strength of my assurance that I already knew it to be friendly.

In this Take I was also aware of further features of the situation that the other members of our party did not know — namely that the tracks in the slushy snow were not those of enemy vehicles, but had been made by an American Task Force which was already at the summit. This superior knowledge might be explained by the fact that I had already been up the same road earlier in the morning, were it not for the difficulty that I could not have made the triple journey — up, down, and up again — in the time available between first light and the climax of Take Two. So it cannot be that the two experiences were consecutive. This throws us back to the other obvious answer that the first Take must have been either an illusion or a dream. Yet, acceptable or not to our present ways of thinking, one of the objectives of this book is to offer a further alternative — that both journeys might have been simultaneous.

Are we confronted here by some sort of fold-back in Time, resulting in two contradictory denouements to a single basic situation, both of which are actual? This, I personally believe to be absurd. Nevertheless it might be possible, according to a more recent conception of the structure of the

A Problem for the Starmen

DURING the Autumn of 1955 a world conference of Astronomers assembled in Dublin, and the local newspapers joyfully opened their columns to reports on their deliberations. There is nothing unusual about a wide popular interest in the lore of the Heavens. Ever since Sir James Jeans pointed a finger at wonders overhead, the Press has always managed to find space for newsworthy disclosures about the latest discoveries of Science—marvels and *bouleversements* in conventional ideas that, rightly or wrongly, are usually associated in the public mind with the name of Albert Einstein.

We have become accustomed to listen open-mouthed to dicta about the velocity of light, and to the bending of its rays under the influence of Gravity. The curvature of Space has been given some incredulous attention while the recession of the Spiral Nebulae and the phenomenon of the expanding Cosmos have each been received with much the same respectful acceptance that used to be accorded in an earlier epoch to the Virgin Birth, to the miracle of Transubstantiation, and to the liquefaction of the blood of St. Januarius. There is indeed a host of other surprises, most of which are available in paper-back form, to bemuse the fancy of even the stoutest of Rationalists.

The occasion seemed too good to miss, so a few of us got together one evening after dinner, and composed a letter to *The Irish Times* that was intended to widen the discussions of the Astronomers in a way that might allow the Public to push into a corner of their deliberations. The operative part of our query went as follows:

> Let us suppose that rocket travel has progressed to a point when it is possible for an Observer to be accelerated in some sort of a manned ship to a speed of c plus One over Two — that is to say, just over half the speed of light, which is not, I suppose, beyond the bounds of theoretical possibility. Let us suppose that I observe such a missile approaching me on a course which is at a tangent to my point of observation on the Earth's surface. According to present-day thinking, it would be true to say that an observer on such a rocket (let us call him "A") would see me approaching him at the same apparent speed.
>
> Now let us suppose that another observer ("B") is also approaching me at the same speed on a course which is in precisely the opposite direction. From his point of view, he will also observe me approaching him at the same speed. So far so good.
>
> But now let us suppose that "A" turns his attention to "B". What is happening between these two? Surely both logic and mathematics insist that, whether or not their relative speeds enable them to see each other, "B" must actually be approaching "A" at a speed slightly greater than that of light? Yet we are

assured by the physicists that such a speed is impossible, not merely as a matter of observation, but in fact. Is it possible to give a clinical answer to the question as to what in fact will "A" see? If he does see "B", will he contradict my observation of his speed, or will he see "B" apparently growing younger instead of older, which seems to be the only answer on the basis of the paradox propounded by Lorentz?

The paradox referred to is the Law of Added Velocities, and is a corollary of the principle discussed by Einstein, that the upward limit of velocity is the speed of Light in a vacuum. This rate of progression is placed at 186,000 miles per second, or if you prefer it in nautical terms, 5.8275×10^8 knots.

In the language of Physics this velocity is conveniently referred to as 'c'. For reasons that are variously given and that will be discussed later, this Olympian speed limit is not merely a figure that ought not to be exceeded, or that holds some contemporary record. It actually *cannot* be exceeded, and in this respect it is an Absolute. It follows from this prohibition that

See pp. 73 and 222 for a note on some recent attempts to cast doubts on this absolute of speed by physicists at Swarthmore and Syracuse.

$$\frac{c+1}{2} \text{ added to } \frac{c+1}{2} \text{ could not amount to } c+1,$$ a peculiarity insisted

upon by Lorentz that was the basis of our question.

It should also be said that the supposed speeds upon which our query was based are not by any means fanciful. In 1960 an object was actually recorded photographically that was apparently receding at about half the speed of light. It is true that whatever this may have been was at a distance from us of about 4,500 million light years. But need this remoteness affect the mathematics of the problem? The fact remains that such velocities are astronomically observable.

A Civil Answer

On the following day, Professor John L. Synge, writing from the School of Theoretical Physics in the Dublin Institute for Advanced Studies, replied with commendable promptitude and gave, not as requested, an account of what 'A' would see, but a description of the mathematical formula that applies to such matters, from which it appeared that the problem was not so simple as one of mere addition. In effect, he attacked the question as meaningless in the absence of any clear agreement as to what precisely is meant by the word 'speed'.

. . . The reason behind Einstein's formula cannot be given in a few words. The first step towards it is the rejection of Newton's conception of one universal absolute time in favour of Einstein's idea that each observer has his own proper time. It is a pity that this tremendous upheaval in human thought should have to remain hidden behind what must appear to many as an impregnable barricade of mathematical symbols, but it is extremely difficult to find any other way of saying what should be said in order to turn mysteries into common sense, and I shall not try to do it, at least not now. This job of translating the most condensed form of poetry into flabby prose remains a burden on the conscience of the mathematical physicist, who prays that more and more may learn to read that poetry for themselves.

So eloquent a tribute to the beauties of Pure Mathematics was more than we enquirers deserved or expected, but his avoidance of the clinical part of the question was somewhat disappointing, though not unexpected. We are acquainted with many of these mysteries enunciated by contemporary Scientists, and with the answer that begins : It all depends on what you mean. Herein lay our reason for presenting our question in a way that demanded a straightforward answer to a tangible point. If the situation could not arise, the query itself would, of course, be illegitimate. But is this a situation that could not arise, and if not why not? If the poetry of mathematics has, here, got hold of something that renders the question absurd, it is clear that we must radically revise our ways of thought. Apart from any formulas governing the matter, to which we respectfully bow, we still would like a plain answer to the query : What would these fellows see?

So a few days later, in response to some further prodding, Dr. Synge very patiently went on to add :

1 Absolute speed (as understood by Newton) is meaningless in the sense that the words do not correspond to anything in the physical world as we now conceive it.

2 Relative to any observer, there is an upper limit to the speed which can be imparted to any body, and the mass of the body (its inertia, or reluctance to change its velocity) increases with its speed, tending to infinity as the speed of the body approaches that of light.

The latter part of this second letter refers, of course, to an interrogatory from us concerning the relative nature of velocity. If the latter has a purely subjective meaning, how can speed have what appears to be an absolute effect on Matter — for example, on its Mass? Or is Mass, too, a purely relative conception, dependent on something in the Observer?

Indeed we may perhaps go on to ask whether, in the prevailing atmosphere of the time, we are being told that everything is entirely a matter of the way we look on it. Are these peculiarities of Science in the same category as the nature of God and, as such, beyond the grasp of the laity without several years of residence at Princeton or in Westcott House? Or are we merely being treated to another example of the Non-Answer?

The Era of Non-Everything

We live today in a slough of negatives — Non-Music, Non-Art, Non-Poetry, Non-Theatre, and in the realm of ideas, Non-Answers. This is largely due to the practices of my own generation — we who were youngsters in the 'twenties, and who were heavily taken to task by our parents for our misbehaviour, libertinism, atheism and general reluctance to accept any ideas that were current before the First War. In this resistance to the generalities of our forebears we were delighted to find that we had some support from the Scientists, and between us we definitely got the Clergy on the run. Now we are being currently reproved by our own children for bringing them up badly — a fact that is self-evident, although it seems a little hard to have to suffer disapproval at both ends of our careers.

What our juniors mean, of course, is that we are incapable of instructing them intelligibly, owing to the enormous success of this very campaign against answers, and in particular against the Absolutes to which intelligible answers seem to point. If so much is a matter of doubt, it is difficult not to convey the impression that there are no tangible facts behind whatever we are discussing, and little in the way of honest conviction to support anything that we say. To this our offspring attribute their sense of 'Insecurity'. It is not the Bomb that has upset them nearly so much as the Non-Answer; and we would be very ill-advised to allow this alarm and despondency to continue indefinitely in a branch of the species that has recently become equipped with a practical means of race suicide. Non-Answers had better be stopped.

Miracles do occur

In the areas of both Physics and Philosophy the time is more than ripe to get back to a modicum of common sense in spite of the fact that phenomena undoubtedly do occur around us every day that cannot really be accounted for in current mechanistic terms, and that often seem to be beyond the reach of our present framework of Thought. One of the most obvious of these is the process of birth to which every fertile creature can contribute as a matter of course — the cell growth of one body within another that can be catalogued and anticipated biologically, but that cannot be explained scientifically in so far as it leads to a sentient mystery that we call the creation of Awareness.

There is even an element of the inexplicable in the commonplace experience that we describe as Movement — the difference in the physical arrangement of the observable scene around us between one moment and the next that seems to contradict the assumption that most of the objects that we see performing are inanimate. Zeno raised this question many centuries ago, and nobody has really answered him yet, however far our Physicists may have gone in describing material behaviour.   See
Nor is there any adequate reply to the question posed by   Appendix
Vitalism — why does anything 'happen' at all? And what do   I
we mean when we say that it does?

These things, and many more of a similar sort, are beyond the reach of satisfactory description in terms of our current vocabulary; but they are not unnatural. Indeed, we are so familiar with most of them that we generally consider it ridiculous to think of them even as worthy of wonderment.

Nobody rises from the dead, and like Hume, we would very properly be suspicious of anybody who laid claim to this unusual feat. But although we cannot without special training turn water to wine, we experience no difficulty whatever in turning wine into water.

So perhaps we had better see whether a different approach to this vexed question of Thought itself might not lead us eventually to something better than the prevailing non-answer.

Drafting the Pleadings

In the days when I was a Junior Counsel at the Bar, I frequently found myself faced with the task of drafting Pleadings for eminent Seniors, much better equipped with a knowledge of the Law than I was, but who sometimes had difficulty in expressing, in a paragraph or two, what exactly they were talking about. So, when contemplating this considerable heap of scientific data that has been accumulating in unsorted bundles ever since the Michelson/Morley experiment, I face a situation that is not entirely new to me. Indeed, the prevailing congestion is not unlike what has happened in some of our greater University Libraries, where shortage of staff combined with the wealth of incoming material has resulted in the storage of many of the newer books according to size.

My own trouble does not basically lie in a failure to appreciate the poetry of mathematics, as Dr. Synge fears. It is to be found in the problem of getting any general picture of what is going on in the Universe from experts who are all specialists. What we are looking for today is not only a mathematical poet, but also a theological physicist, and a prose-writing astronomer. Until these appear, what is the use of continually doubling and trebling the size of Hubble's Universe, without an intelligible statement from some Observatory on what precisely is meant by Size? In other words are we to believe that in the view of contemporary Physicists there is one law for the large and another for the small? Or alternatively, is Velocity now to be regarded as some form of Cosmic Capitalism which, in the realm of Matter, distinguishes the rich from the poor? Due to my professional training I am unsympathetic to magic and magicians, and am addicted to the use of words to convey meaning rather than the reverse. Consequently I am eager to find out whether hard words such as Extra-sensory Perception, Parapsychology, etc., can only be discussed in terms of illusion and a willing acceptance of the incomprehensible? Or whether any and which of our current difficulties can be attributed to the fact that some of our basic assumptions in the fields of Science and Theology are out of step with recent discoveries?

The Trouble with Newton

By the turn of the century, although still engaged in dropping iron balls in moving railway carriages, and expressing surprise at the results, there was a growing suspicion amongst Physicists that there was something inadequate about Newton's picture of a corporeal, three-dimensional Solar System, performing for our benefit in an area called Space by arrangement with a mysterious entrepreneur known as Time — a kinematic setup, the future behaviour of which might be predicted in advance by anybody who had studied the programme properly.

Ever since the Michelson/Morley experiment in 1887 it had been reasonably clear that the Earth and its companions were not on the move in any measurable way, direction or speed through an 'Ether' that presumably filled the emptiness of a great box — the wider Universe. An uneasy feeling was growing that, speaking in terms of Mathematics, there was as much evidence for the mediaeval, geocentric conception of the World as a fixed point around which everything else revolved as there was for any innovation in the ways of thought that had been circulating since the age of Copernicus. Maybe, after all, the Church had not been so wrong in its treatment of Galileo. Or perhaps it would sound better to say that, since Space was turning out to be not so spacious as had previously been supposed, and since Time was no longer strictly temporal, it might be safer to go along with Minkowski who was promoting a union of the Two in some way.

Let there be Einstein

Then, round about 1905, there appeared Albert Einstein of Ulm, with his Special Theory of Relativity which introduced several new fundamentals in place of those that were being nervously swept under the carpet. Amongst these was the formula, $E = mc^2$, which was said to cast a new and interesting light on the relationship between Energy and Mass.

Since the findings of Newton in the seventeenth century, Light had generally been regarded as something in the nature of a stream of particles originating from some ascertainable source, and rushing through Space at a tremendous velocity known as 'c'. According to Einstein, if the square on this non-figure is multiplied by another unarithmetical expression representing Mass — which, of course, is not a statement of weight but has something to do with Inertia — then the result will equal a figure representing an entirely different commodity known as Energy, which, needless to say, has got nothing to do with Speed, but is an aspect of Acceleration.

It seems that the straightening out of such an array of imponderables is a task worthy of Alice's Humpty Dumpty who might be expected to explain the situation in the following way :

> If we imagine an arithmetical figure that describes the reluctance of an egg — such as myself — to move off elsewhere, and multiply this by the square on the fastest speed at which it could possibly undertake the journey, then the final quantity so arrived at will be equal to a further imaginary figure representing how hard it would have to run in order to stop in the same place. Do you follow me?

In such a form it does not sound very algebraic, but it is only through the medium of Algebra that the equation can be said to have any meaning. Further than this it is not possible to go, apart from saying that we are henceforth committed to four-dimensional calculations which have superseded the more familiar three, in recognition of the fact that Space by itself now means no more than Time by itself, and that both must be amalgamated into an entirely new concept known as Space/Time.

But lest so very revolutionary an idea as four-dimensional Space/Time might prove upsetting to any other well loved formulae, Authority was soon on the scene with some important qualifications calculated to take the menace out of this new situation, and to forestall any dangerous speculation from unqualified quarters. According to Eddington of Cambridge (whose directive is still widely observed) the three conventional dimensions (Length, Breadth and Thickness) are still spatial, and are to be measured in yards or metres as before; but the fourth is strictly temporal, and may only be assessed by clocks. Thus we find ourselves more or less back where we started from, with Space and Time separated as before into a Box on the one part and into God-Knows-What on the other. Yet, whatever it actually means, Einstein's difficult pronouncement must be accepted as a formula, because of the fact that it works.

Relativity

The popular conception of Relativity used to be that 'everything in Creation is relative', which means in its turn that practically all unqualified statements are suspect, since whatever you say depends upon something else. In actual fact most of the work of Einstein and his associates (to whom he owed much) was directed, not at the abolition of absolutes, but towards the confirmation of several new ones, the most notable — since the Quantum Theory — being a discovery that the speed of Light in a vacuum ('c') is the upward limit of velocity and, as such, is constant, notwithstanding the speed or direction of the source of the signal.

This unexceedable figure for all forms of velocity (not merely that of Light) was soon to be explained in various ways, the most naïve being that anything receding at a speed greater than that of Light could not be seen at all since its signal could never get to us. So also, if it were approaching, it would arrive before we could see it. So since the object — whatever it might be — could not be examined, it might as well be regarded as non-existent. This rather simple-minded reasoning ignores, of course, the second and most interesting part of Einstein's restatement of Michelson/Morley — that the speed or direction of the source has no effect on the quantity of 'c'. So the other explanation is the more serious one.

Calculations of Velocity depend upon clocks; and since clocks appear to slow down at enormous speeds — not in the eyes of a traveller scrutinizing his own clock, but in his observations of another fellow's clock —

there can be no absolute determination of speed in the face of contradictory instruments of measurement.

This, of course, proves nothing of a positive nature, and simply shows
that estimates of very high speed have no meaning apart from the individual impressions of the Observer, and that every Observer must ultimately regard himself as a fixed point of reference and a final Authority,
if he is not going to go off his head.

The Shape of the Universe

So when Einstein turned to a study of the shape and extent of this four-
dimensional Universe, in the light of all these considerations, he started
off in the footsteps of his Victorian predecessors who held the opinion that
the Universe could neither be infinite in its extent, nor bounded by an
Edge. This means that, like the 'limited but unbounded' surface of the
Earth, it must curve, and is probably spherical, with a measurable size.
In due course he made a rough calculation of what he termed the 'Cosmological Constant'. In so doing, he was acting as a good Realist by making a
wise distinction between what his Universe *is* and what it *does*. Here,
however, he came into collision with a number of his fellow Scientists
who were addicted to the Bergsonian idea that nothing exists apart from
what it does. In insisting on this point, they were prepared to cast serious
doubts on any conception of Creation as being a matter of Fact, independently of being an object of Observation as well.

High Words in the Athenaeum

From this point Einstein's troubles began to multiply because, as a logical
Thinker, he felt bound to go on to argue that a Universe which is factual
must also be regarded as being causative — that is to say that everything
that 'occurs' is a natural consequence of adjacent conditions. From which
it follows that it ought to be theoretically possible to predict all future
events, if one is in possession of all the relevant Data. The reason why we
cannot do this is simply one of insufficient information.

From about the year 1927 Einstein's reputation went into a noticeable
decline. A certain understandable resistance on the part of many of his
colleagues to his enormous and perhaps undeserved reputation encouraged
them to seize eagerly upon the work of Bohr and Heisenberg in the field
of atomic behaviour, where experiments had conclusively proved that the
movement of particles of Matter can only be predicted statistically — that

is to say, on the basis of probability — and that even the present position of a particle cannot be definitely ascertained, because the act of examination itself affects the answer. Therefore — said these Physicists — as the future behaviour of Matter is undeterminable, the whole idea of absolute Causation must be relegated to the nursery. Least of all can human behaviour be conclusively predicted.

This was a conclusion welcomed not only by the Physicists who were getting a little tired of the name of Einstein, but also in philosophical and theological circles. There Free Will is regarded as an essential element in human destiny, and Man must be taken as being a responsible architect of his own future, and by implication, of the future of the World, which his decisions must inevitably affect. To Einstein's scientific and somewhat Calvinistic ways of thought this was an idea that ought to be resisted on the grounds that, if the behaviour of a particle is unpredictable and arbitrary, it means that God must be 'playing dice with the Universe'.

Bragg's Bull

The views of the Heisenberg group were, however, reinforced by a quandary of old standing about the nature of Matter itself. Was it corpuscular — that is to say, did it consist of an aggregate of physical particles? Or was it some sort of intangible wave in Space? Electro-dynamics and other experimental tests offered strong support to both conclusions, and the mere fact that there could be any doubt on so fundamental a question was a serious stumbling block to the whole conception of a material Universe.

So here again, in 1927, the scientific High Table resolved the problem by an ex-cathedra statement through the lips of Sir Lawrence Bragg, who laid it down that Matter is *both* corpuscular and a wave. According to this very English compromise, the passing of what we call 'Now' has the effect of 'freezing' an intangible wave-motion into tangible material. As Sir Lawrence summed it up:

> An advancing sieve of time coagulates waves into particles at the moment — Now. . . . Everything that has already happened is particles. Everything in the future is waves.

So, having discarded Causation because of its determinacy, we have now arrived at contemporary opinion, that the nature of the Universe itself is altered by the passing of 'Now' — whether your Now or my Now or God's Now is not clear. We are all simultaneously engaged in turning

Waves into Substance, with the blessing of Eddington, whose unanswerable dictum many years before had been to the effect that there is no such thing as an ascertainable 'Now' in a Universe where absolute simultaneity is an illusion. Yet absurd as it is, this idea is not out of line with an instinctive way of thought to which we are addicted — that through the mere fact of living, collectively and individually, we are each continually creating a tangible and irrevocable Past out of a Future that has no existence, apart from being a complex of mere Possibilities (however that odd word may be defined).

Whittaker's Non-Curve

Nevertheless, it was generally agreed that although Einstein was wrong in his life-long insistence that the Almighty is not taking part in any crap-game, he was right in adopting Riemann's non-Euclidean Geometry in his calculations. This mid-Victorian mathematical Laputa was originally designed to meet the requirements of a three-dimensional field in which parallel lines meet, and where dropped perpendiculars converge — as they usually do on the curved surface of the Earth. And it was even more appropriate in the field of a four-dimensional Space/Time that was now demanding examination. So if non-Euclidean Geometry implied curvature, then 4D curvature must be admitted. But at this point Authority again stepped in to assert itself before the acceptance of any such heady developments might lead to something worse. Because curvature occurs — announced Sir Edmund Whittaker — don't let us imagine that anything in particular is really taking place. It is no more than a formula of Geometry. Unlike the curvature of the Earth's surface, where straight and parallel lines cannot exist at all, here in this four-dimensional Continuum to which we have recently been introduced, the appearance of Curvature is entirely theoretical —

> because curvature, in the sense of bending is a meaningless term except where space is immersed in another space. . . . What mathematicians understand by the term "curvature" is not what the term connotes in ordinary speech. . . . Curvature has nothing to do with the shape of space — whether it is bent or not — but is defined solely by the metric — that is to say, by the way distance is defined. It is not the space that is curved but the Geometry.

It may be that these verbal gymnastics describe the situation correctly. On the other hand it may be the language that secretes the twist — not the Geometry. Indeed, we may well suspect that most of these difficulties are not intrinsic in the situation at all, but are due to an attempt to apply a lower dimensional metric in the field of a deeper dimension which in actual fact is precisely what they say it is — curved.

Need it be added that all these high words and disagreements were fundamentally German, with only some peripheral amendments added by England. On the whole it amounts to another example of the peculiarly Teutonic liking for answers that make the problem harder. All the same, the contributions concerning uncurving curvature and the corpuscular Yesterday of Tomorrow's waves come to us in English accents, accustomed to the linguistics of the British Constitution, which is not supposed to mean what it says, provided it works.

In the midst of all this shouting, an honest and very endearing man, Albert Einstein, continued his hopeless quest for a General Theory that might reconcile the unavoidable evidence of Heisenberg with a common sense belief in the absolute dependence of the Future upon the Past. Finally under pressure from this combined assault upon his findings, he abandoned his curved, measurable Cosmos (the Cosmological Constant) in deference to the verdict of Palomar that the Universe could be shown to be expanding at a calculable rate, and he never seems to have mentioned it again after 1930. In this readiness to take such a step Einstein displayed his firm attachment to the genuine scientific method. Whenever a theory, however desirable, turns out to be at variance with the evidence, it must be abandoned whatever the Scientist himself may previously have said — whatever the Party may prefer — whatever his Country may insist. For this integrity, no less than for his race, Hitler drove him out of Germany, and even put him in peril of assassination in his exile. A second generation of his colleagues, whose word is still the prevailing one, was not quite so lethal. But in praising him with faint damns, they managed in his later years to spread it abroad that Einstein was out of date, sentimental, and addicted to unsustainable generalities about God. He is called an Atheist because he did not need an irresponsible Deity to account for the behaviour of the Universe. At the same time he was accused of piety and religiosity because, in a period noted for its distaste for Causation, he could not agree that 'might have been' connotes any serious scientific statement.

A Green Hall Door

It was not until after he had gone that voices began to be raised on his behalf. We are only now hearing that Light is neither a stream of particles nor a passing wave, but is a non-material effect in the fabric of Space/

Time that can best be described as a Signal — an offspring of Causation just as Space is an aspect of Matter (see page 90). However correct Heisenberg may be, he is telling us nothing of any consequence about a determined or undetermined Universe. If I invite you to look at my house, and promise you the sight of a green Hall Door, Heisenberg will add that nobody can promise you anything of the sort with certainty. And curiously enough, Heisenberg will be speaking the truth. What you will see is indeed unpredictable until it is clear whether you have decided to look at the front of my house or the rear, or indeed at the inside or the outside. In short, his comment has nothing to do with the absolute quality of my Hall Door, but is about observation, which is something about You — not about my house. It is You and I who are unpredictable.

No Sieve of Time is advancing — we hear today — and all that 'coagulates' at each Man's particular Now are his own individual impressions. Space does not have to be immersed in another Space to permit a three dimensional object to extend in a fourth direction, which no more creates 'another space' than stereoscopic sight does. The Cosmological Constant need never have been abandoned since the apparent expansion of the Universe is merely a drawing apart of the Observer's coordinates (see page 117). And above all, we are being reminded today that whenever reliable Scientists offer philosophical or linguistic explanations of the effects that they have observed, we are, of course, under an obligation to accept their data. But we need not listen with any greater respect to their explanations than we need offer to anybody else who is stepping outside the bounds of his own expertise. For herein lies what is probably the greatest cause of the contemporary confusion — a widespread linguistic difficulty in being able to distinguish between our Nouns and our Verbs.

But, alas, this tremendous old man is no longer here to listen to any such words of comfort and support.

Esse or Percipi?

I suggest that the first thing to be cleared up before entering upon any exegesis of contemporary scientific lore is to find out what views, if any, our informants hold on the distinction between what Is and what Seems to Be. If we persist to the point of rudeness in our determination to discover whether the statement that the Universe is expanding is offered as a description of Fact or of what seems to be happening, we will usually find that a rather peculiar thing occurs. The authorities will tend to divide into two or three categories according to how they choose to treat the meaning of words.

The first of these is represented by one whom we will call Doctor Zophar of the Massachusetts Institute of Technology, who is up-to-the-minute with his Field Equations, and who will approach the subject by enlarging his subdivisions. He will tell us that there are actually several meanings for each of the terms used in the question. In the case of 'expansion' there is 'absolute expansion' as well as 'relative expansion'. And what do we mean by 'the Universe'? Is it the three-dimensional Continuum which is not expanding, or is it the four-dimensional Continuum, which — according to him — most certainly is?

At this point the conversation will probably end, in much the same way as it terminates if we attempt to switch from aspects of Physics to less tangible matters, by asking the Doctor whether his aversion to un-qualified statements also applies to rules of behaviour such as the Ten Commandments? Are these, too, subject to the same nullification by sub-division? Very sensibly, Doctor Zophar will refuse to get himself involved in a problem that is outside his field. But if we are lucky enough to have roused a theologian from amongst his pupils — or better still an Irishman who is ready and willing to discuss, let us say, the shortest Commandment — we will probably be told that there are actually several kinds of killing.

First, there is absolute killing, for our own personal convenience, and with no element of public benefit. The Commandment clearly condemns this expression of private enterprise. But there is also qualified killing, as for example at the request or command of the Government, in which case the Law does not apply. There is also non-killing, as in self-defence, or in pursuit of some approved political conviction, or where other mat-ters of mental derangement arise. Indeed, if one allows geography to have a say in the matter, there may even be justified killing in the realm of race relations, or (in Latin countries) in the event of interference with conjugal rights. All these forms of murder may — on occasion — be allowed. In other words, 'Thou shalt not kill' does not mean that thou shalt not kill, any more than curvature means curved. It all depends.

On the other hand, we have a second type of answer, represented by 'the Rev. Father Eliphaz' of Bowdoin, who is a philosophical mathema-tician. He has at his finger tips the well-known formula advanced in the eighteenth century by Dr. George Berkeley, the Bishop of Cloyne — *Esse est Percipi*. (To be is to be perceived.) He may even be prepared to make

their advanced degrees, so why should they not be entitled to reap their
rewards without the intrusion of Quacks?

And so, what was once the awesome authority of the Papacy passes to
the various Institutes of Advanced Study, and a newer Hierarchy begins
to be as nervous of anything in the nature of vernacular Science as the
Council of Trent was of the vernacular Bible — and for much the same
reasons.

Following this analogy, it may be said that the only proper response of
the public to such an impasse is that of the Lollards. We must be prepared
to look into these matters for ourselves — those of us who have nothing
to lose but our Thirds — dispensing as far as possible with hard words in
unknown tongues that are intended to obscure meaning.

Idealism — No !

So let us approach the Codex from the angle of two or three assumptions
that need not be accepted by anybody who does not actually want an
answer, and see what transpires.

First, let us agree that *Esse* is basically a statement of factual existence
— a noun statement — while *Percipi* is an expression of what it does to
us, or what we do to it, or see it do — a verb statement. To argue that the
one can validly be correlated with the other is as illuminating as to say
that a good glass of beer is to drink it. We drink it, but our consumption
of it is not what constitutes it as beer. So *Esse* is not *Percipi*, and we are
entitled in every case to know whether our informants are talking in
terms of the one or the other. Let us have no more of this Bergsonian
attack on Nouns.

Second, the psychology of the Psychologist is as properly a subject for study as are the reflexes of a famished rat. Professor Bildad's conclusions are the consequences of his own conditioning by a more remote Professor Moriarty, as is also the significant fact that so many of his offspring, when not actually delinquents, tend to be afflicted with an unaccountable stutter. This is a side issue that Although one readily agrees that all kinds of behaviour patterns can be induced by calculated interference (which itself has to be accounted for in terms of a more remote stimulant, which in its turn . . . etc. *ad infinitum*) Heisenberg has shown that predictions based on data, however precise, are merely statements of Probability. The fact that this law is not dependent upon the vagaries of human thought, but is actually derived from an examination of atomic structure provides, I suggest, a valid objection to any purely mechanical view of behaviour. If mechanical, it must necessarily be pre-

Bildad regards as irrelevant; but it is no more and no less a part of the main issue than are the quandaries of life in a box, in which one of our more uncompanionable companions is the Professor himself.

As for Dr. Zophar and his multiplication of categories, we will say nothing against him at the moment for the simple reason that we will shortly find ourselves engaged in the same practice. One must not blame the Doctor for attempting to be precise in his language. The Facts of Life have a complicated structure of many categories and subdivisions. All that we have to avoid is the danger of assuming that this means that non-answers are inevitable.

A Child's Guide to the Solar System

Let us therefore begin a brief survey of the present state of Astronomy by taking a look at the subject in the terms in which many of us first came in contact with it, when our personal frames of reference were in the making. I refer to Arthur Mee's *Children's Encyclopedia* — the foundation of much of my own cerebration on more subjects than that of Science. It was a most influential publication — as many of my generation will agree.

In the first volume of the first edition of this very basic work there is to be found a picture of a number of very primitive-looking motor cars labelled respectively 'Mercury', 'Venus', 'Earth' and so on, driving rapidly around a central ball of fire which we recognise as the Sun, all on circular courses — or as nearly circular as we need care about. In studying this cartoon we are encouraged to feel a certain superiority over our misinformed ancestors who had been foolish enough to believe what they saw — namely that the Sun, Moon and Stars travel around the Earth. For a while there had been some difficulty in determining by direct observation just what the Planets do. Visually, they appear to be a law unto themselves, and to go just anywhere.

But it was Copernicus, I believe, who finally tidied up most of this confusion by pointing out that all that is necessary to make sense of the movement of the Planets is to stop being so damned geo-centric, and to look upon them from the angle of the Sun, whereupon their circular motion in relation to a solar centre rather than to an earthly one, becomes perfectly intelligible, even if it is not visually obvious from here.

QUERIST   Does "*c*" manage to survive as an absolute if we insist on pressing you so far, Dr. Zophar?

ZOPHAR   Ah, but you must realize that "*c*" is only an absolute in this context in a relative sense. It is the absolute limit of speed in relation to a given set of circumstances. Pick a different set of circumstances, and quite a different set of calculations will apply.

QUERIST   With two different absolute limits, each in a relative sense? Is that what you mean?

ZOPHAR   You must understand that the speed in each case will depend upon our reckoning of Time. Time is the basis of all observations connected with Speed, and Time itself is affected by velocity.

QUERIST   So that Time-reckoning is also non-absolute?

ZOPHAR   Better to say a relative absolute. I think you are beginning to understand at last what Einstein means in this connection. Congratulations.

QUERIST   The point being, that we have here two relative absolutes, each alibying the other. Velocity depends on Time, and Time depends upon Velocity, which depends upon Time. Does this mean that we are actually talking about anything in particular?

ZOPHAR   Not unless we can manage to continue to speak scientifically, and clarify our minds from Newtonian presumptions. I hope that you now appreciate the difficulty in making such matters clear to anybody who is not equipped to use the proper vocabulary.

How true: But one may legitimately wonder whether it is not the vocabulary that is itself creating most of the difficulties. Out of this tangle emerges the fact that we *are* only talking about ways of thinking about Appearances, and that Dr. Zophar has, in effect, agreed that — apart from appearances — there is actually no such thing as absolute Speed, or absolute Time.

This is precisely what Dr. Synge said in his last letter. They are 'meaningless in the sense that the words do not correspond to anything in the physical world as we now conceive it'. They both Depend. And what they depend on depends on them. And there the matter rests — with still no answer to the clinical question, nor any further explanation as to what it is that makes the entire query absurd.

As long ago as 1690 Huyghens wrote:

> In true philosophy, the causes of all natural phenomena are conceived in mechanical terms. We must do this, in my opinion, or else give up all hope of ever understanding anything in Physics.

But suppose our difficulties lie in the fact that we *are* insisting on discussing these matters in mechanical terms, when we should not do so? Although certain mechanical laws do manage to prove themselves to be

Bildad regards as irrelevant; but it is no more and no less a part of the main issue than are the quandaries of life in a box, in which one of our more uncompanionable companions is the Professor himself.

dictable. But whatever the odds of probability may be, the existence of any element of the unpredictable defeats this alternative conspiracy which, in effect, is aimed at the sanctity of verbs.

As for Dr. Zophar and his multiplication of categories, we will say nothing against him at the moment for the simple reason that we will shortly find ourselves engaged in the same practice. One must not blame the Doctor for attempting to be precise in his language. The Facts of Life have a complicated structure of many categories and subdivisions. All that we have to avoid is the danger of assuming that this means that non-answers are inevitable.

A Child's Guide to the Solar System

Let us therefore begin a brief survey of the present state of Astronomy by taking a look at the subject in the terms in which many of us first came in contact with it, when our personal frames of reference were in the making. I refer to Arthur Mee's *Children's Encyclopedia* — the foundation of much of my own cerebration on more subjects than that of Science. It was a most influential publication — as many of my generation will agree.

In the first volume of the first edition of this very basic work there is to be found a picture of a number of very primitive-looking motor cars labelled respectively 'Mercury', 'Venus', 'Earth' and so on, driving rapidly around a central ball of fire which we recognise as the Sun, all on circular courses — or as nearly circular as we need care about. In studying this cartoon we are encouraged to feel a certain superiority over our misinformed ancestors who had been foolish enough to believe what they saw — namely that the Sun, Moon and Stars travel around the Earth. For a while there had been some difficulty in determining by direct observation just what the Planets do. Visually, they appear to be a law unto themselves, and to go just anywhere.

But it was Copernicus, I believe, who finally tidied up most of this confusion by pointing out that all that is necessary to make sense of the movement of the Planets is to stop being so damned geo-centric, and to look upon them from the angle of the Sun, whereupon their circular motion in relation to a solar centre rather than to an earthly one, becomes perfectly intelligible, even if it is not visually obvious from here.

But if it is not visually obvious, it ceases to be a matter of sensual awareness, and becomes an exercise of Thought. We do not *see* the Planets going round the Sun. We only think of them that way. So the phenomenon is not one of observation but of informed imagination. It is the thought that makes their behaviour intelligible — not their appearance. But — may one also add — it is not the thought that creates the Planets.

The fact that the human mind is quite capable of shifting from a view based on what the eyes report to a purely theoretical one, and can understand and apply the consequences of such a change, is very encouraging, and it speaks well for our chances of carrying the same process a little further in our endeavour to understand some even more complicated occurrences of which we are aware today. So let us agree that it is only from a particular way of thinking about the Universe that any generalizations about its behaviour can be expected to make sense. From this, some far reaching consequences follow. At the moment, however, it is sufficient to point out that, as a child, I had no difficulty in visualizing the solar system as being heliocentric, in spite of the fact that I was not, myself, sitting on the Sun. My own children, on the other hand, have been accustomed from an early age to regard the Sun as a minor star on the outer fringe of a revolving Galaxy — thereby shifting the centre of their picture to a more distant and totally invisible point.

What we do not usually ask ourselves is what effect this shifting of our imaginary centre of reference has on the geometric picture of the smaller objects that have been left supposedly still circling around a centre that has been discarded. We have managed to satisfy ourselves with an image of two celestial curves: (1) the orbit of the Moon around the Earth, and (2) the orbit of the Earth around the Sun. But having done so, some wrinkling of the brows should occur — as they did in our neighbourhood nurseries — over the orbit of the Moon around the Sun. What sort of figure could this believably follow?

Actually, this is an unfair question, since our Moon happens to be unique amongst the satellites of the Solar System in being more powerfully under the influence of the Sun than of its parent body. But in thinking about these astronomical vagaries, something obviously goes astray when we try

This is partly because of the Moon's unusual size in relation to its parent, and also the fact that it is the nearest planetary satellite to the Sun. This has the curious consequence — neatly described by Professor Krogdhal of Kentucky — that at no stage is its orbit convex to the position of the Sun. Unlike the satellites of the more distant Planets, the Moon does not really circle the Earth at all. Both Earth and Moon may be said to circle around a comto imagine what the actual orbit must be of a satellite of one of the outer Planets, as viewed from the Sun, without any reference to its parent. Sometimes it is moving in one direction and sometimes in the opposite. Sometimes it is approaching, and at other times it is going away. And never at a constant speed. mon centre of Gravity, which has the effect of rendering both orbits a couple of inconstant curves, which cross and recross each other at 1st and 3rd Quarters. We have here what is known as the *n*-body problem. Neither orbit is a perfect ellipse, nor is the velocity of either body constant, since each slows up and accelerates the other in turn.

In fact, if any sense is to be made of its behaviour, we must go back to its parent, and reassume the old geocentricity that we were so pleased to get rid of. The satellite circumnavigates its parent, and this is all that can be said about what it does.

What I am getting at, of course, is the question as to whether, in these circumstances, it is legitimate to talk about Speed, or even distance, at all, in the absence of any fixed point of reference. Knowing the circumference of the Earth's orbit, and speaking of it as if it were a circle — which it is not — we presume to calculate a figure for its orbital speed in miles per hour.

$$\frac{\text{Diameter of Orbit} \times \text{Pi}}{365 \times 24}$$

But we are also part of a family that is revolving collectively with the outer elements of a Galaxy that has a diameter of about 100,000 Light Years, at a supposed Velocity that takes us round one complete revolution in about 200 million years. So, according to both Hoyle and Kake, we may also say that we are moving, galactically speaking, at about half a million miles an hour.

And who knows whether the Galaxy itself is not also on the outer rim of an even greater wheel? In which case the calculable speed may eventually turn out to be far beyond the forbidden limits, in relation to that more distant centre; so proving — not that we can exceed the speed limit — but that we are making calculations that are, themselves, basically nonsensical.

If it is legitimate to calculate and pronounce upon one orbital speed in relation to one centre — as Dr. Zophar has not hesitated to do — then we must be allowed to do the same with another and greater orbit, in relation to a more distant centre. And if this goes on indefinitely, what happens to '*c*'? No good saying, here, that it depends upon the Observer, because the Observer is the same throughout — ourselves.

QUERIST   Does "*c*" manage to survive as an absolute if we insist on pressing you so far, Dr. Zophar?

ZOPHAR   Ah, but you must realize that "*c*" is only an absolute in this context in a relative sense. It is the absolute limit of speed in relation to a given set of circumstances. Pick a different set of circumstances, and quite a different set of calculations will apply.

QUERIST   With two different absolute limits, each in a relative sense? Is that what you mean?

ZOPHAR   You must understand that the speed in each case will depend upon our reckoning of Time. Time is the basis of all observations connected with Speed, and Time itself is affected by velocity.

QUERIST   So that Time-reckoning is also non-absolute?

ZOPHAR   Better to say a relative absolute. I think you are beginning to understand at last what Einstein means in this connection. Congratulations.

QUERIST   The point being, that we have here two relative absolutes, each alibying the other. Velocity depends on Time, and Time depends upon Velocity, which depends upon Time. Does this mean that we are actually talking about anything in particular?

ZOPHAR   Not unless we can manage to continue to speak scientifically, and clarify our minds from Newtonian presumptions. I hope that you now appreciate the difficulty in making such matters clear to anybody who is not equipped to use the proper vocabulary.

How true: But one may legitimately wonder whether it is not the vocabulary that is itself creating most of the difficulties. Out of this tangle emerges the fact that we *are* only talking about ways of thinking about Appearances, and that Dr. Zophar has, in effect, agreed that — apart from appearances — there is actually no such thing as absolute Speed, or absolute Time.

This is precisely what Dr. Synge said in his last letter. They are 'meaningless in the sense that the words do not correspond to anything in the physical world as we now conceive it'. They both Depend. And what they depend on depends on them. And there the matter rests — with still no answer to the clinical question, nor any further explanation as to what it is that makes the entire query absurd.

As long ago as 1690 Huyghens wrote:

> In true philosophy, the causes of all natural phenomena are conceived in mechanical terms. We must do this, in my opinion, or else give up all hope of ever understanding anything in Physics.

But suppose our difficulties lie in the fact that we *are* insisting on discussing these matters in mechanical terms, when we should not do so? Although certain mechanical laws do manage to prove themselves to be useful within the limited extent of a three-dimensional Solar System, they appear to lose whatever is meaningful about them when applied to Space/ Time or to the Cosmos as a whole. Does size, therefore, affect Law? Must we conclude that what is speed for the Poor is not speed for the Rich? Or had we better just drop mechanics when talking about Things?

Natural Measurements

We are told of Planck's efforts about 1900 to meet these difficulties over intelligible mensuration by establishing a set of 'natural measurements' depending upon the nature of the objects under examination, rather than on arbitrary standards of length such as the King's arm, or the size of the Earth. In this way Planck and his successors attempted to get back to a set of universal constants such as the Quantum of Physics and the Absolute Zero of temperature. But although many of these tentative absolutes still hold good, all measurements have once again been shaken by Lorentz's insistence that there is a contraction of measuring rods in the direction of movement. We have also the Law of Added Velocities, under which two and two apparently do not always add up to four.

If so, what useful purpose can come from talking about measurements, if no objective scientific conclusions can result? Indeed, it is not at all surprising that there is a wide sense of discouragement over many of the dicta of contemporary Physics, and that the Physicists themselves are now the repositories of the Great Mysteries.

Zeno and Bergson

Zeno once argued with impressive logic that any movement of inanimate objects must be illusory since it is not in the nature of the inanimate to grow from one condition into another. To this quandary, Philosophy has given many answers, chief amongst the more recent being that of Bergson.

Bergson grasps this nettle by saying that it is only this very process of change that has got any reality. The whole of observable nature is, in a sense, illusory. The only element that can validly be described as 'real' is this very thing that is bothering us — 'Becoming'.

But in contemplating this sort of explanation, to which Dr. Berkeley would have given his enthusiastic blessing, one is inclined to wonder whether it is legitimate to explain the functional meaning of difficult Verbs by abolishing Nouns? Here again, it only seems to make everything harder.

All of this pother is in line with the proposition advanced by the Rev.
Eliphaz, that all aspects of Creation are, in some sense, 'relative', and
amount only to the sum total of the fleeting impressions of each Observer
— an argument popularized by Pirandello and deferred to by Sartre. And
very flattering it is to the Ego, since it means that everything depends
upon you and me. If the Earth seemed flat, it was flat, and who was
Copernicus to insist that it wasn't? What does it matter if the silence of
an earless desert seems a little oppressive? It need not concern us any
more than these paradoxes of Physics which will be paradoxes no more
as soon as we are all individually in our individual graves, and there is
nobody here to worry about them.

The Coefficient of Confusion

And, after all, why should we laymen complain about any increase in
the Coefficient of Confusion? It enables us to apply the same sense of
liberation to matters of social behaviour. So far as the Ten Commandments
are concerned, they all depend, too. The only question about anything is,
Does it deliver the Goods? If it does, it is not only permissible. It is Truth.
This contemporary pragmatic heresy is in the same category of the
absurd as the well-known scientific Limerick about a certain young lady
called Wright . . .

> Whose speed was much faster than light.
> She set out one day
> In a relative way
> And returned on the previous night.

Wright is Wrong

In suggesting that pragmatism can be carried so far as to become as
arguable as that Limerick, I am openly taking sides against a widespread
idea that Truth is the sum-total of our collective personal experience.
This error ignores the fallibility of observation, and the deplorable uses
to which we are capable of putting our faculties.

On the other hand it should not be forgotten that although we are quite
prepared to observe phenomena that do not exist at all, we are also able
to reach valid conclusions — particularly about the shape and nature of
the Universe — that are not based upon personal experience, and do not
depend upon the evidence of any of our senses. They often result from a
sensible return to Locke.

Long before Peary managed to get to the North Pole in person, we were in a position to say plenty about it. We could not be sure whether this locality was on land or covered by the ocean, but we knew that it was there, we could point out its precise direction, and estimate its distance. We knew what the aspect of the Heavens would be when viewed from that latitude, and we could pronounce upon the length of each polar day, and even reach certain conclusions about the temperature. All of this without ever having made the hazardous journey.

In precisely the same way it is within our power to deduce correctly both facts and effects prevailing in parts of the Cosmos where no human eye could ever penetrate, or human body exist. Such knowledge is viable. It can be applied to other problems without the confirmation of any faculty of sensual perception.

How then can we continue to assert that Truth is solely an expression of Experience? We experience our dreams, but we would be ill-advised to offer them as evidence in a Court of Law. On the other hand, Reality is not limited to matters of personal property labelled 'Do not touch', any more than it is a commodity that requires a certificate from somebody who can swear that he has been there, and has taken a look.

In fairness to the good Bishop Berkeley, he never expected us to believe that Matter does not exist (as Swift is supposed to have maliciously put into his mouth), or even that nothing has any reality apart from the phenomenon of human observation (as some of his Idealist disciples would wish him to have said).

This sort of Idealism-gone-mad is what we have learnt to expect from Signor Pirandello — not from Berkeley, the principal difference being that the Bishop believed in God, and that God and Man are quite distinct entities. So whatever Man is not in a position to observe, can still exist in the mind of God. Although Berkeley would insist — as Blake does — that this existence is 'mental', it is not non-existent in the absence of you and me.

What has driven the later application of Berkeley's Idealism off the rails is the fact that most Idealists nowadays believe in Berkeley but not in Berkeley's God. (Indeed, it has been said of Father Eliphaz of Bowdoin that 'Eliphaz believes in every cliché except God.') Remove God from this picture of the Universe, and the entire responsibility for keeping the Mental Creation in continued working order devolves upon Man — which is an intolerable state of affairs.

Speaking for myself, I have enough to worry about in trying to make sense of what I see, without having to admit to the charge of having created the conundrum myself. It is a crass hangover from adolescence to imagine that the visible world depends for its reality upon *our* uncertain attention.

So let us stick to our own business, whether or not there is anybody around to attend to God's, and let us be thankful for the words of Locke, who very sensibly distinguishes Existence from Perception, knowing, as he does, that there is a significant difference between Parts of Speech.

The physical world is not a phenomenon that is 'mental'. Mental experience is the offspring of a happy union between the Noun and the Verb — the objective reality and the subjective perception — the one fertilizing the other. So although we may properly drink and enjoy a good glass of beer, let us avoid causing any confusion by our misuse of syntax — a common result of a surfeit of beer.

Esse est Percipi is terminated by the grim formula: Time, gentlemen, please. As for sister phrase, *Percipi est Esse* — this is an open confession of a literal belief in pink elephants.

The Red King's Dream

So when an intimidating voice from Brandeis tells us that, in default of Field Equations, we must institutionalise our ignorance on the subject of Physics, however fantastic it may seem, we may at least require it to disclose whether it is proposing to talk Einstein or Berkeley. Does an object receding at the speed of light cease to exist, or are we merely unable to see it any longer? This is not a question that may be waved aside with any technical One-Upmanship, or with a heavy dropping of Sines and Cosines. Is the basis of the information, with which we are being supplied, Idealistic or Realistic? Because on the answer depends the crucial question as to whether we are each figments in some dream of Alice's Red King, or whether we are People. Once we allow ourselves to be lured into the bogs of Cloyne, we are out of reach of any rational understanding of the nature of the Universe, and of the laws that govern it. We know too much, and yet too little. The Universe was here before we were, and if we cannot consider it objectively without shoving ourselves into the picture, we may as well accept the Red King as our father, spiritually as well as morally.

The Expanding Universe

The widely publicised controversy between the Abbé Lemaître and Professor Fred Hoyle over the origin of the Universe and its apparent expansion has been one of our best-loved pieces of astronomical Hans Andersen until very recently. As it will be referred to in some detail in a later chapter, it is sufficient to say at this stage that each diagnosis associated with these celebrated names carries us back to the basic question as to what is actually meant by that troublesome word, 'Time'. Indeed, it must have long been obvious that this is the principal mystery guest to be identified.

What has already been said about this supposed product of clocks should make it clear that our difficulties do not arise through any shortage of definitions, but from the fact that there are far too many of them.

In the Bible, the word 'love' is made use of to cover a wide variety of merchandise — from Agape to Eros, from Charity to Bonté, from kindness to animals to the Holy Name itself. Considerable ill-feeling has been worked up throughout the centuries over multiple meanings that have become attached to such words as 'Vanity' and even 'Rock'. It will be suggested here that in much the same way the expression 'Time' is being used by a great many of the Scientists with a reckless abandon that must be got under control as quickly as possible.

Our original question to the Conference appears to have brought to light a number of familiar terms, deeply entangled in a sort of grammatical undergrowth: and one of the most striking of these concerns this matter of Velocity, which depends in its turn on our having some sort of objective measuring rods for both Time and Space — not to mention some intelligible ideas about the significance of both 'Here' and 'Now', on which to base our calculations. Until we know for certain that there is such a thing as Velocity, apart from matters of three-dimensional appearance, we are bound to harbour mathematical doubts — which in their own way are even more sinister today than are the religious variety.

Let us hope, therefore, that it is not Mathematics that are at fault, but certain premises that we have allowed to be opened without a sufficient understanding of their contents. It may be that things are not quite as crazy as they seem. At any rate, let us try to clear some of the ground with the aid of two implements. One is a piece of machinery: the other is a sort of parable.

The Derrynane Effect

Many years ago, at a place in Kerry called Derrynane, I was amusing myself with two sheets of paper in order to relieve the boredom of an emotional talk on Catholic emancipation. There were a number of coloured pencil lines on one sheet, and a slit in the other one, and I noticed a thing that has been a commonplace of optics for centuries — that when I drew the slit across the pencilled page, the visible cross sections of the coloured lines appeared to move up and down the slit, and that the speed of their apparent movement depended upon the angle at which they lay to the direction in which I was moving the upper sheet. I do not propose to elaborate this familiar phenomenon any further. (I have always been annoyed to find out how all my most exciting and significant discoveries have been well known for generations.)

All that I wish to point out is that this effect — which for want of a better name will be called the Derrynane Effect — was brought about, not by any activity on the part of the coloured lines, but by the movement of the upper sheet that contained the slit. It is true that this piece of paper 'moves', and to that extent the process is kinematic. But what if it is? Here we are referring, not to a phenomenon of Physics but of Observation, and what Observation amounts to is a matter that may remain a mystery for the moment. At least we have settled with Zeno, and no longer have to explain how some sections of coloured pencil marks manage to fly about at varying rates of speed without any means of propulsion at all. The answer is that they don't. All that is happening is something that I am doing.

Mercator Men

The other item is the story of two ships that set off together on a cruise on parallel courses, and within hailing distance of each other. Sailing due south (or due north, if you would prefer them to be Australian) they communicate with each other for company's sake from time to time. They have all the necessary equipment to calculate and to hold their courses along true meridian lines, and every few miles they check their direction to make sure that they are not straying.

However, in spite of all the care of the navigators, it grows increasingly clear as the journey proceeds that it is becoming more difficult for their Captains to hail each other. Notwithstanding their skill in the use of their instruments it is clear that something very peculiar is happening to their parallel courses. They are drawing further and further apart. After some mutual abuse that proves nothing, one of the Passengers comes forward with an explanation that saves the face of both navigators, as well as the principles of Geometry. This is our friend, Dr. Zophar, who has already made a name for himself by some observations out of the windows of railway carriages. His law — Zophar's First Law — was to the effect that the lateral speed of objects so seen decreases at a calculable rate dependent on the distance of each. He has worked this out on a graph which has become the basis for an algebraic formula which shows the mathematics of such decrease, on the strength of which he is listened to respectfully when he propounds a second law. This disposes of an absurd suggestion made by one of his students that the phenomenon proves that it is in the nature of parallel lines to repel each other relatively to the distance travelled — which is a plain contradiction of the definition of parallel lines. Dr. Zophar's discovery is much more acceptable than this, and is to the effect that the Earth is blowing up at a rate that can also be calculated. This effect he embodies in another formula which is found to work, which proves that it is true (according to the pragmatic climate of the day). And there it remains in the text books, until the two ships are turned on to courses lying directly to the east, upon which new parallels, to everybody's confusion, it is found that Zophar's Second Law no longer applies, but that an even stranger thing is happening. The two ships are no longer drawing apart laterally, but although precisely the same amount of effort is being applied to the propulsion of each, one of them — the ship further north — is drawing steadily away from the other in a forward direction.

The Lorentz Anti-contraction. One of Dr. Zophar's promising pupils has pointed out another peculiarity of measuring rods. If used in the vicinity of two prominent objects it may show them as being so many hundred yards apart. But if the scientist withdraws the rod to a distance from the measured line, the implement of measurement expands in relation to the distance previously ascertained until a point Zero is reached on the scale. The student has calculated this rate of expansion, and exhibits his results, together with a graph, in his Thesis on the subject.

It might also be mentioned that in the field of Athletics, the data obtained from the Captains of our ships shows that on a hundred yards Dash lying east and west — all other things being equal — the competitor running on the northernmost track must inevitably win the race, except in Australia.

At this point we may leave the nuances of the further explanations to the imagination, because the answer — complicated as it may seem to them — is obvious to us, thanks to our superior dimensional awareness.

These Mercator Mariners are perfectly sound in their geometry and sea-manship, but are sadly deficient in their dimensions — applying their 2D calculations on a 3D field. Explain to them that the surface of the Earth is curved and at once the apparent paradoxes cease to be problems, and reason will be restored in the navigation room. But it will not be long before Dr. Zophar will be causing further confusion by another pronounce-ment to the effect that, because of the Earth's curvature, there are no such things as parallel lines at all, and that it is not possible to connect any two points on the Earth's surface by a straight line. Given an allergy towards the consequences of curvature, the Doctor will be reluctant to consider the possibility of digging a tunnel.

Thought is how we use it

In all things of the mind, a framework of reference is as necessary as a Constitution is to the State, and a highly dangerous situation arises if this does not substantially match up with the Data. We have found Lorentz offering us kinematic explanations of phenomena that are them-selves kinematic paradoxes. Ouspensky consistently refers to a plane as a line that moves, while a cube is a plane that moves — two mechanical definitions of geometrical conceptions that are not explicable in terms of movement at all. They are aspects of Extension. Einstein relates Mass to Velocity in his celebrated equation already quoted — an equation that contains in its terms a purely subjective reference to Speed. We ourselves are travelling at any possible velocity you choose, from the angle of an Observer in a distant Galaxy. Consequently, you and I, from somebody else's point of view must have the enormous Mass insisted upon by Einstein, which we are reasonably certain we do not have.

Does Time Exist?

In all of this we find the same Bergsonian obsession that there is nothing of significance except the act of Becoming. We are supposedly living in a Universe where something is being done by something that does not actually exist apart from the fact that it is doing something. When I asked Dr. Synge the direct question, Is there such a thing at all as Time? he replied: The more I think about it the more I come to the conclusion that there is nothing else.

But suppose the answer lies in precisely the opposite direction and Minkowski's conception of Space/Time provides a four-dimensional solution that is independent of Dynamics, and is absolute in its interpretation? Should we not stop talking about the Cosmos in terms of its behaviour, since whatever it does — apart from possessing quantitative extension — is indescribable in the language of measurements, except in relation to an egocentricity that we have been doing our best to grow out of?

It is easy to accept a conception of Space as a mere aspect of Matter. The idea of totally empty Space, existing apart from Matter, is as non-sensical as a shot that I once put into a Movie script: 'Pan to a cloudless sky.' Without Matter, there could be no Space. Consequently we must not think of it as an empty box manufactured by Rutherford, which has to be filled with Lodge's Patent Ether, in order to enable messages to get through.

Space is not the absence of Matter, but the relationship of Matter to its extension; from which we see that, of necessity, it conditions and is conditioned by the phenomenon of Mass. So also it is ridiculous to think of Time in any of the ways that we have been describing, apart from that of its being an aspect of Action. If nothing happened there would be no Time: Consequently there is nothing at all surprising in the discovery that Time is apparently conditioned by Velocity, and vice versa.

It is when we come to apply these terms to personal experience that we are impelled to recognize that it is one thing to say that at enormous velocities Time slows down. It is quite another thing to state that, were we to leave the Earth at a speed approaching that of light, and could we continue to observe the Earth through a telescope as we sped away, we would receive delayed signals that would give the appearance of slowing down to events in the field that we had left behind. If this is a mere matter of appearance depending on a delay in the post — a Doppler effect such as we get when a train goes past with the whistle blowing — our experiences would be reversed on the return journey, so that on arrival — unlike that lady called Wright — we might find that one effect had cancelled out the other, and that our wrist watches were as much in line with local clocks as if we had never left.

This seemed to provide another opportunity to get a clinical answer to the question as to whether our informants are talking in terms of Fact or of Appearance. Would the Astronauts' watches be wrong on their return, or would they not? Dr. Synge says that they would be wrong, and that the effect is a real one. Furthermore, he offers a diagram to prove his point, together with a calculation that I do not profess to follow, but gratefully accept.

This I am placing in Appendix B in deference to the feelings of those

desirable readers who do not proceed any further when presented with
Geometry in the nude. It may be that it proves that a high velocity has
an absolute effect on our reckoning of Time, or it may not. What it
certainly does not show is what happens if the Space Traveller alters his
direction at some point in Space/Time, and returns to Earth in order to
settle this problem of stationary clocks and portable wrist-watches.

There is no Fixed Point

So far as the existence of any fixed point of reference arises, we are, of
course, far too sophisticated to imagine that either Jerusalem or our own
personal Ego stands at the centre of Creation. Nevertheless, we are prone
to worship two nonentities — 'Here' and 'Now' — because they happen
to be our own. We are perfectly well aware of the cosmic unimportance
of this parasite-ridden speck of dust, but we are none the less certain, as
we sit here on our perishable thrones, that Things are Happening all
around us.

For all practical purposes there is no harm whatever in this amiable
delusion, so long as we know what we are up to, and do not allow any
misconceived consequences to drive us frantic, or into double-think. We
sit in our railway carriage and watch the countryside roll by. But is the
countryside doing anything? Or is it *Sinn Fein* — we ourselves? Might it
be possible that an answer is to be found, not in a kinematic interpretation
of the behaviour of the Universe, but in a dimensional view of its structure
— as was the case with those two ships?

We have managed to reorientate our image of the Solar System in
accordance with the advice of Copernicus, without any additions to our
faculty of sight. The scene outside the carriage window still looks the
same, but maybe there is another way of thinking about it.

But all of this has been rather exhausting, so let us leave   See
Science to its own devices for the moment, and turn instead to   Appendix
a subject that is everybody's pigeon — or should I say Every-   I
man's Paraclete? — the topic of contemporary Religion.

III TENTMAKER ON HIS ASS

Sit gratia pro otio quietis
et pro dolore augescendi.

Brains Trust

A SITUATION where there is no apparent sense in what one knows to be substantially true is as perilous in the realm of faith and morals as it is in the field of science. It tempts us to doubt the evidence of our senses, and leads us into cynicism in the use of our minds.

I had a vivid experience of this a few years ago, in the most public manner possible, when appearing in a BBC Brains Trust programme with the actor Sir Ralph Richardson, the critic Marghanita Laski, and the celebrated proponent of Logical Positivism, Professor Ayer of Oxford.

I had already run into some trouble with Miss Laski's Uncle Harold on an Overseas sound spot, on account of having passed some remark about the fraudulent nature of political arguments — an observation that suggested that the snake-pit of Politics was a good thing to keep out of. It was people like me — Laski said — who had made possible the rise of Fascism through our lack of attention to serious issues. If we are not, all of us — he went on — prepared to shoulder our fair share of political gobbledygook, it serves us right if professional liars such as Hitler get the better of the local amateurs. He did not put it quite like this, but the substance of his complaint was as stated.

In the case of the Brains Trust, the unpleasantness arose over a viewer's question about the historicity of one of the Bible stories, and it culminated in Professor Ayer turning on Richardson rather petulantly, and exclaiming: 'But at this date you surely don't accept literally the story of the Garden of Eden?'

Sir Ralph admitted with some embarrassment that perhaps he was only speaking in a spiritual sense. But I, inspired by an unreasonable aversion towards this sort of answer — a hereditary failing that got some of my forebears into trouble at the time of the Solemn League and Covenant — intervened to say that, Yes, although I was aware that Eden never actually existed, I was prepared to believe in it until somebody provided me with a better image of the mystery of Original Sin. And if we believe in it in any sort of way, we are only liable to be misunderstood if we say that we don't *actually* believe in it.

Miss Laski and the Professor looked at each other and promptly changed the subject, politely assuming that they were here up against a religious fundamentalist whom they had no wish to offend by further argument. But I would not willingly be dismissed in any such way, and I went on to insist that in our present state of ignorance about the facts of life, there are many things that it is necessary to believe, in spite of the fact that one knows them not to be true. There are several important topics that it is best to accept, if one wishes to avoid the alternative of suicide. Amongst these I would place an unpragmatic view of social behaviour, a dislike of Determinism, and an insistence that there is some point in being alive. There are strong arguments against all of these eccentricities that are difficult to answer, but had better be wrong. However, I was told that I was guilty of mental dishonesty, and ought to be ashamed of myself as a member of the Brains Trust.

'What a thing to say to Professor Ayer!' was the rather girlish comment in *The Listener*. And this concluded the skirmish.

Pope or Self-slaughter

I obviously got the worst of this, and I do not bring the matter up now with any intention of continuing a discussion in which there was a great deal to be said for the irritation of the High Table with me. I merely wish to say that the attitude to which I gave voice was, and still is, a very widespread one. Indeed, a friend asked me a few days later what I was bothering about, since I had said no more to Ayer and Laski than what is the essence of Anglicanism. In so far as it provides a working alternative to a grim choice between the Pope and self-slaughter, there is a lot to be said for Anglicanism, whether logical or not. It is better to assure oneself that one believes in the Garden of Eden than to know that one believes in a Nothing that is mechanical. Herein madness lies — a state of affairs that may not have mattered in the bad old days before the Bomb. But what is going to happen when some Logical Positivist (not Professor Ayer, of course) provides himself with the necessary equipment to take us all along with him into some positively logical conclusion?

There is no need to apologise for upholding a myth, provided that it is a good one, and so long as we recognise it for what it is, and do not apply it to illegitimate uses. The flaw in my remarks to the Brains Trust lay in my assumption that it is necessary to make any use of double-think in order to provide a reason for the existence of Original Sin, or indeed for deciding to remain alive. The relevant question is not whether Eden is historical, but whether it is valuable.

I agree now that its function as an explanation for the universality of toil and death is no longer helpful. But there was something to be said for standing up for Eden in the heat of conflict, rather than have it assumed that I was in accord with my pragmatic opponents in their view that not only is Eden a myth, but Sin also.

When talking to Secularists who may be unable to throw out the Myth without also pushing over the Meaning, it is sometimes advisable to take, in reverse, the course that is forced upon us by the pious. When arguing with the latter it is easier to dismiss the Holy Trinity altogether than to have to explain that we can believe in it in terms that are different from those defined at Nicaea. We are told that before the death of Saint Columba, three maidens came to visit him on Iona. Their names were Vision, Achievement and Prophecy — three phases of the saintly life. They might also be related to the consubstantial aspects of the Trinity, an appreciation of which makes it all the more necessary to contradict Athanasius.

Is God Dead?

The cliché of the day is Functionalism, which amounts in effect to Non-Religion. But while Non-Art and Non-Theatre are presently engaged very vigorously in thumbing noses at much in both mediums that has seen the best of its days, Non-Religion appears to have nothing better to do than to disinter a decidedly old-fashioned phrase : God is dead. And in this way it washes its hands of the entire problem.

As in the nineteenth century, when Nietzsche popularised this statement, we are not told what it is that is supposed to have killed him, or whether flowers are expected. Indeed, it may be that he has merely been bored to death with what he has to put up with on Sundays.

But putting aside any flippancy, we do feel a sense of loss in the death, if not of God, of a dogmatic system that, rightly or wrongly, did provide a receptacle in which to place the residuum of our experiences, as well as a rule of thumb to help us in the making of decisions. In the absence of any such code, we find ourselves beginning to wonder whether we do actually make any decisions at all : and next we find ourselves becoming Behaviourists and Determinists, and wondering why we ever bothered to leave the unexciting company of John Knox, if Predestination is going to return under a slightly shorter name in company with Professor Bildad under a somewhat longer one?

Religious Types — uncharming

It is a sign of the times that few of us greatly admire the carriers of placards in the streets that ask the menacing and rather impertinent question: Where will you be in Eternity? Nor do we relish the idea of getting involved with members of Bible Classes and Retreats, which is odd in a way, because there ought not to be anything reprehensible about enthusiasm. Yet we do tend to regard any of our friends and relatives who get bitten by religion with much the same disapproval and regret that used to be directed at members of the family who took to drink.

Maybe Religion *is* a form of intoxication: or perhaps we have some reason to suspect that these conventicles, sodalities and prayer meetings are centres for the intimidation of others by second-rate people who are unable to assert themselves in better ways. Yet we must admit to a certain sneaking sense of envy for those who have a genuine belief in something, and we sometimes allow ourselves to be drawn into profitless discussions about the truth of the Bible story, rather than on the more vital topics that are actually at issue.

The motion at present before the house is not whether Noah had an Ark, but whether the image of a Deity who loses his temper from time to time with his own creatures is an encouraging or a blasphemous one. What is even more pertinent is whether the mass of professing Christians actually believe in it themselves, any more than we do? It does seem a little suspicious, that those who ought to be the most eager to get themselves into that Paradise to which this Life is a mere antechamber, should frequently be the most keen to remain for as long as possible in the Waiting Room—like the Nun on a transatlantic flight who, alone amongst the passengers, determinedly wore her life jacket the whole way across. Does this give the impression of a genuine belief in Heaven? Or was she just a little uncertain about the efficiency and attention of her Guardian Angel? Nor are these suspicions limited to the less sophisticated types. We all know the good-chap Parson — the sporty, drinking type in plain clothes, who does not hesitate to tell us an off-beat story, and to express an interest in a pretty leg. Why should his principal objective be to re-assure us that he is just like everybody else, in spite of the Thirty-Nine Articles? I think it was Dr. Johnson who said that the merriment of parsons is mighty offensive, and maybe this fact has something to do with the failure of these theological modernists to convey the impression that they have any real use for Christianity at all — apart from double-think.

It is an anomaly of the present day that Religious Types are best given a wide berth, but this was not always the case. In the Middle Ages the normal man was a believer, and had what to him was a normal answer. Today, Religion — which ought to be a matter of the gravest concern to those who need it most, namely Adults — has, like Gulliver's Travels, been relegated to the nursery, on the principle that, of course I don't have much time for that sort of thing myself, but after all one has to recognise its importance, and it's a good thing for the kids to know about, isn't it. So let's send them off to Sunday School, while we take a well-earned rest in bed.

Compulsory Piety for the Young

This attitude was amusingly illustrated by an attempt at a College where I once taught, to continue compulsory Chapel in the face of widespread opposition from the Students, many of whom also wished to have a morning in bed. Indeed, this insistence on a religious Draft for the Young was taken to the length of threatening the elected representatives of the girls with academic penalties if they persisted in delivering the views of the student body to the authorities.

'After all,' said our Centrepiece, 'you only have to go so many times a Semester, and sit in a really beautiful Chapel, listen to lovely singing, and hear some of the greatest minds in the country talking to you about the most important things in life. The Trustees and the Alumnae are quite satisfied that you should not be allowed to miss this.'

It seemed a pity, in the circumstances, that so many of us grown-ups were liable to miss it too, owing to a lack of any pressure in our direction : and I must say I wondered why it was so clearly assumed that nobody would go except under compulsion, with all these treats in store.

'Besides,' the Leader went on, 'the services are undenominational, and we will make a point of seeing that nothing is included that might offend anybody's Faith.'

'But I don't want a service that means nothing', objected a distressed Senior. 'I'd rather hear somebody saying something I disagree with than have to sit listening to nothing in particular.'

'Why can't you take it all symbolically?' interposed the soft, reasonable voice of a minor official. 'Like you take a poem, or a great book?'

'Because I don't feel that worship should be just symbolical.'

'Well, it's not enough just to object to something,' the President concluded, as he rose to his feet, chilling the room with one of those mirthless smiles that are usually reserved for official photographs.

'You have to be prepared to suggest alternatives,' he went on. 'I'm always delighted to listen whenever an alternative is proposed. But in the absence of any of these, there's nothing more to be said.'

And before anybody could enquire whether the same rule applied to objections to Suttee or even to cannibalism, the interview ended triumphantly in favour of compulsory Chapel. But as soon as the young were dismissed, somebody asked whether this could be regarded as religious liberty for Atheists? And immediately the conversation became more illuminating.

'Oh, the Atheists cause no trouble at all,' said our Leader. 'They don't believe in it anyhow. To them it's just another social requirement. It's actually the Jews who are the biggest trouble-makers.'

'Not the Catholics?' I asked in some surprise.

'The Catholics don't have to go,' snapped the President. 'Their Priests won't let them, so they are excused.'

Good for the Catholics, was my unspoken reply. Only the Priests stick up for their exclusive right to lecture their own sheep.

In the end it was discovered that, where bullying is concerned, there is a significant distinction between Customers and Employees. It was also revealed in the present case who the Customers were — a detail, one would imagine, that any supposed businessman ought to have known in the first place. So there is now no compulsory Chapel. But a less promising introduction to the spiritual side of College life could hardly be imagined.

Gentle Jesus

In my own case, I was first introduced to a serious study of Religion at a Sunday School. Here we sang *Hymns for the Young*.

> Gentle Jesus, meek and mild.
> Look upon a little child.
> Pity my simplicity.
> Suffer me to come to Thee.

At the age of ten, nobody likes to enquire what this is all about. But it is Religion, and this excuses the fact that it would otherwise be nauseating. Religion is like that, and one has to put up with it. Then there was another hymn that began :

> Oh, what can little hands do
> To please the King of Heaven?

The rest of the verse described what the little hands can do, and the fact that I do not remember what it was, is an indication of the extent to which I felt that it was supposed to be taken seriously.

Attendance at this kind of instruction was compulsory, and I have since realised that in the latitudinarian Protestant spirit of most of our homes, we were very well off, compared to the fate of children in other more aggressive faiths, where it is felt advisable to condition the little minds before the age of puberty. Nevertheless, I am reminded of a story told by Frank Harvey, who alleges that one of his teachers came into class on a Spring Sabbath morning, flushed with excitement, and announced:

'Children, can you guess what I've just seen? A dear little furry thing with a bushy tail, that went skipping across the road in front of me and scampered up a tree. Can anybody guess what it was?'

From the back of the class came an embittered voice: 'Bound to be Jesus!' So then we sang:

> I want to be like Jesus,
> So lowly and so meek,
> For no one marked an angry word
> That ever heard him speak.

This of the man who is alleged to have cleansed the Temple of the money-changers, and who swore that it would be more tolerable on the Day of Judgement for Sodom and Gomorrah than for any city that doubted his miracles! But we did not know enough about the matter to protest, although there *was* the case of a rather shady friend of mine, called Aubrey, who chalked up a lot of trouble for himself by expressing some sympathy for the fox that robs the hen-roost.

'But even if you have no proper attitude towards stealing, Aubrey, surely you must have some feelings for the poor chickens, eaten by that horrible animal?'

'What about the worms?' answered Aubrey.

At which point he was allowed to leave the room. Indeed, he was encouraged on his way, thus putting an end to an engaging discussion that might have got round to the fact that, from the angle of the chickens, it makes very little difference whether they are eaten by the horrible fox or by the kindly teacher. All one can say is, that the earlier the chickens are disposed of, the better, if, like Aubrey, one is a worm-lover.

Blake's Spider

Many years later I discovered that much the same problem had been commented upon by no less a person than William Blake in the first part of his poem, *Vala*.

> The Spider sits in his labour'd Web, eager watching for the Fly.
> Presently comes a famish'd Bird and takes away the Spider.
> His Web is left all desolate, that his little anxious heart
> So careful wove and spread it out with sighs and weariness.

'So you see, boys,' said our Teacher, 'God is Love.' And then we continued :

To the best of my recollection it was this same Aubrey who, patting his friendly Corgi on the head, came out with another piece of memorable orthographical impiety : DOG IS LOVE.

> But O, I'm not like Jesus
> As anyone can see.
> Then gentle Saviour, send thy grace,
> And make me like to thee.

As I looked around afterwards at those faces in the pews, I could see little that suggested Love. If they were all trying their best to be like Jesus, good luck to them. But was he something that I wanted to be like, too? Was there any outward and visible sign that he was either gentle or meek or a saviour; and, if the last, a saviour from what?

This question — a saviour from what, is something that we are inclined to lose sight of, because of our very natural regard for all that seems to be taken for granted in our upbringing. This is embodied in the urgings and prohibitions of Holy Scripture — an expression of human experience that cannot be lightly dismissed. We have there before us a profoundly moving story, whether it be fact or fiction, of a crucifixion, and we can recognise in it something that often illuminates our own sensations — a conviction that the good life itself can be for each of us a crucifixion which, curiously enough, is worth our while to endure.

The Fireman's Fire

But does this mean that we have to agree to the further proposition that we must accept professional assistance to save us from some unspeakable horrors that have been prepared for us in a life to come?

It is to be hoped that we know how to respond when a soft-spoken character drops in and suggests that we employ him to protect our windows and person from certain perils of the City at which he darkly hints. Is there anything substantially different in this proposition from that of the gentleman in the surplice, who also has special abilities to assist us in moments of need, with services which he tells us we are not in a position to obtain elsewhere?

I am pleased to say that at an early age I appreciated the fact that while an Insurance Company does not itself promote the blaze from which it offers protection, the same can hardly be said of those who, in return for a small commission, will undertake to get the Dead out of trouble.

The Heavenly Heretics

There were, however, some other aspects of organised Religion that I found more fascinating than the arrangements for a Happy Death. It was at a later stage of adolescence that I first came across the great Heretics, and discovered what intellectual stimulus can be found in a study of these black sheep, and how on closer acquaintance one grows to like them more and more.

There was Arius with his created Christ — quite intelligible as the son of God, but if co-existent, the son of nobody. There was also Sabellius who denied, with equal conviction, that Jesus was a man at all. Both of these were anathema to that unattractive Athanasius, who seemed determined to have it both ways, with the natural result of raising some doubts on both points.

I loved Nestorius, who could not stomach the idea of providing God with a Mother — surely a great impertinence. And Berengarius, who insisted to the end that bread was bread. I also found great charm in Apelles who argued convincingly that faith backed by good works was sufficient for salvation (surely enough for any God, even if not wholly satisfactory to a Bishop), and who believed in an uncreated Deity — a single Principle — while very fairly admitting his inability to understand it. And then there were the Helkasites, who maintained enigmatically that a wise man will deny with his mouth, but not with his heart.

In the wide and windy acres of Gnosticism one could play with the idea that the Holy Spirit was, perhaps, female. And why not? There is a Basilica that is called after her; and so we know her name — Sophia. I duly remarked upon the Docetists, who said that the Incarnation was only true in a spiritual sense. (Where have I heard that before?) And on the Iconoclasts, denounced at Second Nicaea for insisting that the second

St. Thomas Minor Seminary
130, San Thome High Road,
Mylapore, Madras—4.
(S. India.)

My dear Benefactor,

As the month of November draws near, our thoughts go to our beloved deceased ones. While on earth, they were so dear and near to us; they loved us so tenderly and made such great sacrifices for us. Undoubtedly we owe them so much for what we are.

They are now in the dark prison of Purgatory, attoning of their sins in cruel flames. In their utter helplessness, they raise their hands and cry out with the words of Job: ''Have pity on me, have pity on me, at least you my friends, because the hand of the Lord hath touched me.''

Would you, my good Benefactor, pay a deaf ear to their heart-rending supplication? Would you let them suffer for ages in that terrible fire which, according to St. Thomas, equals in intensity, to that of hell? Blessed are the merciful, for they shall obtain mercy. Be merciful to them and help them in their distress. You will show, thereby, your gratitude to them, gather merits for heaven and secure powerful advocates in heaven.

From the 2nd to the 9th of November, we shall have a Solemn Novena of Holy Masses for Souls in Purgatory. All our Seminarians on these days will offer their Holy Masses, Holy Communions, Rosaries, and Sacrifices for the same above intentions.

Please send your donations and intentions in time, and thereby share in the infinite merits of Holy Masses and offer them for your beloved deceased ones. Fill in your petitions and Mass intentions in the enclosed leaflet and send them to my address above.

God Bless you and reward Your charity.

Fr. Joseph Sandanam s.o.s,
Rector.

Commandment was not meant in a spiritual sense at all. And I thought about the Monothelites who were drummed out of the Church at Third Constantinople for saying that Christ has a single will, and must not be credited with double-think.

For a time I fell under the spell of that most subtle of heresies — the one that emanated from our own islands — that of the reasonable and good-hearted Pelagius, denounced by St. Augustine in unendearing terms. (But rightly so, I fear.) And it was down in the Bar Library one day when I was juggling with some of these things in my notebook, in the absence of any urgent briefs, that a passionate brother Barrister of strongly sectarian views cried out,

'The wind has blown them all away.'

What greater miracle could there be — he went on — than the shining fact that all these great Councils — all those Imperial Popes, in their ex-cathedra pronouncements throughout the centuries, had all been right! Every one of them. Orthodoxy had never once erred in its decisions.

A miracle indeed, if this were so. But were these decisions right because they were orthodox, or were they orthodox because they were made?

But perhaps above all I was fascinated by Clement of Alexandria, who wrote that the first person of the Trinity was the Absolute of the Philosophers, and was not just the 'Father' referred to in the Gospels. From which he went on to argue that we need attach very little value to the human nature of Christ, but very great value, indeed, to the Word.

How up-to-date they all were, writing — some of them — upwards of fifteen hundred years ago. How unblown away, in spite of some shouting to the contrary. How like Bonhoeffer — I have since thought — who is now the talk of the Seminaries.

Myth or History?

Now let me say that I am fully aware of the arguments that have been brought up against the veracity of the Scriptures as a whole by those who hold that the New Testament story is not an embellishment on a substratum of fact, but is entirely mythical.

The reason why these arguments are not more widely known is not so much the superior answers of the Church, as the fact that most of the more informed advocates of Agnosticism write unreadable prose. The Right Honourable J. M. Robertson, for example, was a cabinet minister in one of Asquith's governments, and a dedicated student of Shakespeareana as well as of Christology. His book, *Christianity and Mythology*, is so stuffed with disorganised learning, intolerably expressed, that few can read it through. But the substance of his comment goes further than to point out that the Gospels are so contradictory that it is impossible to ascertain which of the fifteen named Apostles actually constitute the Twelve. (The standard explanation of this is that three of them sometimes masquerade under aliases.) Robertson says — like Schweitzer — that the further one looks for the historical Jesus, the further he retreats until — according to Robertson — nothing is left but a miracle play.

We must not be too impressed by all the circumstantial details of the story. They are there, not in spite of its fictional nature, but because of it. Gulliver and Sherlock Holmes and William Tell ring much more true to us in terms of character than Shakespeare or William Wallace or even Richard III. Historical events tend to be messy and disorganised, and they do not usually lapse into silence for a change of scene, as does the crucifixion drama between the Last Supper and Gethsemane. Here, Robertson says, we have a play compressed into the unity of one night, following a standard five part form — a drama that finds nothing incongruous in a description of the sayings and feelings of the principal actor during a part of the action when there is nobody else present to report him — as is the case during most of the garden scene.

What Ecclesiastical or Praetorian Court, he asks, would sit in the middle of the night except in deference to the economy of theatrical production? And here we have two of them in session. And so on.

But enough of this. I am not concerned with the problem of whether the account would be credible as a newspaper story. I am merely trying to show the multiple causation of ritual, and the way in which history books are sometimes conditioned by the need to account for existing ceremonies. To me this is just another example of what has been done over the centuries to what Joyce aptly calls the Tiberiast Duplex, and no aspersions are being cast on anything except the gift wrapping and the commercials.

I am also aware of the fact that even a non-Christian may come to the conclusion that most of the early Councils of the Church, ridden with politics as they were, were substantially right in their theological conclusions, in the light of the centuries that have followed. That is to say, when they stuck to their own business, and left secular matters where they belonged.

Nicaea was right about the co-existence of all three persons in the

Trinity formula, and it was actually Arius who was in error in trying to make three-dimensional sense of a deceptive father-son image. First Constantinople was right in insisting on the divinity of the Messenger. Chalcedon was right in contradicting the Monophysites (and amongst them, Pope Honorius, who was apparently one of the worst). Whatever we may mean by Jesus Christ, it requires a human nature as well as a divine one to make the conception of any significance to us.

On the other hand, Ephesus was wrong in trying to make confusion out of this notable division by declaring the flesh to be divine in its humanity : and Ephesus was subsequently condemned by the considered judgment of the Church . . . right again.

As for Third Constantinople, was it not brilliantly right in recognising the two aspects of the mind—the instrument of thought, and the Thinker? Speaking in terms of Christ, this Council defined something that is relevant to all of us, contradicting the Monothelites in the process. It did not credit Christ with double-think, but with what we all possess — an inner genius that directs thought.

As for the Iconoclasts, anathematised at Second Nicaea — although there was a great deal to be said for them — what right had they to condemn all images on principle, good ones as well as bad? These implements of understanding need to be assessed on the basis of their aptness and their validity; and while some selective smashing is very necessary from time to time, to reject them all is to be too damned intellectual.

It would do no damage to the importance of William Blake's message to smash about three quarters of his engraven images. His vision of Urizen may be the better of an illustration or two, but no great harm would be done by extinguishing that burning tiger. See Appendix C

Even the First Vatican Council was not so far out in its pronouncements upon Papal Infallibility. Theological statements that are genuinely based upon human experience have a way of turning out to be sensible enough, and what harm is there in having them defined by one or two authoritative persons? If so, they may well be *ex cathedra*. On the other hand, if merely concerned with matters of historical fact (such as the Assumption) they may be true, but they are not *ex cathedra*. And in neither case should it be open to the Speaker to determine the category for himself. This is too much of an assumption.

Bonhoeffer and Bultmann

But to return to our major point, what I find myself coming back to again and again is Bonhoeffer's argument that it is the Myth itself that is the important part of the Gospel story — not any question as to whether this or that detail has been fabricated. If we recognise it as honest Myth, and use it as such, we do not have to waste our time examining and throwing out accumulated rubbish in order to acquire a conception of historical and scientific Truth that needs neither lies nor apologies to support it.

Bultmann, on the other hand, was a determined thrower out of this and that, to an extent that amounts to Belief based upon Unbelief. But we cannot turn the latter into the former by saying that we believe in a lie symbolically. If we allow ourselves to be drawn into any arguments as to whether or not Jesus performed conjuring tricks at weddings, it will only serve to distract attention from the shining fact that life itself is a miracle in which we all partici-

This phrase 'honest Myth' may need some clarification. According to the Bonhoeffer school of thought, Myth should be an expression of Truth in terms of a story that illuminates and clarifies human experience. Its literal truth or falsity is irrelevant, provided the point is a valid one and is being made in a legitimate manner. But when Myth is symbolically fraudulent or has been fabricated to support some lie by alleging that it is not Myth but History, then it becomes necessary to denounce it. Thus it matters tremendously whether the founder of Christianity said: 'Upon this rock (Peter) I shall build my Church' if the incident is to be used as a means of enslaving Christendom to the Roman Pontiffs. On the other hand, if the crucifixion story is regarded as an expression of the dignity and universal quality of human suffering, it is a good story, whether or not somebody called Jesus actually died on a cross.

pate. We probably know that Lazarus was never raised from the dead, but we should not allow this scepticism to make us forget that we, ourselves, are raised to what we experience as life usually once a day.

What is objectionable about the Lazarus story is not the fact that it is a Myth, but that its serious contemplation may have the effect of distracting our attention from a real miracle that deeply concerns us. To this extent it should be disposed of — not by saying that it is true in a spiritual sense, but by calling it a lie. Thus, we can still follow the admirable example set by the early martyrs, in delivering public insults to nonsense, not merely as an expression of our scepticism, but as an averment of the fact that we believe in something better.

We realise, of course, that when an intelligent Greek cast his incense upon the altar of Zeus, it was not because he really thought that such a being lived up there on Mount Olympus. It was more likely because of the fact that he felt it was better to believe in Zeus than in the Government. Why then need the early Christians kick up such a scene over so innocuous a social statement? Wasn't this in rather bad taste?

They did it, of course, because they considered that they had something better to support than either Zeus or the Government, a state of affairs that made it necessary to run the risk of openly offending both. Today such a demonstration could be dismissed as an expression of mere crankiness, but only because Zeus is Out. But the Government is still with us — and with it, the Flag and the Credibility Gap, and our various Irrational Anthems, and the fable of 'liberty and justice for all'. So the occasional little protests (also in bad taste) of our children and grandchildren may have some point after all, provided they are smart enough not to tear up too much wheat with the trash.

If the story of Adam and Eve is going to be forced upon them as a rather mean trick played by Bluebeard on his gardener, it is just as well for them to fling it in the fire along with their draft cards. But as a picture of a considered choice on the part of Man not to remain behind those gates in a state of bovine ignorance, but to get outside and start digging, it may have considerable value.

God is neither Love nor Dead

So let us retain our regard for at least one of the heretics by denying with our mouths, but not with our hearts, for it is in the second denial that many of the immediate dangers of the World are to be found. The fact of the matter is that the Theologians are frequently using lies to tell us, for rotten reasons, what is substantially the truth, while the Pragmatists are usually throwing out the bath water without first making sure that they have removed the baby.

Nevertheless, whether young or old, learned or ignorant, rational or sentimental, the paradox propounded by William Blake and Aubrey is still with us, although their expressions of it are unequal in literary merit. And it is not solved by telling us that God is Love. Nor is it illuminated by shouting down sensible enquiries as happened to me in that same Sunday School, when I raised my hand and queried a passage in the Epistle to the Galatians in which we are instructed:

Bear ye one another's burdens.

A few pages on I had distinctly read that, 'Every man shall bear his own burden.' What was to be done about this? Isn't Saint Paul able to make up his mind?

I was brusquely told that the question was a stupid one, that would never have been asked if I knew any Greek. So I never went on to enquire about the four different and conflicting accounts of the Resurrection.

No Names, no Pack Drill

In spite of my very poor showing both in Sunday School and in the presence of Professor Ayer, what I am trying to point out is worth mentioning. Theology, for all its disreputable practices, is often well in advance of our current ways of thought. Solutions to most of these perplexing problems have been bandied about by sensible authorities for centuries past, although they have been generally lost sight of in the common practice of preferring explanations that make the problem harder. In this, the Parsons are just as guilty as the Scientists.

When we Rationalists say that there is no 'God', nor is it a 'He' who can be found 'up there', we are saying no more than does the Shorter Catechism of the Westminster Confession, where this mystery is described as being without parts or passions, infinite, eternal and unchangeable. Could anything be more up-to-date than the age-old insistence of the Jews that, whatever It is, it ought to have no name at all, lest we fall into anthropomorphic ways of thought? It has no proper name that should ever be uttered. In short, it is 'X'.

How many seers and poets have told us that Eternity is not a Time that goes on for ever, but a Time that is All-Time? Heaven and Hell are neither places nor illusions, but Non-places, outside Space as we know it— or alternatively, everlastingly within it. They are not resorts of rewards or of punishments, for whatever Is, is its own perpetual reward and punishment. If we want Peace in our Time, we can get it at once, in the grave. But if we decide to keep on living, we are governed by the inevitability of Conflict, and we will find ourselves sooner or later killing Aubrey's worm, and regretting our behaviour. The idea that we can live without killing is a delusion, as even a good Vegetarian will have to admit. Yet we feel guilty: and by the Gospel according to Sartre, we must feel guilty not only for our own sins, but for everybody else's too. And so we insist on being punished.

The Criminal's Thirst for Punishment

Paradoxically enough, Man on the whole approves of punishment, and particularly so when it applies to himself. Abolish punishments and we also abolish prizes. But much more subtle than this is the widespread view that the payment for Evil by penance, or better still, by the repetition of the offence upon the offender, whether on Earth or in Hell, has the effect of wiping out the crime and leaving the record all square. Or maybe the evil-doer derives some satisfaction from the assurance that, thanks to punishment, he must be a person of some consequence rather than an outcast. Indeed, punishment, as such, shows that he is at one with God and the Courts in his practices.

This may be why criminals so often are more interested in penalties than in reformation; and the way in which this works out is strikingly illustrated by the peculiar service that the Government of Israel performed for the killer Eichmann, by kidnapping him, and putting him through the form of a year-long ritual murder.

It is reasonably certain that Eichmann was an exceedingly guilty person, and few would have felt greatly disturbed if he had been killed in hot blood by some infuriated victim of his abominable prison camps. However, the procedure actually adopted — modelled, one presumes, on some of the precepts of the Old Testament — had the effect of leaving the score, as between Eichmann and Israel, in the nature of a draw, a fact that is not very inspiring to others who may not have undertaken the liquidation of Nazi Germany and the opening of its Dachaus with the object of ending up all square.

It is only fair to point out that the Jews were doing no more than follow the example set by Jahweh. So somewhere in this area lies the source of a deep issue between modern Man and his Command Post (as visualised by the Christian). This seems to have troubled Saint Thomas Aquinas almost as much as it troubles us. For all our fuss about Penance, who wants to serve a God whose answer to Evil is the perpetration of a greater Evil? What sort of a divinity is this? We have surely enough to do in explaining the existence of pain and misery in this world under circumstances that cannot be prevented — circumstances to which we each contribute our quota whether intentionally or not — without being expected to admire a vindictive Creator of a Hell after death, and from our comfortable seats in Paradise, applaud the fact that the damned are being tortured.

The root of the quandary lies, of course, in an assumption that Evil is a flaw in the facts of life as they were originally intended by a well-meaning Deity — an error of construction that binds the Creator as perilously as it binds us. (An interesting parallel is to be found in the arguments offered to Athena by the Furies in the third part of the Orestean Trilogy.) This misconception of the nature and purpose of Evil produces a tension in Man's attitude towards Heaven that cannot be remedied by double-think, and is very bad for him. It is unusually acute at the moment.

This last feature of the logicality of the Christian position, is a reluctant conclusion of Aquinas that most normal believers have long since rejected together with any great regard for the Book of Esther.

> Why is the sheep given to the knife?   (Blake continues)
>   the lamb plays in the sun.
> He starts ! He knows the foot of Man !
>   he says, take thou my wool
> But spare my life, but he knows not
>   that the winter cometh fast.

Here we have Blake propounding, not one human quandary, but two.

The Hell of a Heaven

To the mediaeval mind, the existence of misery in this world was a matter of minor importance. We deserved it as the children of Adam; and in any event, this life was but an ante-chamber to a better or a worse life to come.

Our forefathers did their best to avoid calamity, but if they failed to do so — and in particular if they failed, like Job, under circumstances for which they could not possibly be blamed — they did not think the worse of God on that account, or question his Justice. Nor was this submissiveness merely due to a fear of mentioning the matter. Actually earthly sorrow was not of much importance, since there was always the possibility of an eternity of bliss to make up for any present inconvenience. Indeed, some immediate discomfort might make this all the better.

But today a great part of the race has no belief in a life to come of the kind envisaged as Heaven. Even more significantly it realises that it would probably not enjoy any such paradise of inactivity as is promised to the Elect in the theology of both the Christian and the Mohammedan faiths. It was Shaw who pointed out that eternal rest was a hellish conception of Heaven that could only have been dreamed up by an overworked community. No Sartrean Inferno could ever equal the horrible prospect of an eternity of Time in a Paradise where lambs lie down with lions, while (God save us) a little child leads them.

My daughter at an early age was heard to make an enlightening comment on this prospect of the after-life, and it deserves some serious thought. She said that she didn't think that she would care to go to Heaven, as she might get stuck there. So, too, my mother on her death bed, in one of those moments of complete candour that often occur on such occasions, bitterly denied any belief in a life after death — a thing that she would never have dreamed of saying in her younger, church-going days.

Conditioning for Happiness

But there are even stronger objections to Heaven than a feeling that one might get stuck there. There is an awareness of the fact that so hedonistic a condition is based on an erroneous idea that happiness is a wholly desirable thing, and that sorrow is something to be avoided at all cost as a matter of principle.

In a moment of great inspiration, Cocteau opens the printed version of one of his plays with the following couplet :

> What is ugly is the happiness for which we long.
> What is beautiful is the sorrow that we have.

We must surely be aware of the fact that the normal man seeks most earnestly for something that cannot be described as happiness, but more accurately as a sense of Fulfilment. In this life he usually looks for work and danger quite deliberately, and nothing oppresses him more than the total absence of either. The rich seek both in all sorts of fantastic ways. The poor get more and more bloody-minded — not more and more contented — as they escape from the burden of labour and long hours through the power of collective bargaining.

My point is not that we should desist from bettering ourselves. That would be as absurd as the proposal that we should all bash our heads against walls in order to enjoy the pleasure of not doing so. The proper conclusion is that happiness, although desirable, is not in itself an objective. Like the Music Hall joke, it is a state of mind that is dependent on whatever has gone before — the Conditioning, the latter, of course, being natural and not fabricated. More significant, however, is the fact that no man can say for certain that his life has been better or worse than that of another, if happiness is to be the criterion. A woman lying in the sun on a Riviera beach is just as likely to be miserable as a woman scrubbing floors in London. The man on the pier and the man on the departing ship may have equal cause for envying each other, and for wishing each were in the other's shoes.

Life's greatest menace after Fear and Pain is not misery, but Boredom, and both Sartre and the Subconscious will agree that there is no Hell like a jail where there are no opportunities, and nothing to do but torture others. Boredom is the principal spoiler of middle age, of married life, and even of world peace. In our generation it has been the peculiar curse of the English who deliberately threw away an Empire after experiencing the boredom of winning two wars —two intolerable victories that only appeared to have the effect of justifying an idiotic social system.

'We always muddle through, you know. I suppose it's just part of the British character.'

Boredom grows, rather than diminishes, with efforts to alleviate it through organised entertainment. It is the bane of happily married women, and — genealogically — the eventual ruin of prosperous families.

We cannot be expected, willingly, to go back to overwork and

'I don't want to have a dreary life like father's — going into an office every day. There's more to life than money.'

underfeeding, yet without at least the threat of both, young men and women only get angrier and angrier. Our wives were not really worse off during the war, standing in fish queues, than they are today, being taxied once a week to and from Supermarkets. Or at any rate, they complained less about their fate.

The Return to Pelagianism

But whatever may be the reasons for this general sense of unease and disbelief, not only in a life to come, but in the existence of any intelligible system of rewards and punishments, we have here the same highly menacing situation that heralded the end of Classical civilisation, and a doublethink that was rightly denounced by the firm of Ayer and Laski. We do not believe what we feel we ought to believe in — a state of mind that easily degenerates from double-think into a specious acceptance of Professor Ayer's pragmatic and apparently sensible solution, which — when we come to think it out — is only a return to the heresy of Pelagianism in terms of current philosophy, and is no more satisfactory than the Idealist fallacy. The objection to crime is not that 'it does not pay'. Actually, crime quite frequently does 'pay', on the short haul; and so far as honest merchandise is concerned, many shopkeepers will assure us that it is much easier to prosper by selling the glossy rather than the good.

Where are those Field Equations?

Nobody in his senses is denying the considered wisdom of the race as embodied in a sensible theology. But this does not answer the question as to what existing congregation is offering modern man a frame of reference, based on contemporary experience, into which he can fit everything that he knows to be true (which is not necessarily the same thing as profitable or smooth) and into which everything that he does not know as yet, might be fitted? — a view of life that provides an alternative to the dreary conclusion that existence has got no particular purpose, that there are no rewards or punishments apart from those that happen quite by chance, and that we have a problematical future and an inescapable past, presided over by a God who is either a demon or an incompetent. Or a corpse.

Perhaps it might be said that it is not the business of any Almighty to concern itself overmuch with what in my own profession is laughably called 'Justice'. It ought to have larger calls on its attention than the duties of a Shop Steward. But it is not comforting to arrive at the conclusion that the Divine Image — whatever it is — is quite uninterested in what is generally described as 'Fairness', as appears to be so under present conditions. We gird at the apparent cruelty of a God who seems to lose patience with his dear children from time to time in a very arbitrary way — yes, and in the end slaughters us all quite wantonly, whether in the bloom of youth or at the end of a disillusioned old age.

Meanwhile, throughout our Mortal life, he robs us of a perishable store of years in a way that even a good Catholic like Alexander Pope can take exception to. To Pope, a child begins with everything, but Time filches it all away. Yet — one may reasonably ask — does Time actually steal anything from us, or does it give?

We resent the cruelty of nature, while ignoring the extraordinary generosity of nature — the prodigality of life that pours itself out in fantastic waste all around us, and invites us to do so too.

How often do we ask ourselves what this world would be like without its terrors — and above all, without the acquisition of our father. Adam —

the gift of Death? Or without the services of that worthy scavenger, Aubrey's worm? An Earth crammed with the aged — cluttered with the corpses of the centuries that will not — that cannot — disappear? This is the horror that the medical profession and the embalmers would force upon us permanently, if they were more competent in their jobs.

Our distemper over certain aspects of the Universe around us is understandable in many ways, but it can hardly be described as having been fully argued — least of all if the answer is going to be that our first requirement is to implore forgiveness from some Old Nobodaddy up there, not only for our own inadequacies, but also for the facts of life, which are his affair.

I am fully aware of the riposte, that many of us cherish serious doubts about the existence of any Old Nobodaddy up there. But if elsewhere — in some depth behind what we regard as Here—there is something else— some unnamable 'X' — this might lead us to quite a different set of conclusions.

IV   THE ERYMANTHIAN BOAR

Et spero utrumque venturum esse
in ordine proprio.

The Market for Definitions

BRONOWSKI tells us that he had a small daughter who was attended in her early youth by a doctor who wore a hearing aid. Because of this experience she acquired an unshakable conviction that the badge of a reliable medical man was an apparatus behind the ear — an understandable mistake of a kind to which we are prone at all ages.

From this amusing illustration of one of the problems of Causation, Bronowski goes on to distinguish between the didactic methods in use in the United States and in Great Britain, pointing out that the Englishman tends to arrive at synthetic conclusions after having defined all his terms, while the American is not usually interested in By-laws, but prefers the practical method of asking, Does it work? And if so, How?

Although the death of many a good discussion can be heralded by this demand for Definitions (e.g. What exactly do you mean by Fish?) it seems probable at this point, that we have gone as far as we dare go in the use of undisciplined terms without the permission of Bertrand Russell. (Or maybe I am still just entangled with Cambridge.)

The Statute of Uses

As a law student I was warned many years ago to look with distaste at what is termed a use upon a Use. As a playwright I have sometimes suffered the consequences of trying to make a joke upon a Joke. Probably the soundest objection to Sentimentality lies in the fact that it usually amounts to feeling about Feeling; while the Philosophers offer us a grave example of what occurs if we allow ourselves to be drawn into arguments about Arguments.

So when Heraclitus invites us to discuss with him the problem of whether it is possible to step into the same river twice, let us politely decline the invitation. We know what happens when we step into a river, and we do not need any further information on the matter from Philosophers. Whether it is the same river or a different one, the result is the same. We get our feet wet; and to get tangled up in any discussion as to whether the flow of water gives us the same cold or a different one, is a matter of words about Words — which is what a great number of philosophical bull-sessions amount to.

But when we come to consider what it is that Parmenides means when he avers that nothing changes, or what Robbe-Grillet is getting at when he says that the Past is Now (if, indeed, it is he who is responsible for that particular paradox), it becomes necessary to think about Thought. And the first thing that ought to strike us as peculiar is the fact that it is possible to think about Thought, and that there is evidently something that does so.

We are all acquainted with the situation in which we say to ourselves: Now what will I think about next? After something has decided this question, the obedient mind — sometimes reluctantly — does what it is told. This Something does not appear to be in control during sleep, in consequence of which some mechanical mental operation continues to cerebrate nonsense. When we awake, we find this rubbish encumbering our memories, and we call it Dreams. We may also be acquainted with an even stranger experience in sleep when something becomes aware of the fact that misbehaviour is going on in the abandoned classroom, and intervenes to say: Stop this nonsense at once! Wake up — you are asleep! And one does wake up, so putting an end to these shenanigans of the undirected implement. The vacation is over.

Does this mean that there are two implements for Thought—the bodily machinery that can be conditioned by experience, as the Behaviourists love to insist, and also an inner, master mind that directs the workings of the other, when it is there to do so, and that will occasionally confound the Behaviourists by inducing us to do things that are not under compulsion, and which cannot be accounted for by conditioning?

We know that the part cannot comprehend the whole, yet the Psychologist can contemplate himself. Evidently the person to whom we are expected to pay those extravagant fees is not the whole. Who or what thinks about the Psychologist's psychology? There is clearly a Pentagon behind the Headquarters in the head, that is not concerned with tactics, but with strategy.

We will go into this further at a later stage. In the meantime, let us merely relate this phenomenon to Hegel's view, that there is a universal and absolute Mind to which our individual, physical grey matter pays its humble duty. But although it is not helpful to proceed from here to a discussion of Quantum Mechanics — as Sir James Jeans does — it is appropriate to spend a few moments in considering what precisely we mean by this observation of Observation, and what is implied by the word Absolute, which is insinuating itself more and more into the conversation as a result of our investigation of the Observer.

The Observer — a Cosmic Nuisance

As all Observers with whom we are likely to be in touch are in substantially the same cosmic location as that in which we are ourselves, it is not unreasonable to make didactic statements that are based upon our common experience. We can agree with our neighbours, for example, on what 'c' amounts to in miles per second, and this figure is, in that sense, an Absolute. But it is what we must call a Qualified Absolute, since another Observer, elsewhere (or close at hand but with a markedly different direction to his world line) might report otherwise — if we were in a position to hear what he says. This divergence of opinion, however, is usually concerned with verbs — with what an object is doing, rather than what it is.

If we agree with Bergson that there is nothing to any object apart from what it is doing, we must stop at this point, since everything — being a matter of some aspect of Becoming (according to Bergson) must be in the qualified category. But if we are rude enough to push the Observer off the stage, and to insist — as I have been suggesting — that all objects exist independently of the fact of being looked at, we may then validly describe ourselves as Realists, and regard their qualities (as distinct from their behaviour) as Unqualified Absolutes. They *are*, and that is all that can be said about them.

This distinction between the qualified and the unqualified is not limited to objects that might be described as being 'in action', but applies to the vagaries of observation itself. A catastrophic change in the position of the Earth's Pole would alter the respective latitudes of London and Edinburgh, but it would not affect their distance apart, or their geographical relationship to anywhere else on the Earth's surface. These are unqualified Absolutes, but their respective coordinates, which depend upon a frame of reference between Pole and Equator, are qualified.

No particular virtue should be attached to either adjective. His Lordship of Cloyne was perfectly justified in arguing on behalf of the egocentricity of observation. The Looker-On has nobody except himself, and there is nothing absurd in his regarding himself as the centre of his universe of Awareness, so long as he remembers that he is not at the centre of a universe of Fact. Much of our confusion is caused by our failure to make this distinction, and by denigrating out of habit either the qualified or the unqualified. But it will have been noted that even Dr. Zophar of M.I.T. made use of the distinction when driven into a corner in Chapter Two.

The Fallacy of Postponement

Another expression that will require some definition before we pass on to obligatory matters, is the word 'Postponement'. By this is meant the dialectic trick of pretending to solve a problem by repeating the original dilemma in other terms that leave us precisely where we were to begin with. One of the examples that immediately come to mind is the answer that some of our flat-earth ancestors used to give when enquiries were made as to what it is that holds up the Terra Firma?

A giant, said some inspired cosmologist. What is more, we can tell you his name, which proves that we know what we are talking about. It is Atlas. He holds the Earth upon his shoulders, and this is what makes the Terra firm.

But then some tiresome sceptic came along and wanted to know what is making Atlas firm? What is he standing on? Nothing daunted, an answer was produced. Atlas is standing on the backs of two elephants. (At least I think that was the reply.) But whatever it was, it is of little account, as it only led to the further enquiry, what are the elephants on? On the back of a very large tortoise — and so on, through an endless zoological garden, without any prospect of ever finding a way out, since each answer continued to harbour the essence of the original problem.

In more recent days the idea of a Heaven elsewhere, with a Time outside Time that we call Eternity, presents us with much the same kind of non-answer as to what was before 'Time' and what will be after it — each interrogatory carrying in its mouth a time answer about Time, and a place answer about Place.

Serial Time, as described by Dunne, is largely a repetition of the same trick, with an escape hatch called Infinity. Indeed, it is fair to say that any answer with a practical application in which Infinity is required, below the level of what will shortly be described as a Sixth Dimension, should be regarded with the same suspicion, in so far as it is supposed to convey any actual information outside the realm of mathematical theory.

It is true that a reasonable objection may be made to this objection to double-talk by asking whether the conception of Dimension behind Dimension that is being advanced here is not itself an example of Postponement? Is Postponement not Postponement if we choose to call a halt to the progression after a few briskly incomplete explanations of the explanations?

The reply to such a question depends upon whether a series is actually leaving us precisely where we began, or whether it is leading us to an ultimate level at which the question itself becomes unnecessary. The fact that we object to the use of Infinity as a way out from a mathematical impasse in some theoretical, lower-key situation, does not mean that the expression is inadmissable in a dimension where, being an Entirety, quantitative measurements have consequently become pointless.

So also, when it is suggested that Activity is not an expression of Mechanics but of Observation, the fact that this remark does not answer the further enquiry, What is Observation?, does not affect the validity of the original statement that has been made, not about Observation, but about Activity. Most answers to problems concerned with matters of large significance invite a further question that we may or may not be equipped to face. Actually, Man should never expect anything in the nature of final knowledge from the reply to any of his questions: so if he solves one problem only by coming face to face with a more difficult one, he is not being guilty of postponement by going as far as he can go. All that is being objected to here is the circular solution that simply leads back to the original query.

How Many Dimensions?

This point having been made, let us now turn our attention to the matter of the dimensions of the Cosmos, and of how many of them are necessary. Our school geometries used to stop at three, for reasons presumably dictated by Euclid. These were Length, Breadth, and Thickness. But from an early age, an interest in the tantalising subject of Axioms, Cuts and QEDs, included some speculation on our part as to why there should only be three different right-angle directions from any given point — if indeed this was the case. As the years passed and

Geometry has always struck me as being a subject filled with useful information and intellectual excitement. Algebra, on the other hand, is about nothing in particular, and consequently has been for me, a field of enormous boredom that cannot be enlivened even by Dr. Synge. It is merely a game with adjectives.

we progressed from the third to the sixth form, rumours began to filter through that, according to the latest view, there was indeed a further right angle in which a more subtle and fourth dimension might lie. A new and necessary feature of the landscape had appeared in the calculations of the Wranglers and of the pioneers of a new Physics.

But before discussing this number Four, it should be pointed out with regard to the more familiar dimensions, that an evolutionary element applies to our appreciation of each of them, and that what the Observer comprehends of each depends upon his faculties. Whatever he is un-equipped to observe, he calls 'Time'.

Vegetable life, which has no faculties for vision or for volitional move-ment, exists in a Universe of no dimensions, in which the only awareness is of the passage of Time. A sightless creature, burrowing through the earth, or moving through the depth of the sea, may be conscious of dis-tance travelled and of a change of location, but not very seriously of Right and Left or of Up and Down — a one dimensional condition, where linear progress may be measured, but where all the rest is Time. A creature endowed with flat sight can see in these last four directions — a two dimensional picture to which we can limit ourselves by the act of closing one eye. But if such an animal could express any idea of the distance to that hill over there, its description would have to take the form of an estimate of how long it should take to get there — five minutes trot — a Time statement, that may still be seen on signposts in certain parts of the Continent : — HAFELEKAR — 3 St.

But man, with his stereoscopic sight, is equipped to see in depth, and can give a rough estimate of the breadth of a river without actually swimming across with a tape measure between his teeth.

This enigmatic information means that there is an estimated three hour climb to the summit. It has a peculiarly irri-tating effect upon those of us who propose to take our leisure on the journey, rather than be hurried by energetic Civil Servants.

Nevertheless his organs of vision can take him no further than to a third dimension, and any more subtle extension of what he is looking at — for example, the previous conditions of the object of his attention — is regarded as being related to Time. Indeed, he probably does not consider that these non-contemporaneous states constitute a physical dimension at all. If he is an unrelenting Idealist he will even have difficulty in conceiving of them as existing because they are not Now, and are therefore unassisted into the realm of reality by his necessary attention. So he will usually regard any extension beyond the third as something mystical — another world inhabited by memories and dream figures. Or else he will concede enough to the Mathematicians to admit it as an algebraic formula, described as Space/Time.

On Comprehending a Fourth Dimension

However, if we are in agreement about the mutual independence of existence and perception, it ought to be possible for us to comprehend the nature of this unfamiliar 4D field without the depressing intervention of any mathematics at all. We can regard it not merely as a formula, but as a fact, thanks to the assistance of the late Mr. H. G. Wells in one of his earlier works of Science-Fiction called *The Time Machine*. That there is a good deal more fiction than science in that book must be admitted. Nevertheless Wells does offer an argument that is good enough to start from.

A line — we are told — which has length but no breadth and a square which has length and breadth but no thickness, are mere geometrical expressions of quantity and shape that, however informative they may be, do not exist in any physical sense apart from the object to which they apply, and should not be confused with it. Semantically speaking, expressions such as length, breadth and squareness are not nouns in their own right, but are merely adjectival. If we add length to breadth, and thickness to length and breadth, we are in each case adding a dimension, not to the measurement, but to our conception of the object itself.

The question must then be answered as to whether three assessments of size and shape are sufficient to give a complete quantitative account of whatever it is that is under observation? Wells says No, because of the fact that, so far, all that we have been describing is what he would call an 'instantaneous solid'. And by making use of four dimensional symbols in their calculations, the Mathematicians are apparently supporting the view that three dimensions are not enough.

What then are they measuring when they add a fourth? Wells takes the view that an 'instantaneous solid' has got no more practical reality than has a line or a square. In fact, whatever is observable at all, even if only for long enough to be measured, must have a Persistence in Space/Time in addition to its lower dimensions, for without this element, even a too-too solid Cube remains in the category of a purely Euclidean proposition.

Mathematically speaking, this is entirely in keeping with Minkowski's insistence that a set of spatial measurements limited to three dimensions only is as incomplete as is a mere quantitative assessment of an object's capability for persistence. These two elements must

Minkowski stated in Cologne as long ago as 1908: 'Henceforth Space by itself and Time by itself are doomed to fade away into mere shadows and only a kind of union of the two, will preserve an independent reality.'

be combined in order to give the object 'independent reality'. In going on to apply the expression 'world line' to this combination of four components — Length, Breadth, Thickness and Persistence — Einstein is in effect answering the question as to what it is that is being measured when four dimensional calculations are in use. It amounts to a set of four extensions, the last of which is just as much a physical quantity as are the other three, in spite of the fact that we are unequipped to study it visually.

A celebrated effort was made by a painter called Duchamp to break open the aperture that we call the Present, and to express four dimensional extension in terms of visual Art. His picture is called *Nude descending a Staircase*, and it can be seen in Philadelphia. It is not wholly successful in attempting to give a composite view of more Nows than one, for the obvious reason that the artist is trying to represent on a field of two dimensions something that we have no means of seeing at all — even in three dimensions. It requires a new form of perspective that cannot be expressed visually, and for which no conventional method of depiction has yet been worked out. Possibly the best model for such an extension is to be found in a strip of cinematograph film — a series of pictures of the same scene in a directed order of Nows, which we can hold in our hands and view as a series of States, rather than place it in a projector, thereby limiting ourselves to one frame at a time, but giving this the appearance of motion.

But this, too, gives an inadequate idea of the nature of 4D, since its extension is presumably no more a series of disconnected conditions than is the length of a line. It has a continuous existence, making it impossible to insist that at any particular point one state ends and the next begins. Any variations of state appear to us as the phenomenon of motion, thanks to the changing position of observation. This semblance of what we call movement in the physical world is brought about by the fact that the world lines of observable objects do not necessarily lie in the same direction as that in which our observation is proceeding. The greater this divergence, the greater the apparent activity, until beyond an angle of 90° the latter reduces itself again, the difference being that what has been an impression of movement developing into the Future, now becomes the culmination of a series of conditions that we may have already experienced in the past. (See the Stuckelberg Effect as discussed in Appendix D.)

MARCEL DUCHAMP
NUDE DESCENDING STAIRCASE NO. 2
Philadelphia Museum of Art. Louise and Walter Arensberg Collection.

This absence of visual assessment is probably at the back of Eddington's determination to confine yards and metres strictly to statements about the first three Dimensions, while presenting the fourth in terms of what it *does* rather than what it *is*. Herein lies another source of much of the confusion of thought that follows in the whole field of dimensional measurements. For surely to switch our standards from extension to performance in this arbitrary manner is rather like saying that one gets out of bed in the morning with three things — two legs and a cramp — a couple of centrifugal statements that do not add up at all. The first is anatomical while the other is therapeutic, and although both pieces of information may be true, they are no more related to each other than are ten miles an hour and a horseshoe, which do not add up to eleven. A schoolboy asks what is it that has four legs and flies? The answer — two pairs of pants — makes a joke out of the same comic shuffling of parts of speech.

See also *Particles beyond the Light Barrier* by the Physicists Bilaniuk and Sudarshan of Swarthmore and Syracuse Colleges respectively, in the issue for May 1969 of *Physics Today*, together with a number of interesting comments in the December number. Also see the marginal below in Appendix D. The existence of Tachyons (superluminal particles) is not inconsistent with the views expressed by Einstein on the upward limit to velocity. On the contrary, it confirms them.

If a World Line is an extension — and for what else was the expression coined — it must surely be measured (if measurable at all) by the same standards that apply to the other three: and if this means that our own World Lines extend by so many Parsecs to our respective births, we might be well advised to accept this statement realistically, since the fact that our telescopes cannot be turned in that peculiar direction is no reason for an arrogant assumption that what we cannot see, cannot exist — particularly when Mathematics insists that it must. All that we see is whatever is visible through the Derrynane Slit — the Present. So, like other Observers even less equipped than we are, we apply the word 'Time' to a physical extension that we cannot see and report on visually, but which nevertheless has got to be recognised if we ever hope to make head or tail of the current evidence.

The standard view at the moment is that a World Line is merely a graph or diagram showing the course along which a three-dimensional object is supposed to be 'moving' through Space/Time. The host of problems that immediately springs at our throats from this sort of jungle has in its forefront the obvious objection that any sort of 'Movement' implies Time, and as Time is already embodied in the definition of Space/Time through which this 'movement' is supposed to be taking place, the word is being used twice in two ways at once, which makes nonsense of the remark.

The probable reason for this type of absurdity is an understandable fear that if it is ever agreed to regard a World Line as a tangible extension stretching back into the Past, it will not be long before we are being told— following the same argument — that it extends into the Future too. And then where are we? Back into Rutherford's discarded receptacle, if not into Bildad's abominable box — chained hand and foot to a determined Future — a conclusion that is not only undesirable, but is 'contrary to human experience'.

It seems to be essential to our sanity to regard the Past as fixed and beyond the reach of any rascality promoted by Signor Pirandello & Co., while the Future must remain open and unpredictable if we are to account for the phenomenon of human choice that we all experience, and for the responsibility that most of us desire, outside the slum areas of the Psychology Departments. Therefore — as Bragg insists — something must be happening to our World Lines at Now — some process of change from intangible Possibility into irrevocable Fact, rather than a grim unveiling of the Inevitable.

It is in the midst of this thicket of Philosophy-cum-Physics that we find many perfectly reasonable Scientists abandoning the hard-won concepts of Space/Time and clutching vainly at the retreating coattails of Sir Isaac Newton. Others give it a second thought — amongst them Mr. Martin Gardner who, in *Relativity for the Million*, makes the following frank admission :

> Strictly speaking one should not say that an object moves along its World Line because "movement" implies movement in time, whereas time is already represented by the World Line.

Yet he goes on to commit something very like this offence which he has warned us against when he adds :

> An object moving in a random, unpredictable way can be graphed by a world line just as easily as an object moving in a predictable way. After an event has occurred its Minkowski graph does indeed freeze it in a timeless "block Universe", but this has no bearing on the question of whether an event had to happen exactly as it did.

Without spending any more effort in attempting to analyse these earnest manoeuvres to keep World Lines out of the future, let it be emphasised that Science is doing no more than trying to avoid horrendous conclusions. We hope, however, to be able to show that there is actually no occasion for any panic in our pursuit of this admirable end. Nobody is going to suggest in these pages that the human performer has no say in his own destiny. Heisenberg has effectively placed a road block on the route to any such undesirable destination, as we have already seen. And we can thank God for Heisenberg, notwithstanding any distress that he may have caused to our friend Albert Einstein.

As it turns out, there is nothing at all inconsistent in the latter's determined Cosmos (which is an expression of fact) and the former's description of the unpredictable behaviour of the Atom (which is a feature of observation). So we need not allow any philosophical or religious qualms to drive us into talking nonsense.

If we take the trouble to collate some further information from the current output of the Laboratories, we may discover that what we are faced with is not the bleak and hellish face of a single Fate, but a Future that may be regarded not only as real but also as multiple. It is not the multiple extension of World Lines into a 4D Future — and indeed, back into the Past as well — that is unpredictable, but the more personal question as to what channel of the delta of Alternation we choose to select for our wandering attention.

Remove that Man !

It is probable that most of the Scientists of today will find little that is unacceptable in this realist description of four-dimensional extension, except possibly my insistence on the importance of an absolute statement that is not dependent on the presence of an Observer, and the suggestion that it should be measured in linear terms like any other extension. Most of the instinctive opposition to my evident distaste for the intrusion of 'appearance' where expressions of independent Fact are being called for, is not really a scientific reaction at all, but has other considerations behind it.

Most people have no aversion to the idea of a permanent, physical existence for the Past. We probably like the Past, and it is a not unpleasing thought that the days of our youth, as well as the Dead whom we feel have been taken from us, are just as real as we are ourselves. They just happen to be elsewhere in Space/Time, and any difficulty in our enjoying them here and now is not a matter of total disappearance, but is merely a problem of communication — something that might remedy itself under certain circumstances.

But more of this later. It is the grim prospect of a predetermined and unavoidable Future that we are entitled to be leery about, as it calls in question any purpose in life, and makes nonsense of all our efforts to arrive at intelligent decisions.

But suppose we refuse to halt at the four dimensional terminus indicated by Minkowski, now that we have been got on the move — perhaps we might find that the facts of life have an encouraging way of turning out to be not so crazy after all, and that Responsibility can be rediscovered just around the next corner. Having been led by the Mathematicians to accept the idea of a further dimension against our natural inclinations, suppose we pay them back by insisting on taking it seriously — not as an exercise in Algebra but as a tangible fact? Suppose we ignore the circumlocutions of the High Table on the subject of curvature and, sticking firmly to the simple axiom that curvature is curved, proclaim a common sense view that this element is a necessary element of extension? (Aren't we behaving very like those abominable Lollards?) Not for us — we state — is there to be any return to a twentieth century repetition of Dante's Geography with its absurd Edges or meaningless Infinity.

Suppose instead we revive that intelligible concept of Einstein and his friends—following in the footsteps of the great Copernicus — that the shape of all Creation is spherical. (And let it be remembered that Copernicus did not limit his remark merely to the shape of the Earth.)

As long ago as 1543 Copernicus wrote thus : First of all we assert that the Universe is spherical; partly because this form being a complete whole needing no joints, is the most perfect of all; partly because it constitutes the most spacious form which is thus best suited to contain and retain all things . . . or because all things tend to assume the spherical shape, a fact which appears in a drop of water and in any other fluid bodies when they seek of their own account to limit themselves.

Shape

It is not easy to conjure up a mental picture of four dimensional Space/Time, but it is not impossible. And it is certainly easier to grasp than is a phenomenon that only exists as an expression of its own measurements. The only other alternative offered so far by the Laboratories is a curvature that is not 'positive' (that is to say, that turns in on itself), but is 'negative' — meaning that the Universe is 'saddle-shaped', which so far from avoiding a problem of Infinity, presents us with multiple Infinities, all curving away in multiple directions.

This must be a prize example of an answer designed to render the problem quite insoluble, and the cause of this reluctance to approach anything fairly obvious is probably rooted in the fact that a Sphere is not merely a round surface, as it is commonly supposed to be, but is a solid. And if so, of what does the thickness consist? Has it but one surface — the 4D Universe? Or, regardless of the length of its Radius, should it be regarded as the aggregate of a series of concentric surfaces extending outwards from the centre, each presenting the features of a curved Continuum, as the segment of a sliced Cube may present that of a two dimensional square? However this is not the place to go into such matters, when Appendices are available. (See Appendix G.) What I am suggesting here, as being the most obvious basis for objection is the fact that a four dimensional Universe of spherical shape clearly requires the recognition of a Fifth Dimension.

A Fifth Dimension?

There is nothing new about this further step. Indeed we are told by Bonner that Einstein was toying with it nearly sixty years ago as a means of solving some of the outstanding calculations that were encumbering his General Theory. He only abandoned this glittering denouement to his investigations — we are told — because he felt that, like his Cosmological Constant, it was liable to lead to another situation 'contrary to human experience' — as indeed it does, at first blush. Had he not already been induced to abandon quite enough in the face of evidence that the Universe is expanding? And if what we are wandering in now is no longer a realm of factual extension at all, but is truly one of Pure Mathematics — an Inferno of measurements of Nothing, how dare we complicate matters still further by introducing a Fifth Dimension? This is truly what only Alice could recognise — a smile without a Cat.

But just a minute: Is this not just another difficulty that is creating itself by the form of its own question? Let us pause and consider what the consequences would actually be if the Universe should indeed turn out to be a five dimensional Sphere. Would the outstanding issues be simplified, or the reverse?

The Poles of the Universe

To begin with, we will see that on this basis, the lower Derrynane sheet on which World Lines extend, is not flat as we assumed it to be, but is curved, and the analogy of the movement of the slit in the upper sheet over its surface could be better expressed by considering what happens when a sphere is dipped into a bucket of water. The plane of the surface of the water, as it travels up the curved surface of a sphere, represents the movement of the slit of Observation that we call Now, while a cross-section of any particular Meridian that it has reached is what we know as Here.

The important thing to note in this new model of the Derrynane Effect is that the whole operation has now been given an element of polarity, created at the point on the sphere which first touches the water, and from which it continues to descend. In simpler language, a spherical Universe in the eyes of the Observer, has now got a Pole, the position of which is determined by the direction in which the plane of his attention is moving over its surface.

While applying the same geometrical laws to 3D, 4D and 5D that we are accustomed to apply to 1D, 2D and 3D, it is important to remember that a World Line is a four dimensional phenomenon, and that its direction in that field must not be confused with any 3D angle at which its cross sections may happen to lie in the visible World. The 4D angle of a World Line takes visual form to us as the apparent velocity of the System concerned.

Alternation

There are two other matters that immediately come to mind when considering this image of a 5D Cosmos. The first is the need of a name for the extension in depth of World Lines in the 5D fabric of the Cosmos, which has been referred to briefly on page 77 and will appear again in greater detail in Appendix G. At the moment, it should be sufficient to say that, to avoid confusion with lower forms of solidity such as the thickness of the Earth, it is here proposed to use the word 'Alternation' to indicate five dimensional extension in depth — or in less elevated language, into or outwards from the belly of the Cosmos.

The other matter is about something that is far more pressing. In dismissing Time as defined by Wells, and relegating this conception to that of a 4D linear extension, we have not managed to dispose of it altogether.

Indeed, all that we have done so far is to postpone the answer to another dimension. It is true that in doing so we have settled some of the difficulties raised by Zeno and Parmenides,
who desired an answer to the question as to how inanimate Matter can be said to 'move' at all? We have now replied by saying that it doesn't. But even if nothing is actively taking place outside the carriage window, we cannot ignore the fact that something is being done by the train. We must not fail to comment on the movement of the slit. Observation moves.

This 'movement' may also appear as Growth or Decay in a World Line that does not move elsewhere, but remains substantially in parallel with that of the Observer.

If we continue to insist that any sort of activity is an aspect of angular extension in a further dimension, we have still to provide a dimension for the movement of observation. If 'Time' requires time in which to operate, it is certain that we have not as yet arrived at an understanding of what it actually is. We have probably managed to pinpoint some of the problems presented by the apparent behaviour of the physical cosmos, by separating them from quite a different phenomenon — the activity of observation. But we have not yet accounted for either Time or the Observer. The countryside may no longer be in a state of inexplicable liveliness; but what about the Engine Driver?

Indeed, I am afraid that we are going to require a sixth dimension, in order to deal with these outstanding matters, which are otherwise unescapable.

The Sixth Dimension

We dare not call any such further extension a Continuum, although we can happily make use of the expression in connection with the other five. At the moment all that can be said about 6D is that it is logically and mathematically necessary to account for the phenomenon of Happening. We have now reached the Olympian level at which it is necessary to put in the verbs — not as a description of the physical Cosmos, but of the most miraculous aspect of life, the 4D behaviour of Awareness.

The sixth dimension may be described as the level where all Times are Now and all Places are Here — the realm of Dunne's Ultimate Observer and of the all-embracing Infinity that is unmeasurable as a Continuum, because it is a Totality. Ouspensky touches on this conception of a final dimension, though only briefly, and without any real analysis of its implications. It is actually something so like the definition of God as given in the Shorter Catechism, that we seem to have got back again to Theology by a route pointed out to us by the Mathematicians.

This is a very odd state of affairs, but it may explain why, heretofore, I have made a point of avoiding the common 3D expression, 'Movement' altogether, when referring to whatever it is that Observation does, and have suggested, instead, that — like the Holy Ghost — it 'proceeds'.

It will also have been noticed that, for the sake of clarity, I have already been using different words to distinguish the fields of physical extension themselves. When speaking three dimensionally, we shall continue to refer to the *Earth*. The *Universe* is a convenient expression to employ when referring to the 4D Continuum — the extension that curves, and to all that extends in it, including the countless number of world-lines. As for the more subtle extension enabling its curvature, I think that we had better continue to use the word *Cosmos*, when speaking of the 5D globe, and in particular of its solidity.

Why Stop at Six?

It will have been seen how 4D is necessary to account for the anachronisms of 3D, and how it also becomes essential to add a fifth to the fourth, and even a sixth to the fifth. But there is no need to continue this process of piling up dimensions indefinitely. Six dimensions, I would suggest, turn out to be quite enough to encompass the physical nature and behaviour of all things so far as Homo Sapiens is concerned, together with the all-encompassing awareness of an Ultimate Observer. As a description of any 'going on for ever' of any lower dimensional phenomenon, Infinity is a meaningless alibi that is usually trotted out to get the Mathematicians out of an impasse. But there is not the same objection to its use under circumstances that are not amenable to measurement at all. In fact there is no other word that *could* be applied to the condition of All-now and All-here that we find in the all-comprehending Sixth Dimension. Such a condition implies the only really intelligible description of Infinity, and the same point may be raised in connection with the absurdity of giving a Proper Name to 'X'. To do so, implies that 'X' is a person who it is necessary to distinguish from other persons by means of a name. (The same fallacy is intrinsic in the verbiage of the First Commandment, which assumes that there *could* be any 'other God before Me'.)

If there are any further dimensions applicable to experiences that are beyond the comprehension of our faculties, they have nothing to do with us, and are none of our business. The God of Yesterday we may confidently discard. The God of Tomorrow we may prepare to welcome with Faith and Good Will. But he who presumes to investigate — much less live with the God of the Day after Tomorrow, will be lucky if he keeps his reason.

Order versus Direction

The Cosmos as unashamedly presented so far in terms of quantitative extension must be regarded not only as linear but also as reversible — as all unqualified Absolutes are. By this I mean that whatever way we look on it is a matter of convention, and an expression of Order. This is a term that must be distinguished from its opposite number — Direction.

If we take the series A-B-C-D-E we will agree, I am sure, that nothing is expressed apart from Order, which is, in effect, no more than a list, and as such harbours no mystery. The Russian alphabet has got some letters of its own, and those that are common to both the Russians and ourselves are not always in the same order in each tongue. Yet both series are alphabets, and neither can be described as intrinsically right, or 'better' than the other. We can put B between D and E if we choose, without altering the essential nature of the series as a list. The only thing that can be said of the arrangement is that it is an expression of Order.

On the other hand, if we take the series 0-1-2-3-4 quite a different condition prevails. For whatever these figures may represent or are related to, their order is not a matter of convention (apart from the element of inductive definition), and cannot be altered without destroying the nature of the series. Whatever it stands for, three must always come between two and four. There is a quantitative and unescapable difference between four and zero. Therefore this series must be said to have Direction, and whether this quality be diminishing or increasing or even oscillating, the fact of direction is absolute. It is this feature that puts us on safer ground with a quantitative statement than with a kinematic one.

It should be noted that Direction, in the sense in which the word is being used here, does not necessarily imply anything in the nature of movement. If we consider a meridian on the Earth's surface, it may be said that all locations that lie along it show a general direction from the arctic to the tropical, or vice versa, according to the way *you* are going. It will also be noticed that in this very analogy, the conception of Direction is being used in two different ways. It may refer to the quantitative changes in temperature at various points of the extension. This is objective, and has nothing to do with any journey. On the other hand we have the Direction in which an Observer is proceeding, while studying the above. This is subjective, and clearly has got a lot to do with movement. Consequently another word is necessary to distinguish the new familiar direction of Procession — a 5D operation — from the less obvious process of change — the non-moving but altering qualities in a series that extends in 4D.

If this sounds unintelligible, imagine yourself climbing a mountain. First of all there is your own general direction, which is one of movement — Up. There is also a different form of direction — that of a series representing the various altitudes at which you stand on the mountain itself. These tend to be higher as you go up and lower as you go down. In other words these figures have a quantitative direction that is not simply an expression of movement on the part of the mountain or of yourself. What is more important still is the fact that such Direction is not an unalterable rule, but is governed by Probability. You may go down for a while but your general movement, and the numerical altitudes at which you are panting, are more likely to be rising.

The name that we will here apply to this type of Direction was invented by Clausius in the middle of the nineteenth century and was defined by him as 'the transformation content of a system'. The word is Entropy, and we will hope to have a less formidable description of what it means before we have gone very much further. Eddington attempts to clarify it by using the model of a pack of cards. When it comes from the manufacturers, it is organised in suits and numbers. But then some divine hand commences to shuffle the pack, so introducing disorganisation. Eddington then applies this analogy to an observable quality of the Universe — that it appears to be changing under the influence of Entropy from a highly organised and concentrated state to a greater and greater condition of dispersal.

This is not stated as a matter of logical necessity, but of observable fact; and if you do not agree, Eddington will invite you to unburn a piece of paper. It is quite correct to say that you will find great difficulty in reorganising it.

This illustration from a pack of cards is not actually as specious as it appears to be at first sight. It might be said that the original organisation of a pack of cards is as arbitrary a matter as the order of the letters in the alphabet. But although it is a matter of indifference in what order the suits are placed in the pack, there is at least a grouping of the cards in four categories, and within these categories they also follow a direction based upon their numbers. So there is an organisation in the original arrangement of the pack, which may be based upon arbitrary principles, but which is none the less an organisation.

But can it then be said that, once one starts to shuffle the pack, dis-organisation not only appears, but also increases? Can one say that it becomes more and more disorganised? I think that one may — again on the basis of probability. The pack may for a time display the wreckage of order: 'This pack is badly shuffled.' And although there is a mathematical possibility that one might reshuffle it back into the original order, this eventuality is not very likely. It is more probable that repeated shuffling will continue to have an effect until no card has any organisational con-nection with either of the adjacent ones. This state of affairs illustrates, with a fair amount of validity, a phrase that we will be applying to the condition of disorganisation at the level of the Cosmic Equator — 'an ultimate state of dispersal'.

We must admit, however, that the possibility that we might happen to shuffle the pack back into order makes it clear that Entropy is not unreversible. In climbing our mountain we may find ourselves going down from time to time. So in the words of Boltzman (1872) the individual steps of Entropy are governed, not by inflexible law, but by Probability, which makes no difference to the fact that there *is* a general sense of direction. It is even possible temporarily to reverse Entropy by mechanical means — a feat that we perform whenever we make ice cubes for our cocktails. Refrigeration is a reversal of Entropy — a truism that is indicated by the fact that it requires much less complicated apparatus to cook than to freeze.

Entropy in Human Experience

I have gone into this matter at some length because of the fact that, in our various attempts to discuss the nature of Time, we are only too ready to use that word when what we are talking about is Entropy.

If Time were a mere matter of four dimensional extension in the Well-sean sense, measurable not in inches but by clocks as Eddington would have it, our experiences would be reversible, which they are not. When a politician tells us that we 'cannot put back the clock' and we ask him why, he will probably answer 'Because of Progress, which we are all in favour of.' A more correct answer would be, 'Because of Entropy, which we cannot permanently avoid.'

Before my first son was born, I remember sitting in the Nursing Home and gazing at his vacant cot. What ought to be more melancholy than the spectacle of the empty basket of my son and heir — a baby that is not? Were he lost to me through death, I would probably be in tears over the sight of this receptacle. Yet, in a sense, he was also lost to me through not yet being born. If Time-order were reversible, how distressed I would feel. But it is not reversible, thank God, and so the occasion was quite a jolly one for everybody, except of course for the mother.

The reality of this absolute difference between the Past and the Future — as unescapable as the difference between 2 and 5 — is familiar to us in terms of human experience in that sense of inevitable change that we all know — the change being in a direction over which we are fully aware that we have no control.

It is also interesting to note that, while Procession has no known beginning and no known end — probably because it is available permanently wherever an instrument of Observation is functioning — Entropy may originate from Zero or terminate in Zero, and may to this extent, be closed at one end, as in the series 0-1-2-3-etc.

History may seem to repeat itself, but never quite in the same way. Like the orbit of a 4D particle, its world line does not circle, but follows, instead, in 4D, the locus of the point P Sine Alpha, which I understand from Father Eliphaz of Bowdoin is the correct definition of a corkscrew (and much good may it do him the next time he wants a drink).

Anyhow we have in Entropy a useful word to apply to the phenomenon already described as 'the running down of the Universe' — a sinister expression that seems to imply a slow and lingering death for everything. What it more cheerfully amounts to is the simple fact of 4D direction on a probability basis, from a state of concentration at the Cosmic Pole, to one of ultimate dispersal at the Cosmic Equator, with you and me observing the process somewhere in the middle.

Entropy distinguished from Procession

For reasons that should become clearer at a later stage, I would like to underline now an important difference between Entropy and Procession, and show why the advance of the former from Pole to Equator must present the effect of slowing down, while the latter can proceed at a uniform rate. This is largely a matter of understanding the dimension in which each operates. A diagram is offered below which may help to make the point clear.

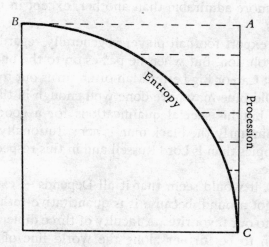

Visual perception, being dependent upon Light signals, does not conform to the curvature of the 3D surface of the Earth. Hence the horizon. Light waves, like Radio signals, lie in space, and curve with the medium in which they lie — which is in 4D. In the same way, Procession, being a 5D phenomenon, does not conform to the curvature of 4D, the continuum of which is represented by the curve BC. Entropy, on the other hand, is an expression of Direction on this curve, and its apparent speed is conditioned by the projection of the speed of Procession (down the line AC) upon the curve BC. It will be seen at once that the speed of such a projection is much greater in the neighbourhood of B (the cosmic Pole) than at C (the cosmic Equator), where its rate of advance conforms eventually to that of Procession.

It should be kept in mind therefore, that Entropy is slowing down, which means in turn that all expressions of movement (including the speed of Light) taking place on the 4D continuum (BC) are qualified by the Observer's position on the line AC, or in other words by his cosmic Latitude.

Entropy as a Yardstick for Evolution

Entropy, apart from its scientific importance, has got a social aspect that is of interest. It is the only viable yardstick that can be applied to what we like to think of as evolutionary progress. We realise nowadays that it is very questionable to lay down the law on the topic of what type of human being is more admirable than another, except in the most crudely functional terms.

At school, an expert football player is generally regarded by his chums as the goal of Evolution. But when he passes on to the business of earning a living, the First Cap or Big Letter Man often turns out to be a very lowly specimen. The Old Blue may have done well enough in the hey-day of the Colonial Office, but his special qualifications for a good job are not so obvious today. Similarly the black man is constitutionally better equipped for life in the tropics than is Lord Russell and in this respect he is definitely the superior type.

So here again, it would seem that it all Depends — except in one way that cannot be got around, because it is quantitative rather than a matter for prize-giving to our favourites. A faculty of three dimensional awareness is almost certain to be further along the world line of a species in the direction of Entropy than is an awareness of only two.

In this respect it is more 'advanced'. No moral judgements need be attached to this distinction between one form of life and another. I am not even suggesting that the fact of being further along in the direction of Entropy is a good or a bad thing. I merely say that it imports a distinction that cannot be ignored as a fact, any more than the fact that it is a characteristic of adolescence (early Entropy) rather than of Maturity (later Entropy) to be unable to distinguish between Reality and Appearance, and indeed, to show a certain complacency over this form of myopia.

Time Out

As a result of these distractions, we have not yet got around to the major problem of deciding just what is meant by 'Time'. This may partly be due to the fact that we have been plagued with too many contradictory meanings by the various authorities, who are often quite ready, in parallel with their own information, to hint that the word is an unscientific expression in any case.

It is only too easy to dismiss Time as something that has been wound up by God at the beginning of all-things, and that can now be bought at so much a unit at any good clockmaker's.

We have found the word being used by Wells as an aid to Science-Fiction, in a sense that corresponds to the extensions of Einstein's World

Lines — the persistence of all objects through their Past, Present and Future states. But this is a linear conception, and should be given its precise description — namely 4D Extension.

Nor should we use the word when what we mean should more properly be described as Entropy — the directional quality that makes an absolute difference between Events in our past and those in our future — a distinction that relates to relative positions on World Lines, and is only incidentally concerned with clocks.

Thus in 4D we find Extension masquerading as Time, while in 5D it is Entropy that is being referred to under the same obtrusive pseudonym. Finally, in 6D the word Time turns out to be an unnecessary expression altogether, except in reference to the unknown speed of Procession. In an all-here condition one can hardly be expected to measure anything. An Entirety cannot be analysed in linear terms, as if it were an Extension — which by definition it is not; and the same impossibility arises in connection with any attempted description of Continuity in a condition of all-now.

In fact, Time *is* an unscientific expression in so far as it cannot be measured meaningfully in any cosmic context, so long as there is no known unit of mensuration that applies outside the local field of vision.

In effect, this is just what Dr. Synge told us long ago; but with this difference, that the Doctor added a rider to his statement when he said that it was his own personal conviction that 'there is nothing but Time'. The conclusion to which the present thesis seems to be leading is just the opposite — that Time is non-existent, except as an expression (like 'God') to be applied to matters that we are unequipped to comprehend, and apart from its special use (of importance only to an Observer) to indicate the mysterious movement of his own Procession in a fifth dimension.

A Poet of genius

Jean Cocteau—a man of genius in more ways than one—summed up this view of Time when he wrote: 'It is possible that Time is only a mirage of our defective senses.' This is precisely what the facts suggest, although the language of Science is neither so succinct nor so poetic.

Time is an expression that should not be flung around recklessly or without adequate definition. Colloquially, the word is obviously needed to describe dynamic processes in the lower dimensions, and for that sort of purpose our stop watches may legitimately be produced. But we must agree upon the limited application of the word when we so use it, and prevent our uninstructed perceptions from fooling us into the notion that anything is actually occurring, apart from the procession of our Observation. And even this probably cannot be expressed in terms of arithmetic, for reasons that will shortly be discussed.

For here is the Golden Rule: All kinematic statements concerning Action, will eventually resolve themselves into statements related to the direction and speed of Procession.

Much of this has already been discussed in works of a scientific or philosophical character — and in that earlier work of my own, I have described how this geometrical conception was first opened to me in a Paris hospital, on the basis of seven dimensions. I accepted this figure at the time, probably because of the attraction of a mystical number. But the more I have thought about it since then, the more it has become apparent that six is the required figure, so far as we are concerned. There is no geometric need for a separate plane of observation apart from the 5D continuum mentioned above, and only one further dimension is needed in order to enable Procession to operate.

What this implies, of course, with regard to the universal consciousness which is in 6D, is a matter of considerable importance. It would seem that the existence of the imponderable already described as 'X' does not have to be proved by the use of Archdeacon Paley's watch, but is a mathematical necessity. One cannot avoid the conclusion that what is experienced as activity in each dimension inevitably leads us to 6D — the realm of the unchangeable and only Infinity, which is 'X'. This is not only a theological conception, but is also a scientific one — unless we are prepared to submit to the fallacy of Postponement and go on serialwise to unscientific conclusions.

As we advance, dimension upon dimension, Time — like the historical Jesus — retreats. We have found it masquerading under the guise of Order in the fourth dimension, and under the guise of Direction in the fifth. Now when we eventually try to corner it in the sixth, we find that the term becomes superfluous, except as an expletive — 'About time too!' — a useful and expressive phrase, but just about as meaningful as 'God dammit'. So now perhaps we can go a little further than Dr. Synge in describing it as unscientific, and agree with Cocteau that it is a mirage of our defective senses.

When we use the word at all, we are probably referring to something else, and as a rule it is something about Procession. So Time and its dependent appendage, Velocity, must be consigned to Limbo, and with them goes the kinematic interpretation of the Universe, except in so far as it is helpful in a purely subjective sense, for use in the lower dimensions.

If most of the above can be expressed more eloquently in the language of poetry than in the dreary verbiage of prose — as is the generous desire of Dr. Synge — we need look no further than T. S. Eliot's prophetic statement in *Four Quartets*, where he says:

> Time present and time past
> Are both perhaps present in time future,
> And time future contained in time past.
> If all time is eternally present
> All time is unredeemable.
> . . . .
> What might have been and what has been
> Point to one end, which is always present.

The Unmechanical Corkscrew

In the final analysis, no kinematic description of nature is necessary, since the apparent behaviour of the Universe does not depend upon Energy or upon Mass (two subjective, and therefore qualified Absolutes) but upon Angle.

Push a tightly held sheet of paper downwards upon a corkscrew, and imagine that you are observing only what is going on at the changing point of contact. From here you will report that a whirling is taking place, not unlike the behaviour of the celestial bodies, or what is to be found in the interior of an atom. But no whirling is going on at all. All that is occurring is the downward drive of the sheet of paper. At the point of contact matter is not moving in the locus of a circle, but is extending in a spiral, like a corkscrew. The apparent speed of the whirling is not dependent upon anything energetic about the corkscrew, but upon the closeness in which the twists of its spiral lie — slower and slower as the loops are pulled out, faster and faster if they are compressed into a circle — no revolutions at all if the implement is stretched out into the shape of a skewer, but instantaneously fast if it is squashed into a ring. Here we also have a model of the nature of wave-length. The closer the spiral the shorter the wave.

It is also interesting to note how a system such as a corkscrew has, on the whole, a general direction (at a right angle to its head) that bears no reference to the changing direction of its component cross sections. The direction in which a corkscrew may be said to be pointing is at no stage the direction of the turns of the screw. This is just another aspect of the word popularised by the late Jan Christiaan Smuts — Holism — a term that is made use of here to indicate the principle that the behaviour of the component parts of a system does not necessarily bear any resemblance to the behaviour of the system as a whole.

What are Signals?

But before putting away our corkscrew, it should be noted that as it proceeds through the plane of our piece of paper, its apparent rotation causes a shiver or vibration in the paper that may perhaps contribute to a crude understanding of the next phenomenon that it is necessary to define. I refer to something that we know as a Signal.

A signal must not be confused with whatever causes it, and for the purposes of the present discussion it might be defined as a modification of Space/Time (the 4D Continuum) that is brought about by a material Happening. It is not itself an extension of the Cause, but it has an extension of its own in Space/Time that appears to have some of the pulsating qualities of a wave.

If we accept the statement that Space is merely an aspect of Matter, it is not very difficult to see why all Systems have the effect of modifying Space — which is probably a more accurate way of saying that they 'emit signals'. One of the most striking examples of this modification occurs in the neighbourhood of the Sun, where light rays extending from a more distant source, appear to bend, as was successfully predicted by Einstein in mathematical terms. It is not any gravitational 'pull' on Light that results in this effect, but an actual geodesic curvature of the medium in which Light extends, which is due to the happening of the Sun.

Indeed, Gravity which we popularly regard as some form of attraction that draws Matter in a particular direction, has got many of the characteristics of a signal, and can more readily be thought of as one of the consequences of 4D curvature, than as a celestial magnet.

The Variation in the Speed of Signals

All signals, unless rendered directional by some kind of interference, extend in all directions from their source, like the ripples on a pool into which a stone has been dropped. But this ripple in the medium is a 3D effect which, in 4D, is an extension, only one section of which impinges on the Observer's faculties at the particular point where it lies across his meridian.

Given this wave effect, it is not very surprising to learn from Professor Lebedeff of Moscow that a light signal seems to have a detectable beat upon its terminal target (indicating weight), whether this target be a beach, a mirror, or some other type of instrument capable of measuring the pulsation. Weight, however, does not mean Mass — as they are fond of reminding us. Mass is something that is related to Inertia. A signal has no Mass, having no Matter or Inertia; nor does the Lebedeff effect mean that any knocking on doors is being done by a messenger who has personally travelled with some good news from Ghent to Aix. It simply means that a pulsating effect is being produced Here by something that is occurring There — the source having a spiral world line; hence presumably, the pulsation. It is an example of that much-frowned-upon misdemeanour — Action at a distance; which is indeed difficult to assent to, intellectually, so long as we continue to regard Space as a separate and negative commodity that can be purchased at so much a quart, probably at Greenwich.

We know that a speed boat has passed by when a wave slaps upon a beach, although nothing except an impulse has actually travelled from the boat to the beach. We are aware that a shot has been fired when an atmospheric impact crashes against our eardrums. But these are 3D effects. What we actually mean is that the pistol shot has conditioned an area of the 4D Continuum around it — an area that is funnel shaped, and that is progressively larger in the direction of Entropy, until the area becomes so large that the effect becomes unnoticeable. The apparent rate at which this area appears to expand depends upon the texture of the medium that carries the effect. In more intelligible language all that this means is that Sound appears to have a faster speed when it extends in water than when it does so in air, because water and air have different qualities as mediums.

Light, on the other hand, can be carried in the extension of Space/Time itself, and when it meets with no interference, as in a vacuum, its effect would be instantaneous were it not for curvature, the consequences of which will be discussed shortly.

Our more advanced data in the realm of Physics has now long persuaded us to discard the old image of the four Elements — Earth, Air, Fire and Water — which are no longer capable of meeting our need for viable, scientific information. However, we are still confronted today with some tantalising aspects of Science for which we need the help of other and better images, if we are ever going to comprehend them and their relationship to each other in a way that is not purely pragmatic. Prominent amongst these is the nature of Signals, which in its turn is closely bound up with the related phenomenon of Causation.

It would seem that neither Matter alone nor Energy alone can have any causative effect upon Space/Time. But wedded together, they have. Jointly they create a Happening, which is causative. What we see as sunlight is a consequence Here and Now of something that has 'occurred' There about eight minutes ago. Why it should be eight minutes ago rather than Now depends upon the shape of the 4D Continuum (the medium). The Signal is an aspect of Causation, in the same sense that Space is an aspect of Matter, as we have already pointed out. And it should be added that an even more striking example of the kind of effect that we are talking about is to be found in what we know as Gravity.

Only a limited number of Signals can be appreciated through our existing senses, although they may govern our behaviour, as Gravity does. Nevertheless, a signal of which we are sensually unaware, such as Radio, can be transmuted by means of apparatus into the form of Sound and Vision, which we *are* equipped to apprehend. So, also, the fact that we are not capable of expressing intuitively what precisely we mean by either Mass, Energy, or Signals may be got around by translating what we know of them into terms of a more familiar experience — possibly even a theological one — in order to clarify their relationship.

Take the Holy Trinity — the consubstantial Father, Son and Holy Ghost — a mystery in its own right about which we may have our doubts, but which, nevertheless, is intelligible as an image through long familiarity. In terms of communication, it is not hard to align such a conception to the grammatical relationship, already mentioned, of the Noun, the Verb and the Message.

Let me put it this way : (a) The word 'She' alone, is a noun statement, signifying nothing but the reality of Matter. It is an Event. (b) 'She died' adds a verb to the primal reality, and Action to Matter. But it is still no more than a news headline, without interpretation. Nevertheless, the union of the two diverse aspects of communication is sufficiently important to turn the Event into a Happening. (c) But if we go on to say 'She died for want of love', we find that the intrusion of the element of causation has turned the Happening into a Statement, to which considerations of beauty and of artifice apply, and which is capable of producing an Effect elsewhere. The Happening has acquired a significance that can make it a Message.

'And so abideth these three — consubstantial and coexistent, neither confounding the Persons, nor dividing the Substance. And in this Trinity none is afore, or after other; none is greater or less than another : Unity in Trinity and Trinity in Unity.' And so on.

May we not apply similar language to the enigmas confronting us in the field of Science, in order to illustrate the relationship of Mass, Energy and Signal, or in 3D terms (to which we are instinctively attached) Matter, Velocity and Effect, or more subtly still, the interdependence of 'X', the Word and the Kerygma, (i.e. the Message)?

Further than this it is difficult to go in our attempt to define a Signal. It has got all of the mystique, beauty and importance to man of the Paraclete. To appreciate its nature we must be prepared to show the same readiness to make the shift from a kinematic 3D view of a travelling wave pattern with a measurable length from crest to crest, to the conception of a 4D extension, the pulsating appearance of which is due to a Doppler Effect caused by the spiral world line of its source.

Systems and Events

But before turning our attention to the consequences that flow from such a conception of the Universe, let it be added, that by a System, we mean any collegium with a joint, physical existence, capable of a continuing identity as such, in 4D. Some of the writers call this quality 'Genidentity'. An astronomical Galaxy is a System. I am a System. The genealogical chain in which my flesh is a link is a System of a different kind. Whether or to what extent the State is to be regarded as a System is a political question that has long divided Whigs from Tories. As a hereditary Whig, I personally deny that the State is a System — but this is a matter that is open to very violent argument.

An Event — already referred to as a Noun — is a 3D cross-section of a world line at some particular point. If extended four-dimensionally, so that it appears to 'do something', it becomes a Happening, which is liable to be causative.

Open Future and Open Past

What we describe as 'Now' is usually visualised as the sliding zipper of a fastener which, in proceeding into an open Future, leaves behind it a Past which becomes closed as it passes. This endows the prevailing image with a shape rather like that of a wine glass — Y — with Now at the junction of the stem (past) with the bowl (future). I am suggesting that this is a deceptive view, in that it implies a physical difference between Past and Future, brought about by the passage of the Zipper 'Now', for which there is insufficient evidence.

If we profess to believe in a Future which is left open for individual choice, why should we not as readily accept the idea of a Past that is no less open? What is there about this moment of individual attention that, in its passing, should be able to turn a gaseous condition of many possibilities into a frozen stem that remains closed for ever? Why should we insist that there is something structurally different in the fabric of the Universe according to whether we regard it as Past or Future?

The reply that first springs to our lips is that we remember the Past but not the Future. Therefore the one exists, but not the other. This might perhaps be regarded as another consequence of the working of Entropy — that which makes an absolute difference for us personally between what is behind and what is before us. But although Entropy does indicate a difference between Past and Future, it is only a directional change, usually showing itself to us as a decrease in organisation. It is not so fundamental as one from the undetermined to the determined — a change of structure. Granted that the 4D world lines extend in multiple form in both directions, — as is normally the case with our individual genealogical trees, — what justification have we got for insisting that they are any more or less fixed in this direction rather than in that?

For what, after all, is Memory? A reading today of certain brain traces or cells written by the events of Yesterday on certain tangible tablets within the cranium. How do we know that they contain the whole story, rather than the spoor and droppings of a particular continuum? Indeed, how *could* the cells of this continuum contain a record related to another? Unless . . . ?

We will go into this question further, when we come to discuss the working of Alternation. It is sufficient to suggest at the moment that the limitations of Memory do not provide an answer that disposes of an Open Past. 'Now' is more likely to be at the focus of an X than at the junction of a Y. See Appendix F

Owing to our restricted view of Past, Present and Future, we tend to regard 'Now' as a temporary and passing phase in the course of a perpetually disappointing journey in search of something that we hope is going to be more to our taste later on. If we are Evolutionists, this prob-ably means that we are dissatisfied with a lamentable present day, which we trust is going to be improved upon by Nature in some happier by-and-by. Nature has not been so obliging in the past. Had this been so, we would now be living in the Paradise earnestly worked for by earlier generations. The fact that we are in no such Paradise need not cause any particular disgust with the Present. It is those who express a belief in 'Progress', and a hope for something better around the corner, who are its real detractors. Now is not a temporary expedient undergoing repairs. It is a cross-section of the Universe, presenting a 3D field of vision to the human observer at a particular latitude of the 4D continuum. It is entirely natural as it is, and will not be any less or more natural next year after Progress and Bernard Shaw have had their way with it. Its quality is vulgar, for it has none of the glamour of the Past, to which we look back with some nostal-gia, whatever miseries it may have harboured in its day. Nor has it any of the excitements of the Future, to which we usually look forward with hope.

The Present, for all its stresses and anxieties, has none of these qualities. It is crass. It is commonplace. It is crudely familiar and it always will be so. Yet it is all that we have, all we ever had, and all that we ever will have. When we sing:

> I'm but a stranger here.
> Heaven is my home,

we are expressing a natural distaste for Now, wedded to a conclusion that is not in accordance with the facts. Wherever the soul may reside, the Present is the proper and appropriate home for the flesh, in which the flesh is no exiled stranger.

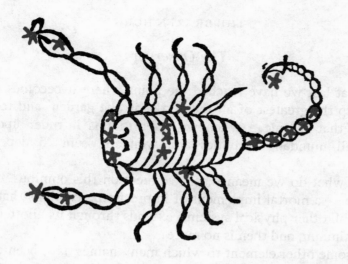

V   AN APPLE
FROM THE TEACHER

Laudo cupiditatem
et fructum cupiditatis
qui amor est.

The Observer

SO now at last we have reached the point where it becomes necessary to grasp the greatest of all the nettles in the garden, and to consider what it is that we mean when we refer to this intruder upon whose presence all mundane activities and wonders seem to depend — the Observer.

Who or what do we mean when we mention this omnibus? Is it Man in the flesh — a mortal implement of imprecise perceptions that, in company with all other physical systems, extends through its allotted segment of the Continuum, and then is no more?

Or is it some other element to which many names have been applied of varying respectability — the Soul, the Elan, the Life Force, the Conscious Mind, and an Incarnate Intelligence consubstantial with an unnamed Infinity?

Or is it all of these?

Don Man the Mammal

Suppose we begin this part of the investigation by taking a dispassionate look at Homo and Mulier Sapientes — a couple of Systems, low in the upper range of biological size, and about a million years old in the shape in which we can substantially recognize them today.

Quantitatively these mammals are larger than most other forms of life with which we are acquainted at present, although they are not by any means the biggest. They have, however, been growing bigger through recent centuries, as a visit to the armour in the Tower of London will confirm.

The significant period of about a million years during which they have been at large in their present shape suggests that, as a species, they are at present probably ripe for either mutation or extinction in the foreseeable future. In fact they are at rather a dangerous age.

For some reason, probably connected with physical prowess, or maybe with some picture of an anthropomorphic deity, they are collectively referred to under the description of the male partner, although this member appears to be in a slight overall minority. A good deal of effort — principally for social reasons — goes into emphasising the differences between the sexes, although in western communities at the moment this distinction is not as evident as it usually is. Actually, most of the obvious differences can be put down to education and conditioning, apart from certain unescapable physiological demands.

The males are popularly supposed to be dominant, while the females are recessive. One sex is said to be reasonable, while the other is intuitive. One is regarded as being domestic and greatly concerned about the welfare of its offspring, while the other is adventurous and provides the provender. But actually, whenever we cast a candid eye on the examples that we know in each category, we have every reason to doubt the accuracy of these generalisations.

The point is that, nature having endowed both sexes with the rudimentary organs of the other, it has been felt necessary to counteract this inexplicable and rather irritating trick by creating artificial differences. Clothes, mannerisms and other forms of adornment, as well as an air of mystery induced by segregation, are all valuable instruments for keeping alive a strong awareness of sex. These practices go under the name of Morality, without which a lack of interest in the matter might long ago have endangered reproduction.

But whether or not these distinctions are valid, we will here continue to refer to both varieties as Man, partly as a matter of convenience, and partly in recognition of the fact that the ladies seem to have no special objection to being called tomboys or to wearing trousers, while normally their supposedly dominant partners show extreme fussiness about being considered feminine, or being seen around in petticoats. In fact, the boys are much more sensitive about their sexual image than are the girls — which suggests that they are less certain of it.

Some Competitive Statistics

There is a lot to be said for Man in comparison with other forms of life on this particular planet: It is true that he cannot run as fast as the antelope, but he can dance with greater grace, and indeed outdo all local competition in this accomplishment, including that of both the monkey and the bear. He can sing more pleasantly than the birds — or at any rate with greater range — and although he cannot use his feet as cleverly as the mule or the chimp, he is magnificent with his hands, and is unsurpassed in his use of implements.

The universal stimuli of Fear and Pain will be found to motivate most of his activities: nevertheless there are occasions on which he displays a certain social sense that can modify both these reactions. And although he is like the squirrel in being an economic animal — an inveterate storer up of rubbish as well as of nuts — his behaviour is often more dictated by a sense of Pride and of 'Face' than is generally supposed by the Economists.

He can see better than the lion, and his sense of hearing is unusually wide and selective — although not as wide as that of the dog. There are peculiarities and an uncertainty in his sense of smell that make it unreliable, but his stereoscopic sight and hearing put those particular senses in the forefront of the field. He also shows signs of interest in the problem of widening the slit through which his present faculties are operating, and his growing historical sense, combined with some limited ability to anticipate, shows that he has already got, in embryo, the rudiments of 4D perception. His awareness of the future cannot wholly be explained away in terms of the salivation of dogs at the ringing of a bell. And with this rudimentary pre-vision, combined with a comparatively good memory, he may fairly lay claim to certain features that are unique in the present biological range.

He has also got a genealogical memory, as distinct from a purely individual one, by which I mean that he can be greatly influenced in his opinions and in his behaviour by what can best be described as a 'family subconscious'. Occasionally he shows a surprising awareness of the probable course of his future, which he sometimes describes in mystical or religious terms, although actually there is nothing supernatural about it.

His Endwaffe

Perhaps it is just as well that Man should be acquiring these further evolutionary faculties, since, in the course of the present generation, he has also acquired the technical ability to exterminate himself in bulk. This perilous know-how means that, without some early widening of his perceptions, he is liable — with growing over-population and discouragement — to put these new practical accomplishments to their inevitable use, thus following in the trackmarks of the Lemmings.

It seems to be one of the peculiarities of many forms of life that they tend, after a prolonged period of growth, to become tired of themselves, and to commit a form of race suicide. The Lemmings are not the only species that provide an example of this cleansing urge. Indeed, self-slaughter is practised on occasions by social classes as well as by particular races — classes that have been doing too well for too long. Or, alternatively, that have never managed to get started.

Symptoms of acute self-boredom are in evidence at the moment amongst certain sections of the white race, possibly as a reaction from the fact that 'Aryan' has been turned into a dirty word by the behaviour of the late Adolf Hitler. This active dislike of self, and of self-preservation, takes some very curious forms both socially and politically, which it is not our present business to discuss, apart from pointing out that it may well be part of a wider movement, sponsored by a sinister Death-wish party, to arrange for the discontinuance of Man altogether.

The Three Brains of Homo Sapiens

According to Arthur Koestler, who in turn speaks on the authority of the biologist, Paul MacLean, Man is still encumbered with the remnants of two primitive brains that are relics of earlier stages of Evolution, and that have not yet substantially vanished, as has been the case with his tail. These, Koestler describes as the Archicortex and the Mesocortex, of which the former is reptilian — that is to say, it has some of the characteristics of the brain of a crocodile — while the latter is that of one of the middle-class mammals, resembling, shall we say, that of a horse.

Each of these primitive pieces of undiscarded machinery can on occasion take over and crowd out the maturer operations of the reasonable brain (the Neocortex) of Homo Sapiens. To this dangerous survival of earlier members, Koestler attributes much of the hysteria and irrational behaviour of Man in moments of stress, and the even more peculiar fact that he appears to find a certain perverse pride in these occasional reversions to the habits of the jungle. Even Yeats has been known to exalt emotion over considered common sense, as when he wrote:

> God guard me from those Thoughts men think in the mind alone.
> He who sings a lasting song, thinks in the marrow bone.

The Cistern of Nature

In addition to an acute neurosis over Sex that is given voice to by SS. Paul and Augustine — from some experience, one would imagine — Man shows a distinct aversion, not merely to Evil (which would be understandable), but to certain of the ordinary facts of life, that are in no way tied up with any aspects of proper behaviour. Unlike the lower fauna, which have no such inhibitions, he seems to regard some of the arrangements of the Creator as being in bad taste.

A New England Puritan called Cotton Mather expresses some of this disapproval in an amusing passage in his diary for July, 1700:

> I was once emptying the *Cistern of Nature*, and making *Water* at the Wall. At the same time, there came a *Dog*, who did so too, before me. Thought I : "What mean, and vile Things are the children of Men, in this mortal State ! How much do our *natural Necessities* abase us, and place us in some regard, on the same Level with the very Dogs !"

We may laugh at Cotton Mather's snobbish aversion to being at one with Fido in his need to micturate, but his attitude towards Nature — which he clearly regards as letting him down — is only part of a wider difficulty that Man at present finds in forgiving Heaven for the facts of Life. To Society as a whole — as represented by the Policeman with the flashlamp — both sex and stool are urges that are to be regretted. Indeed, if it were not for the fact that the Church in its great wisdom has invested the former with an aura of naughtiness that enhances its desirability, Cotton Mather and the Manicheans might have had their way, and put an end to Man long ago in the quiet of sterility and the pains of constipation.

In fact, Man may be regarded as in an intermediate stage of his development — sufficiently aware of aesthetics and of his rational power of selection, to be upset by the mechanical urgings of the flesh that have kept the race going throughout the ages. The desire to indulge in so inartistic an act as copulation must obviously be due to the prompting of a demon.

Look, says Saint Augustine, how uneasiness of conscience impels us to do it in secret. In which conclusion he is gladly supported by the professional dispensers of heavenly antidotes. What really upset the late Dr. Buchman over me was an innocent remark to the effect that I did not happen to have any particular sex difficulties. I meant, of course, that I found no special difficulties in it, but he assumed from what I said that I was 'unconvicted of sin', and he never spoke to me again. Without that disability I could not be morally rearmed.

Maybe he was right, because my personal conviction is that Man should thank his God for Desire. For when that leaves him he is done for, as surely as was Goethe's Faust when he made that poignant compact with the Devil :

> If ever I lay me on a bed of sloth in peace,
> That instant let me from existence cease . . .
> Then will I gladly perish, then and there !

Evolution as a Fact

We are told that the Earth is at present still pulling out of an Ice Age, but it is hardly legitimate to express an acceptance of this theory by saying: There was much better skating in Grandmother's day. Nor can we truthfully allege in terms of Biology that Man is a different animal now from what he was when written records began in bulk, about four thousand years ago. Planck tells us that, in the brief period that may be regarded as historical, there has been no significant change in the make-up of Homo Sapiens that can properly be described as evolutionary. Conditions are different; that is all. Man's education and environment have changed from those of the days of barbarity, but fundamentally, whenever circumstances revert to a rough and tumble, he is quite capable of behaving in precisely the same way as those whom he is pleased to regard as barbarians.

This particular generation is unusually well-informed on such a point, because of events that have occurred during the twentieth century. Take away our civil institutions, and in a decade we are capable of returning to torture, to unrestrained brigandry, and indeed, to new enormities such as genocide, that have been made feasible by technical know-how. Even, quite possibly, to human sacrifice — though probably it would take a little longer to get back to widespread cannibalism. There is, in short, no marked physiological difference between Sir Winston Churchill and a reasonably informed Visi-Goth. What makes the apparent difference is Harrow and the House of Commons, neither of which are physiological.

On the other side of the coin there is, of course, the fact that even in the darkest ages Man has also displayed intellectual and social qualities just as fine as any that we know today. Wessex had its Alfred, and Charlemagne had his Alcuin. India had its Asoka, and even Imperial Rome had its Antonines. On the other hand, it is not at all certain that Socrates would be awarded a Guggenheim Fellowship today. He might have trouble in finding suitable sponsors, and his programme would certainly be regarded as much too wide. But he would be more than equipped to join in the after-dinner jokes at All Souls.

But if we take a long enough view, it is true that an evolutionary change does take place in the realm of our capabilities for perception. The Yellow River follows a well-established course, but it does alter it from time to time. So does the human animal — although not over a period that offers any significant difference between Trevor-Roper's material and that of Herodotus.

Nor is it necessarily a change for 'the better'. It is a change towards a condition that is further along in the direction of Entropy. Also it is of importance to remember that the historical span covers a very short part of our genealogy, and that this pertinent figure of about one million years might turn out to have a significant bearing on our future prospects. There is evidence to suggest that, at about that interval, many species tend to disappear, unless — on the other hand — they manage to develop some new, quantitative faculty by the operation of Mutation, which gives them a new span of life in a more effective form. This must have happened to *Homo Sapiens* before, and it would seem that, in his present condition, he is again approaching a critical stage in his career.

His Fear of Death

So here we have Man — a creature no longer dazzled and confused by his capability for three dimensional vision, but still bullied by several mechanical, but fortunate instincts that have helped him to survive, to the present. Sex is only one of these. More subtle still is his inrooted belief that he is afraid of Death.

In actual fact the normal Man is not at all averse to Death, provided that it comes at the right time, and he shows this fact quite clearly in his urge towards a personal maturity — which is only another way of describing Death. He wishes to 'complete himself', and directs much of his energy towards this fateful task. Yet he is probably not mature enough to be safely relieved from this purposeful illusion that Death is something to be avoided purely for the sake of avoiding it. This instinct keeps him from suicide in moments of despair or exhaustion, and as such it is highly important. But it is a delusion, none the less. Man would be frantic without the gift of Death.

As it is, he normally lives for something less than a century, and he does his best to make sure that this natural span is not enlarged into too long a senility, thanks to the efforts of his medical advisers.

But perhaps most interesting of all is his sense of oneness with the rest of sentient creation, which manifests itself in a feeling of personal incompleteness, and in particular in a desire, somehow or other to enlarge this slit of the Present into a wider awareness of the Universe through which his faculties are passing. He loves to recreate the Past by means of various tricks, however much he may have disliked it when he was there; and his efforts to foresee the Future are endless. As for his oneness with his fellows — this may not always be evident, but it is of interest to note that solitary confinement is widely regarded as one of the severest forms of punishment.

His Sense of Guilt

It would be inappropriate to conclude this survey without some comment on a matter that is only part of a deeper and more sinister neurosis in contemporary Man — his curious sense of Guilt. Man has every reason to feel some dissatisfaction with his personal performance in many of his undertakings; but what I am referring to goes much deeper than this. It amounts to a deep-seated distemper about something that he calls his Sins — for which his conditioning and his metabolism are usually as much responsible as is any wilful misbehaviour.

The orthodox view of this mystical fall from Grace, which is regarded as the cause of the prevalence of Sin (the unescapable lot of every Man), is best explained in the words of Saint Thomas Aquinas, as summarised for us by Bertrand Russell:

> By mortal sin a man forfeits his last end to all eternity, and therefore eternal punishment is his due. No man can be freed from sin except by grace, and yet the sinner is to be blamed if he is not converted. Man needs grace to persevere in good, but no one can *merit* divine assistance. God is not the cause of sinning, but some he leaves in sin, while others he delivers from it. As regards pre-destination, St. Thomas seems to hold, with St. Augustine, that no reason can be given why some are elected and go to heaven, while others are reprobate and go to hell. He holds also that no man can enter heaven unless he has been baptised.

The fact that this dogmatic outline of the irresponsible working of the divine arrangements is not universally accepted today, does not affect its orthodoxy, or its accuracy as an expression of the Christian view of Original Sin. Any questioning merely throws doubt on the status of the doubters as Christians.

What Man's quandary amounts to is the fact that it is clearly impossible to go through this mortal life without contravening the divine Law — which disobedience is what is meant by Sin. Although the Christian does not openly admit that the Law demands the impossible, he does so in effect by insisting that Man is born under the curse of Adam, and is bound to sin, even in his efforts to perform good works, if he approaches these without Grace, which he cannot earn by any merits of his own. Or, more significantly still, without the assistance of those who have invented the trap.

Worse than this, Heaven has got Man on the spot in every way. The newly created soul does not merely inherit the infected nature of its first Father. The orthodox view is that once a new Soul is created, it is then deliberately encumbered by the Creator with this burden of guilt. So the situation is not simply Adam's doing. Guilt is actually created by the Almighty itself and inflicted as a curse upon every new Soul — a fallen condition that can only be remedied by a panacea which Man is not entitled to demand as of right. So far as Heaven is concerned, the issuing of a Visa is entirely arbitrary, as is the case elsewhere.

It is against this monstrous idea that Man must endure eternal punishment unless his God arbitrarily decides otherwise — the decision, needless to say, having been influenced by favourable reports from the clergy and the saints — that most normally compassionate people revolt today. And the usual form that their objection takes is to begin by denying that God is the universal author of Evil as well as of Good. A God, in fact, limited to the Summertime of Experience.

They then go on from this point to doubt the existence of any penalties for evil-doing whatsoever, except purely pragmatic ones, and to question Sin's inevitability. Finally they ask sceptically for some further particulars of this 'Soul' that we hear so much about, but which nobody has ever actually seen. And in the absence of any answer, they dismiss the Soul as a fraud, together with that box of returned empties, in the shape of which they visualise the moral Law.

In following this beaten track, we Agnostics display our usual obtuseness by condemning Christianity for insisting upon certain fundamentals on which it is substantially right, while we raise few, if any, objections to a number of undesirable trimmings on which it is not. For instance, no truly orthodox Christian should deny for a moment that God is the first cause of all things, including 'Satan', as personifying Evil, and all else that Satan is supposed to stand for, if for no other reason than that in Holy Scripture, God says so himself. Secondly, we Rationalists are in very deep water whenever we attack the idea of Original Sin, which states in effect that breaches of the Law are inevitable for all rational creatures who have accepted the burden of Life itself. That such breaches are also punishable is doubted too, although equally undeniable.

But where we get deepest into the mire is in our assumption that questions of justice or injustice play any part in this Harlequinade. Nobody is forced to take part in these activities, but if we do so, any question of justice or injustice is rendered irrelevant by the fact that, in our evident readiness to live, we indicate an awareness that, painful or not, the game is worth the playing. Besides, whatever penalties for lawbreaking may follow, they are not everlasting, even when they affect other people. If the Church appears to insist on this everlasting quality as part of its exaggerated view of the perils of Sin, it is because it is professionally concerned with the remission of punishment and — like the medical community — it had better not minimise the ills in the curing of which it manages to prosper. The Church needs to have its customers, as does the Bar, and it can hardly be expected to flout the reality of Sin any more than my own brethren at King's Inns can be expected to work for an end to litigation, however devoted to justice we may be.

As for the existence of the Soul — here at last we find ourselves face to face with the real question at issue : What do we mean by this expression? When we speak of Man, do we mean the telescope or the astronomer? — the implement or its operator? — or both? For each has a separate existence, as distinct as the noun and the verb, and as the locomotive and the driver.

In general, what we have been discussing so far is what is referred to as the Flesh. As as physical implement, the Flesh is a system, extending in temporal continuity from birth to death. It did not exist before conception, and after death it disintegrates, notwithstanding some insistence to the contrary on the part of spiritualists and readers of *Dracula*. Let us face it — Imperial Caesar may well be found stopping a hole to keep the wind away.

But in doubting the existence of a life for the Flesh-after-Death, we must not fail to recognise the corollary — that the passage of Time (or should we not say, the advance of Entropy) has no effect whatever on the physical reality of the Past, of the World Lines of which the Flesh-before-Death is a part. Between the limits of its actual extension, the body has the same everlasting quality that the Universe itself possesses. Whatever may happen to Observation, the telescope is indestructible within its proper temporal limits which, on the other hand, are not interminable.

But what good is that — we hear somebody say — if I am not aware of it any longer? But this is not the point. The flesh is not what is 'aware', and the wailing that we are being treated to at this particular Wake is for the telescope — not for the Astronomer. What we are taking exception to is an irrational lamentation over something that has not in fact been destroyed, but is merely elsewhere.

Besides, who knows whether or not we will be aware of it, or that an eye may not be applied again? Even before death, the implement was not in continual use; but do you ask, of what good was the body to me throughout the darkness of last night, when for eight long hours it was asleep, and nothing was observed?

If we have anything to feel concern about, surely it is the fate of the Astronomer. And him we will not find inside any four dimensional coffin into which he does not fit — but somewhere in 5D and 6D, as a function or a manifestation of 'X'. And 'X', one feels sure, can be relied on to look after itself.

Buridan's Moke

Clearly, *Homo Sapiens* is a complicated Field Equation involving multiple causation, and a control beyond the comprehension of the Monophysites. He is evidently everlasting, but he is not immortal. Let us agree so far with the Behaviourists that this sort of Man makes no choices, and as such, incurs no responsibilities. But not even a donkey starves to death if placed exactly equi-distant between two hay stacks — as Buridan has pointed out.

There is another thing that makes the choices, and that suffers, and that in suffering, as in rejoicing, demonstrates its dignity and its immortality.

VI   THE CURVING PARACLETE

Et in heredio meo
vitae miraculo delecto
et aeque in vitae corona
quae fines sunt.

Onwards from Copernicus

I hope that I have made it clear that the facts are the inviolable property
of the laboratories, and so far as I am concerned, that there is nothing
about any of them that is in the slightest paradoxical if regarded from a
realistic angle. But although the Uninitiated may not lay a finger on the
Data, I do respectfully suggest that the interpretation may properly be
anybody's business.

So, while happily inviting any corrections from our academic comforters on points of peripheral detail, we may quietly insist that a survey of
what is already known is not inconsistent with the model of an unkinematic, four dimensional Continuum (the Universe) which forms a curved
surface of a five dimensional Sphere (the Cosmos), on which a great many
observable genidentical Systems extend as durable World Lines. If we
then go on to add that the direction on this Sphere, of the movement of
the Observer's Entropy must add two subjective Poles and a notional
Equator to the globe, we are not saying anything outside the bounds of
reason. These co-ordinates are our personal property, and do not affect
the absolute nature of the Cosmos itself. But the fact that any other
Observer with whom we are likely to be in communication has substantially the same co-ordinates, does manage to give these Cosmic Poles and
Equator a special significance in all our experiences and calculations.
Indeed, for all practical purposes, they may be regarded by us as
absolutes, too.

In so far as observable systems lie in the general direction of our own
Procession or across it, they appear to us either as Matter, with its correlative Velocity, or as Energy, with its correlative Mass. Which direction
produces which effect is for Authority to tell us, but Carnot is commonly
supposed to have laid it down that the product of both is constant, which
confirms the proposition that all Systems *in Esse* are unquali-   But see
fied absolutes. In other words, any change in their aspect is   Appendix
merely an expression of 4D angle.   E

Activity — a matter of Appearance

From this it would seem to follow that the phenomenon of physical
activity in the Universe is a matter of appearance, since the only actual
kinematic movement is that of the Observer's point of view, which
activity is not in the 4D Universe at all, but in a fifth dimension, where
its behaviour is made possible by the existence of a sixth.

The atomic structure of each system — including that of the material body of the Observer himself — takes the form of a series of spiral world lines, that bear no necessary relationship to the 4D direction of the system as a whole. Hence the appearance of the interior of an Atom as an aspect of whirling energy.

If this general picture is at variance with any of the admitted facts it is, of course, subject to correction. But it would be interesting to know whether it is logically impossible, and if so in what respects?

The apparent Speed of Light

The first phenomenon that has to be fitted into such a frame-work is the apparent speed of Light, upon which so many of our astronomical calculations are based. And closely related to this is the expansion of the Universe. Is there any logical reason why, if Light has any speed at all, it should move in a vacuum at 186,000 miles per second? Why not more or less? And why is the Universe expanding? From what to what? Did this peculiar behaviour originate in an explosion out of nothing, and will it go on for ever? If not, what will stop it? And in any event, if the Universe is universal, what can it be regarded as expanding in relation to? Maybe we should send for Aubrey.

Lemaître's Exploding Universe

It was in 1927 that a Belgian astronomer, the Abbé Lemaître, already mentioned, propounded his 'cosmic egg' view of the Creation, which has later been pictorialised by Pfeiffer in the following terms.

> The evolution of the world can be compared to a display of fireworks that has just ended : some few red wisps, much of ashes and smoke. Standing on a well-chilled cinder, we see the slow fading of the suns, and we try to recall the vanished brilliance of the origin of the world.

A melancholy picture, especially if we relate it to an equally depressing expression of Eddington's — 'the running down of the Universe'. But it need not depress us unduly, for the Abbé and his associates, while being more informative about the details, are by no means so emotional in describing our prospects. According to them, the explosion took place between four and six thousand million years ago — an estimate that is much too short if we accept more recent ideas on the subject.

We are told that at the date of this beginning, all matter was tightly packed into a sphere about five hundred miles across, from which congested parcel of first causes everything has since been expanding. No theory is advanced as to where the contents may previously have been, or as to what was the cause of these first causes, or as to who or what saw to the packing.

Does not this bear a significant resemblance to the statement of Archbishop Ussher that is enshrined in the margins of our Victorian Bibles? According to this, God created the Firmament in 4004 B.C. and all else may be calculated from this significant date. There are ample grounds for suspecting that we are now being treated to a different example of Postponement. Nevertheless there *is* observable evidence to show that the 4D Continuum is actually behaving very like the surface of a balloon that is being blown up. On the basis of probability, every point on it appears to be getting further and further away from every other point.

Hoyle's Static Universe

On the other hand, there is Fred Hoyle's alternative picture of a balanced, self-creating, self-destroying Universe which manages to circumvent the problem of an advertised starting time by introducing the mathematician's panacea — Infinity. This thesis gives stability to the general conception, and a brighter outlook for our descendants. We may, however, look askance at a theory that postulates the Universe as creating itself, by an odd coincidence, at the same rate at which it disappears into Limbo. We hear, too, that Hoyle has since discarded much of his diagnosis in favour of yet another alternative that was supported by Allan Sandage and the Palomar astronomers down to the year 1974. This took the view that the expansion is followed by contraction after an ascertainable period of time, and that the Universe oscillates between these two extremes of concentration and dispersal. This thesis manages to reconcile Lemaître's positive evidence of expansion with Miss Bath's distaste for a definite beginning followed by an undefined ending. But it will be noticed that all these three bases for a cosmology are similarly grounded upon the old conception of Time as an independent commodity, and are not strictly relevant to the problems raised by the newer ideas that have been circulating since the coming of Space/Time. Like Whittaker they accept the idea of Space/Time theoretically, but they do not as a rule apply it practically.

In reply to an enquiry as to whether this section correctly describes Hoyle's present view, the Professor replied, under the pseudonym of 'Miss Bath', that he was too busy to consider the matter.

Indeed, it must be plain that we are all inclined to regard Time as a separate entity whenever we refer to the speed of Light, and attempt to estimate the significant distance at which the growing recession of the retreating nebulae approximates to the absolute limit of speed that we are already acquainted with as 'c'.

Hubble

It is quite feasible to work out a rough figure for such a distance by means of a graph. We do not have to keep peeping and prying into greater and greater depths of outer space, because — thanks to Palomar and Jodrell Bank — we already have a sufficient number of reliable figures for both distance and speed, applying to the nearer galaxies, to give us a line on a graph. Having tried to plot such a diagram myself a number of years ago, I had a lucky opportunity to put the question to the celebrated astronomer, Professor Shapley of Harvard, who recognised at once what I was enquiring about, and gave me an immediate answer in terms that confirmed what I had already suspected, that the diagram followed a straight line so far as it had then been possible to plot it. He also added that the feat had already been performed by Hubble as long ago as 1929.

This was a little galling to my pioneering hopes, which as usual had been soaring far beyond my qualifications. But it was more than exciting to learn from such a source that the increase was evidently a simple arithmetical progression, because this meant — as far as one could judge from the direction of the line already known as the Hubble Constant — that it should cross the level reading 186,000 miles per second on the speed scale, at a reading somewhere between nine and ten thousand million light years on the distance scale.

Since then I have heard Professor Sandage put the Hubble figure at 13×10^9 which is thirteen thousand million light years — somewhat further than had been expected. But what are a few thousand millions to Palomar? The subject is further discussed in Appendix G.

The question arises then as to why, beyond this distance, nothing more can be seen? Is this because there is nothing there? Or is it because of the fact that, with a greater speed of recession, it would be impossible for light or radio signals (the fastest messengers of observation) ever to reach us, regardless of the fact that Einstein assures us that the

This peculiar quality of light signals is not so odd as it at first appears. All that Einstein is actually saying is that the Now at which the Observer is made aware of a signal from an Event on another meridian is not conditioned by the direction of the 4D World-line of speed of light is not affected by the speed of the source of its origin?

Actually I do not believe that we can answer such questions while still clinging to a set of assumptions that are not really aspects of Science at all, but are ways of Thought. The whole conception of recession implies a beginning, not only of the physical Universe, at a specific date, but also of a Time before which there was no Universe and no 'Time' — whatever 'before which' may mean in such a context. What then is happening? since it must also be agreed that Recession is something that is not only observable, but that can actually be measured. Measured by what? — we may reasonably ask. And at once we get the expected reply: By means of the speed of light signals — which answer takes us back at once to the unresolved problem: What do we mean by the 'speed of light'?

the source of the signal (i.e. its apparent speed). If an unkinematic view of the situation is taken, Einstein's principle becomes obvious. The curvature in 4D which governs the apparent time taken by a signal to reach an Observer on another meridian must not be confused with the Doppler Effect appearing in the pitch of the signal (Wave Length), which is a 3D phenomenon, and which in fact *is* governed by the direction of the World-line of the source. This is how the principle enunciated by Einstein is not contradicted by the 'tired effect' that is to be observed in the wave length of light coming from a very great distance. This has nothing to do with the apparent speed of the signal, which is an effect occurring in a different dimension.

A velocity for this phenomenon is usually calculated by aiming a flash at a mirror that has been placed at a measured distance from the source, and by timing the interval that elapses before the signal returns. This would be fine if the signal returned to the same location. Such, however, is not the case, and the fact that there is an interval at all merely shows that, for some reason, the return limb of the extension does not reach the Observer until his procession has taken him to a later point in Space/Time.

I am aware that the earliest known calculation of the speed of light — by Ole Röemer in 1675 — was not carried out by means of a mirror. But I hope to show that the same principles apply to data obtained from signals derived from the occultation of Jupiter's moons, as from a reflection.

If we agree that the unbeatable velocity of the light signal indicates that it must lie away from the meridian of the source at the unexceedable divergence of a right angle (90°), and if, presumably it is reflected by the mirror at a similar angle from the meridian of the reflector, it would seem to follow that it ought to return to its precise point of origin without apparently taking any time on the double-journey. And so it would, of course, if plane geometry applied. But it does not apply except — and this is important — except at the Cosmic Equator. The medium in which the signal lies is curved, and this is the reason for the interval.

As a practical illustration of what this amounts to, let us return to our terrestrial globe as a model for the Cosmos, and select an Observation Point somewhere on Longitude 0° from which an imaginary light signal is flashed to a far-off reflector. I suggest an easily identified Latitude in the temperate zone — shall we say the 50th Parallel, where it intersects Meridian Zero, a little to the south of Greenwich, and not far from where I am as I write.

A thread extending from a pin inserted at this O.P. and stretched along the surface will, of course, have to curve to the south, following a Great Circle, if it is to hold a direction that sets off at a right angle to the Meridian. If we follow it as far as Longitude 31°, we will find that at that distance it has swung as far south as the 45th Parallel, at which level let us suppose the mirror has been placed.

This corresponds, in terms of the geography of the Earth to a point in the English Channel, north of Le Havre. The suggested Parallel is also the closest in round figures to the estimate of our present cosmic position, as will be offered on page 125.

Here we shall loop the thread around another pin, and carry it back again on another Great Circle lying away from that Meridian at a similar angle. This represents the return extension of the signal, and its course will be found to intersect our familiar Longitude Zero at about the 40th Parallel, or to continue the terrestrial comparison, somewhere close to the east coast of Spain, near the town of Castellon de la Plana.

Again, applying these coordinates to the map of Europe, it will be found that such a point corresponds to one in the Black Sea and not far to the east of the mouths of the Danube. On a Mercator projection the course of the signal will appear as a curve. To check its substantial accuracy, the pin and the thread should be abandoned, and a straight line drawn on a Gnomonic map from Long. 0°, Lat. 50° N. to Long. 31° E., Lat. 45° N.

Now, however accurate or inaccurate our stop watches and other implements may be, it will be seen that they are not telling us how far or how long it takes for Light to fly from the Channel to the Black Sea and back, but the 4D distance and the 5D Time taken by the Observer in proceeding from the original O.P. directly southward to Castellon. This is just another application of the truism mentioned in an earlier chapter: All kinematic statements of Speed in the physical Universe (including that of the ultimate speed of Light) resolve themselves into statements related to the direction and speed of Procession. The light signal never returns to the Channel. What happens is that we meet it again on the other leg of its extension, further on in Space/Time, and we wrongly express this fact in terms of an unshakable attachment to a travelling signal in an imaginary lower-dimensional time that is independent of Space.

It is also of importance to note that if the experiment described above were to be carried out at the Cosmic Equator, the returning signal *would* be instantaneous: from which we may conclude that the apparent speed of light signals in a vacuum is dependent upon the latitude, and that 'c' is quantitatively what it is because of where we are. At the Equator, Entropy and the speed of Procession coincide, and thereafter the former goes into reverse — a phenomenon that accounts for what Sandage described as the oscillation of the Universe, from a state of expansion into one of contraction. Why this reversal should take place at the particular parallel at which it does occur, is simply a matter of the quantitative size of the Universe. Indeed, we have in 'c', as we measure it, a clue to a method by which an accomplished mathematician might calculate our present cosmic latitude; through which in turn the radius of the Cosmos might be accurately ascertained, and compared to all those other estimates that have been made by a series of distinguished astronomers during the past fifty years. Apart from this, if the above diagnosis is substantially sound, it also offers us a simple explanation of the data upon which the observed recession of the galaxies is based.

Expansion is not expanding

The apparent expansion of the Universe does not have to be related in any way to effects in the Spectrum. Nor does it depend upon the blowing up of a balloon in relation to nothing, any more than do the experiences of the two Navigators in our parable in the second chapter. No mechanical assistance is required to explain the obvious fact that all Spheres expand quantitatively between their Poles and their Equator, and

As to Ole Röemer's calculations without the use of a mirror, the same principles apply whether or not such an implement is there. By the latter part of the seventeenth century it was possible to predict with some accuracy a time for the eclipse of each of Jupiter's moons. Noting a discrepancy between the calculated times and the actual moments when a series of these phenomena were visible from the Earth, Röemer maintained that the lateness of each eclipse was not due to an error in the calculations but to a further element, hitherto ignored — the time taken by the Light of the signal to travel to the Earth from the known distance of Jupiter. At that date, and that the distances between meridian and meridian grow greater as one proceeds from a higher to a lower latitude. There is no mystery about the fact that at the tenth Parallel, any world lines lying along Longitude 35° (as seen from Longitude 0°) will literally be farther away than they were at the twentieth Parallel. Thus the expansion of the Universe is not being caused by an explosion, but by the procession of observation from a higher to a lower latitude.

for many years afterwards, a light signal was regarded as something in the nature of a stream of molecules projected like bullets from the source. On this assumption, Röemer was able to give to the Astronomers of his day a reasonably workable figure for the speed of Light, and so restore the correctness of their calculations. Here, no mirror was necessary, but the principle of using the delay in the receipt of the signal as a means of estimating the time taken on a journey over a known distance was, in effect, the same as in the method of reflection in present day use. A calculated time for the actual occultation on Jupiter took the place of the outward limb of the signal's extension.

In this respect it is a real and measurable expansion, and not merely an optical illusion, provided we are prepared to recognise the actual nature of kinematic movement in the 3D world, and agree that it is a misconception of this that is causing the problem.

The Now Curve

Now let us try another experiment with our globe and our thread, to see how these results fit in with what we know as the Hubble Constant. This time we will plot on the curvature of our model Cosmos the positions on other meridians of a number of supposed Events, the signals of which, extending from their respective sources at the maximum 'speed', will cross our Longitude 0° (Here) all at the same Now — let us say for the sake of clarity on the diagram, at the 30th Parallel. In other words, at what levels on the higher latitudes does each Event respectively lie that is observable at that particular Here and Now?

The signals from each of these Events will extend to us here on a series of curves, all convex to the Pole if plotted Mercatorwise, and it must be clear that the further away from our meridian the point of origin lies, the higher the latitude must be. This is only another way of saying that the further off the Event, the further back into History it must be regarded as having taken place. But this is not because of the 'speed of light'. It is due to the curvature of the Signal.

After having ascertained the position of a number of these points as accurately as may be with our primitive instruments — say, one at every fifteen degrees of Longitude — let us draw a line on the sphere connecting them all up with Lat. 30°, Long. 0°. This should turn out to be a semi-circle with Meridian 0° as diameter, at one end of which is the Observer, and at the other end, his Pole. This we will call the Now Curve. It is in effect another graph, indicating the respective positions in Space/Time of everything that we observe Here at one moment of Procession.

The Now Curve must not be confused with the course of the signals. It is merely a diagram, this time on a spherical surface, indicating latitude of origin in relation to distance. And the first fact to be noted is that when an event occurs as far off as Longitude 90°, it must be at the Pole, since at this distance the extension has curved as far north as it can go. At the Pole all meridians are one, and at this distance the extension of the signal no longer follows a Mercator curve, but lies along Meridian 0° itself.

In this geometric fact we find a new and exciting reason for the impossibility of observing any event beyond a certain, specific distance, whatever instruments of visual enlargement or of radio receptivity we may employ. It is not because the system is receding so fast that its signals would have to exceed the absolute limit of 'c'. It is because of the fact that, owing to the curvature of the Universe, at a distance of Longitude 90° we would be observing the Pole. To put the matter in more obvious words, the further we penetrate into Space with our instruments of observation, the further we go back in history, until at a distance of one quarter of the way around the Cosmos we can only observe what could be described in theological terms as the Creation. Beyond this we can never see, not only because there is nothing to see, but because the Now Curve cannot reach beyond this distance. The Universe has not ceased to exist, but we must recognise the fact that, above the Pole, observation, if it could penetrate so far, would not be in contact with the Cosmos at all. Beyond the Pole — or if you prefer it, before the Creation — there is nothing to see. And this is not because of something connected with the speed of light, or for any religious reason, but because of geometry.

The Causal Curve

Lying in the opposite direction — into the Future — we can imagine a similar line, the Causal, which represents the final limit of signals originating Here and Now. This will be found to follow a Great Circle from wherever we are, to a point on the cosmic equator, 90° east or west.

The positioning of these two lines has a significant relation to our

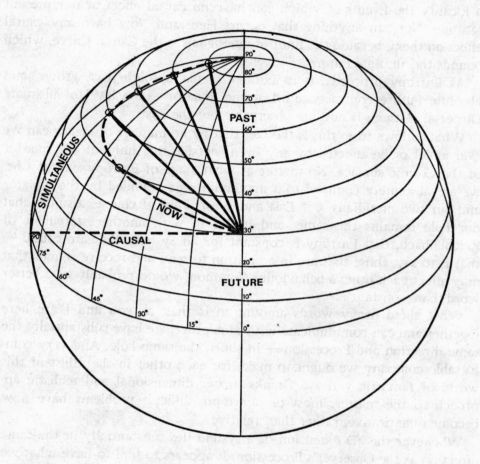

This attempt to show approximately the course of the Now and Causal lines on a plane surface is no more than a picture, drawn in simulated perspective. An accurate diagram of such a subject would have to be drawn on the surface of a globe.

powers of observation. Above the Now Curve is absolute Past. Below the
Causal Curve is absolute Future. Between the two is an interval that has
been described by Eddington as the Simultaneous area, by which he means
a locality the Events of which can have no causal effect at our present
latitude. Nor can anything that occurs Here and Now have any causal
effect on them, because the limit of our signals is the Causal Curve, which
bounds the absolute Future.

As Entropy proceeds, it is axiomatic that absolute Past grows, and
absolute Future contracts, until at the Equator — the level of ultimate
Dispersal — there is nothing observable but the Past.

What follows from this is the fact that by no manner of means can we
ever affect or be affected by any Event outside the limits of one quarter
of the Cosmic surface. No matter at what stage of Entropy we may be,
we are absolutely confined to a maximum area bounded by the Equator
and our two meridians, 90° East and West. This, of course, assumes that
our Pole remains the same, and it ties in with another statement of
Reichenbach, that Entropy is constant for all Systems that are causal —
that is to say, those that are in a position to send and receive signals that
may affect each other's behaviour. 'Common' would probably be a better
word than 'constant'.

What these heavy words amount to is that, as you and I are here
together and can communicate with each other, we have substantially the
same direction and Procession — in short, the same Pole. And very comfortable company we ought to make for each other in the midst of this
world of fantastic variety. Thanks to our dimensional and realistic approach to the matter, most of our more difficult problems have now
become quantitative, rather than relative.

Whenever the 4D extension of a system lies substantially in the same
direction as the Observer's Procession, it appears to him to have what we
call Inertia. If, through the alteration of its angle, it comes to lie away
from the Observer's direction, it appears to acquire Velocity and Mass,
and with them a gravitational field of its own.

This divergence of direction may be due to the fact that at a distance,
its own meridian, although related to the same Pole, lies at an angle to
the Observer's meridian. Alternatively, it may be due to Energy, which
amounts to a change of 4D Direction, and which is related quantitatively
with Mass — the formula being the familiar $E = mc^2$. This equation
holds good notwithstanding the fact that two of its terms are relative,
and the third is virtually meaningless. Oddly enough, it is the imaginary

quality of the supposed speed of Light (which is dependent upon relative Latitude) that makes the equation workable, and indeed, obvious enough to be made use of by the advertising business.

Finally, it might be added, that following the same conception of the Cosmos, Gravity — which has already been classified as a signal — may also be regarded as an expression of a tendency of all observable systems in the same neighbourhood to lie in parallel, in the absence of the contrary effects of Energy. Alternatively, it might be said that they are open to observation because of the fact that they *do* lie in parallel. This phenomenon is probably not so much a compulsive law of Physics, as an aspect of the fact that, while smaller systems have their own individual characteristics, they are nearly all components of greater systems, to the direction of which they in general conform, as members of the same family. As a constituent part of the system we know as the Earth, my ponderous flesh would require a considerable application of Energy before it   See could be persuaded to transfer its allegiance elsewhere, and fly   Appendix off into space.   E

Back to the Abbé

But to return to our vision of the beginning of all things, what we have already heard from the Abbé Lemaître about his cosmic egg and its contents is far from being all that we are told about the features of this primaeval bang, although the authority for the figures is not always disclosed. According to Bronowski, it seems that the parcel of first causes was at the fantastic temperature of about 15,000 million degrees Centigrade during 'the first moment of Creation'. By the end of the 'day' in which dispersal began, the heat was down to about forty million degrees, and it had further decreased to a modest ten million 'on the evening of the sixth day', by which time everything was really spreading out.

There appear to be some overtones from the Book of Genesis in this account: indeed, one almost expects to learn next that on the seventh day the Lord rested, as well he might. This, however, is not included as part of the programme, and in spite of some other touches that seem to recall further aspects of a familiar myth, we must accept the fact — in terms of appearance — that there must be some form of celestial Fourth of July, although the actual date has now been put back by some thousand millions of years. (As in the case of taxation, we usually tend to be very free and easy with the open end of any arithmetical series, which begins at Zero but has no limit at the other end except the sky, unless it converges.)

An alternative View of the Big Bang

As an alternative to this terrifying upheaval, let us go back to our geographical globe — still being used as a model for the Cosmos — and imagine ourselves placing this ball into a bucket of water, the surface of which represents the 5D plane of Procession. The first point of contact of this globe with the water becomes the Pole, for the purposes of the experiment, and the speed at which the sphere descends — which is presumably constant — represents the speed of Procession, while the movement of the surface of the water up the meridial lines relative to that Pole, indicates the behaviour of Entropy.

It will be seen that, for a moment after touching the water, the surface flies outwards, up the lines of Longitude from an instant of absolute velocity (Simultaneity) to a speed that immediately decreases, and which continues to slow down as the contact of the surface of the water with the globe proceeds up the meridians, until finally at the Equator the speed of this movement corresponds with that of the descent of the sphere itself.

Have we not here an intelligible model that explains geometrically the two principal problems that are puzzling us: first, the primal explosion, and secondly, the expansion of the Universe? Were observation, as we know it, possible at the Pole, it would report a fantastic flying apart of all the genidentical systems along their divergent world lines, beginning with a speed of unexceedable violence, but immediately slowing down into more reasonable velocities, that finally accord with the speed of Procession at the moment of ultimate dispersal.

Yet this apparent explosion does not originate, as supposed, in the blowing up of a parcel of first causes. It comes literally from nothing. What is created at the Pole is neither Time nor Space, but the possibility of observation. So both the Abbé and Hoyle are right to this extent, that there is an absolute Beginning, not in terms of so many years ago, but so many Parsecs away along our meridian. And in spite of the apparent effect of this enormous activity at the moment of first contact with the Cosmos, the latter is a perfectly stable and unaltering extension.

Oscillation

What is more significant still is the fact that Sandage, in his advocacy of an oscillating or pulsating Universe, was probably nearest of all to an answer, until he decided to go back to Newtonian conceptions of Gravity, in the company of Caltec and the University of Texas.

In recent years it has appeared to the authorities at Palomar that there are signs of misbehaviour on the part of Hubble's line at very great distances that are now open to more accurate observation through the analysis of radio signals — or the behaviour of Quasars, if a more up-to-the-minute mystique is preferred. It would seem that observable phenomena in this area are showing signs of falling short of their expected Hubble positions, a fact that is taken as evidence in favour of the Abbé's Big Bang at the expense of Hoyle's balanced state. (If the latter were the correct interpretation, any discrepancy should be the other way, towards an increased displacement rather than the opposite.)

See Appendix G

From this it may be taken that the Hubble Constant does not follow a straight line after all, but that of a very elongated curve, unnoticeable close at hand, but with a curvature that increases more rapidly as distance increases, until the point is reached where recession reaches the velocity of 'c', beyond which the Universe contracts to its original condition of absolute concentration, at which point observation can function no longer. It has even been considered possible to put a Time estimate on to this entire period of expansion followed by contraction.

Eighty-two thousand million years was the figure given by Sandage, from Egg to Egg.

This oscillation is explained by some as being brought about by imbalance on the part of the forces of Gravity, and a more dynamic and kinematic conception of the Universe could hardly be conceived. But this need not be accepted as the only possible view. Indeed, we have every reason to feel excited and even elated at being provided with the estimate. Interesting as it is, its importance does not lie in the fact that it offers a Space/Time figure for the linear distance from Pole to Pole. This is a piece of information of very doubtful value, in the absence of any standard of measurement for 5D Time. What is exhilarating is the fact that it presents us with a possible means of calculating our own cosmic latitude. As a basis for all future astronomical calculations, what could be more useful than a reasonably accurate fix of our present 4D position? Whatever the speed of Procession may be, this Time estimate of the distance from Pole to Pole can be related to the Time estimate of our own distance from one Pole, that has already been provided by the Hubble Constant. From these figures, our latitude should approximately be ascertainable.

Furthermore the geometry of the whole performance becomes glaringly clear. Our 5D plane of Observation is proceeding from a Pole (where we have never personally been) towards an Equator (which we need never hope to visit). However, our valuable presence is not required to make the model work.

Beyond the Equator, were the plane of Observation to continue to move down the surface of our cosmic sphere, what would appear — were we there to see it — would be a contracting Universe with Entropy in reverse. Finally, at the other Pole, the Universe would seem to disappear altogether, for precisely the same reason that had caused it miraculously to appear at the Creation — the operation of Procession.

In short, what we have to do is to look in the opposite direction — away from a Past which is being anxiously scrutinised by the Astronomers, and into the Future, and towards an explanation that does not depend upon any cosmic breathing in and out, but that relates solely to the advance of Procession, through a geometric expansion of the field, until Entropy arrives at the Equator.

Our Present Latitude

The figure originally given by Sandage for the entire double process is a Light-Year estimate, and not one of strictly linear distance. And it will also be remembered that the figure of between nine and ten thousand million light years as our distance from the nearest Pole is also an estimate in similar terms. Relating one estimate to the other, the accompanying diagram has been kindly worked out for an unmathematical father by my youngest son. From this it appears that, if the Data is substantially correct, our present latitude on the Cosmos is about 50°, while the 'radius of Space' is whatever linear distance is represented by Sandage's figure of forty-one thousand million years.

This measurement is only valid at the 5D level of the Observer's Continuum. It is not an absolute otherwise. See pp. 231-232.

These measurements are trigonometrical ones, and do not depend on or disclose the speed of Procession. Indeed, it is not at all certain that any such figure can be arrived at at present, without a firm unit of Space/Time to give it quantitative value. So we are merely assuming that it is constant — a fact that there is no reason to doubt until

The Light Year is, of course, a useful unit of Space/Time — the distance covered by a light signal in a vacuum in the course of a year. The trouble is that, for reasons already given, there are grounds to suspect that this unit only applies to observations taken at

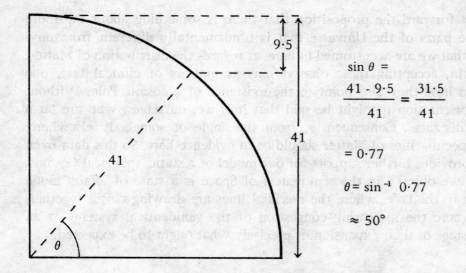

$$\sin \theta =$$

$$\frac{41 - 9 \cdot 5}{41} = \frac{31 \cdot 5}{41}$$

$$= 0 \cdot 77$$

$$\theta = \sin^{-1} 0 \cdot 77$$

$$\approx 50°$$

some evidence to the contrary appears.

The resulting latitude is not inconsistent with Reichenbach's estimate of the relative proportion of organisation and dispersal in the visible world around us, and it places us on the Cosmos in a middle latitude corresponding roughly with that of the English Channel on a terrestrial globe. But of course if the original Hubble figure is too small, as has been suggested, the calculations will merely push us somewhat further towards the Equator.

our present latitude, and that it probably varies with the quantity of 'c' at other cosmic locations. (We have seen how 'c' reaches the ultimate speed of simultaneity at Latitude 0°.) An alternative unit of astronomical measurement is the Parsec, which has a purely geometrical basis (the distance at which the diameter of the Earth's orbit subtends an angle of two seconds of arc). This has the advantage of being an absolute measurement of distance, and in our present location it corresponds to 3.2 light years. But does it always do so? As an unvarying yardstick for lower dimensional measurement it is excellent. But is it any use for statements concerning Space/Time?

Conditions in Farthest Space

There was a time when some Astronomers were puzzled by the fact that the further one probes into outer space, the more signs of congestion appear. One would imagine that, if the Universe were expanding, it should become more tenuous in what, to us, are its outer limits, rather than the reverse. But according to Ryle, this is not so. Indeed, Ryle was so impressed by this evidence of a certain thickening-up at a distance that he put forward the proposition that there is something about the more remote parts of the Universe that is fundamentally different from anything that we are accustomed to here, as regards the distribution of Matter.

Again, accepting these observations as matters of clinical fact, one notices how they also point to the existence of a cosmic Pole. Without such orientation it might be said that it is we, ourselves, who are 'at a great distance'. Consequently, from the angle of somebody elsewhere, these peculiarities of Matter should be in evidence here. So this data from Ryle provides further support for our model of a static, spherical Cosmos. What we observe in the remoteness of Space is a state of affairs much nearer to the Pole, where the meridial lines are drawing closer together, and where the increasing congestion of the genidentical systems at an early stage of their expansion, is precisely what ought to be expected.

Butterflies and Bicycles

Yet even in the speculations of the unpopular Ouspensky, who contributed something to our formulation of a model in six dimensions, we still find this curious inability to avoid Newtonian three dimensional conceptions when discussing 4D phenomena. Considering the enormous velocities involved, we find Ouspensky speculating on how he could catch the end of a ray of light 'that has not yet reached its destination'. This would present no problem at all if he would only apply his own principles. Accepting the nature of Space/Time as a 4D extension, how — one may ask — can there be such a thing as a ray of light that 'has not yet reached its destination'? A light signal has not got an 'end' to it that is winging its way towards some 'destination' in peril of Ouspensky's butterfly net. He is trying to lasso an extension in Space/Time with a three dimensional implement and he ought to know better.

Nevertheless, it is fair to say that expressions such as 'Time', 'Velocity', 'Energy' and 'Mass' are perfectly valid where they belong. In discussing phenomena that occur in the lower dimensions they work successfully, and all we have to do in order to justify their employment is to keep them there.

If I am caught by a policeman while speeding at seventy miles an hour, I will not do myself any good by telling him that there is no such thing as Time. To him, the offence is unarguable, because he and his watch are in a qualified state of rest, and it is in relation to this that the law applies, and the summons is issued.

Similarly, the fact that the mechanical sciences manage to function with a set of ideas that are quite illusory when applied to the more subtle conceptions of Space/Time, does not prevent us in any way from constructing motorbikes, and from going on enjoyable, subjective rides on them.

The Answer we Deserved

So this might be an appropriate moment to pause and ask whether we may now have reached a point at which an unequivocal answer might be given to the question that we ourselves presented to the Astronomers. It would seem that a workable reply is substantially an elaboration of that already given to us by Dr. Synge, namely that the question is an absurd one.

It postulates, not merely one, but three absolutes — my velocity, A's velocity and B's velocity. But no question of added velocities can arise, because so far as the Observer is concerned there is no velocity, except that of his own Procession. The other two speeds are merely expressions of 4D angle. The fallacy lies in confusing the angles of these respective extensions with the speed of Procession, and in attempting to add what we observe as 4D angle to what others observe as 5D Procession. If we are going to talk about what *we* observe, we cannot have it every way by talking in the same breath about what others observe. What we observe of others is their direction, and not their observations, and no statements regarding the appearance of the Universe in the eyes of other Observers can have any reference to our own data, unless they have the same Pole, which is probably not the case in the problem offered.

If I still have not answered the clinical part of the question, let me add that neither A nor B will see anything of each other, since no system can be observed that is moving at such enormous velocities, except at very great distances.

Furthermore, even if it were possible for either A or B to see each other before the point where all three courses meet, it would not be from the direction seen by the central character that they would see each other approaching, but from the opposite 4D side of the meeting point, which would place their approach velocity at less than 'c'.

So the paradox of Added Velocities is really a fraud, and need not alter our old-fashioned conviction that two and two make four. Indeed, the expression itself is a contradiction in terms, since for each Observer there is only one velocity, which is based on his own Procession. There is no other velocity to which it may be added. This fact is fundamental to the thesis being suggested here, and if we stick to it we shall probably find that it ultimately makes sense.

Although the Authorities usually take it as a matter of course that the Observer's point of view changes in relation to his field of vision, I have not so far come across any discussion as to whether this process takes place at a measurable speed. In these pages the movement of Observation in relation to World Lines is referred to as 'Procession' which, in the absence of any reason to the contrary, is assumed to be constant. More significant still is the fact that it is a 5D phenomenon, which is probably why the subject is usually ignored. (A fifth dimension is not, as yet, generally accepted.) So in default of any professional opinions, we can only speculate that the Speed of Procession is not technically a 'Speed' at all, but will probably turn out to be related to an Absolute of Acceleration, and that this mysterious figure of thirty-two feet per second, like that other arbitrary stopping point known as 'c', is dependent in some way upon the Observer's Cosmic Latitude. But this can be no more than a guess until the subject is examined seriously by some inspired Mathematicians.

VII MUSICAL MANGERS

Quae omnia laudentur
et ingenium quo illis laetor.

Cross-Examination

AFTER having devoted so many pages to didactic pronouncements, it is only right to assume for a moment the opposite rôle of *Advocatus Diaboli*, in order to ask a few of those reasonable questions that are calculated to put a diagnosis to the test.

How much of what has been said is a matter of logical necessity, and how much is speculation? Is it based upon experiment, intuition, or only on symbolic information? To what extent is this reiterated claim to unoriginality justified by the earlier statements of experts?

In the course of all these references to observation and appearances, have we taken into account the fact that the instrument of observation is, itself, a system, and as such is subject to Entropy, and is unable to contemplate itself by its own unaided efforts?

In so far as we have been discussing what it is that the instrument should observe at the Cosmic Pole, or under the general conditions of dispersion and inertia that are said to exist at the Cosmic Equator, has it been made reasonably clear that any such diagnoses are purely theoretical? No mortal instrument could possibly function under the fantastic conditions that must be present close to the first contact of a plane of Observation with a Pole, or during the last stages of its approach to an Equator. The area open to the functioning of human observation might, by analogy, be compared to the temperate zones of the surface of the Earth.

The more one considers the matter the more unique both Instrument and Conditions seem to be. It is not just a matter of cosmic latitude, although this obviously plays an important part in enabling our existence. Sentient life, as we know it, is dependent for its operation upon medial conditions of heat and cold, and upon constant protection against radiation and other forms of spatial violence. Parasitic as we are, where else but on a small, overripe planet could we exercise our functions, or would we be likely to meet with our kind? Even if there are millions of examples of similar conditions scattered around the Galactic System and out in the greater depths of Space, they are still relatively rare. Even on this Earth, life of the kind that we are referring to has only extended since the Protozoic, which is but a fraction of Space/Time when compared to the age of the Earth itself.

Systems are as Mortal as Men

I think that it was Hoyle who pointed out that practically all Systems have only a limited extension in the Continuum, and are only remotely connected with a first Cause, even when of astronomical proportions. Our own Sun is described as a third generation star, and is by no means as old as Creation. Hoyle would probably add that this fact is in line with his picture of a balanced production of matter. But we need not so regard it, as the same point might be made when we contemplate the phenomenon of human birth. Conception is another example of multiple Causation — not of the creation of matter, but of the manner in which systems grow out of conditions that have gone before.

This bundle of sensibilities that is typing these words is a collegium of atoms that began to build itself into a system round about the cosmic latitude that we describe as September, 1900. From this level it has extended as a genidentical phenomenon, in which the molecular content has not remained the same throughout. I have got somewhat stouter in recent years, I am sorry to say. I have also pared my nails and had my hair cut at irregular intervals. But the System has remained. At some lower latitude, not very far off, the System will disintegrate, and although its molecular subscribers will not disappear as a consequence of this break-up, the System will be no more. Its constituents will have taken themselves off to form parts of other, and quite different systems — maybe as part of a tree that I would very much like to have planted on my grave, as an indication of the fact that even my debris may still be turned to a living purpose.

There is no intelligent cause for complaint about this process. Nothing goes on for ever, in the sense of an interminable extension — not even the Sun — and to wish that it might do so is a childish fear of the dark. On the other hand, nothing can affect the factual and permanent reality of any System between its terminal latitudes. This is neither an expression of immortality, nor of that ghoulish conception, the resurrection of the body. As between its proper dates, while the Universe itself remains, this particular System is available for the immortal purposes of the Elan — or as the Orient would put it, for the use of the ultimate Awareness — which is 'X'. But not thereafter or before.

All systems, whether sentient or not, are alike in this — that they form, they mature, and they die. They all have multiple causes, which fact may, perhaps, be regarded as an expression of the Open Past. Whether they are significantly causative themselves is a matter of degree; but one and all,

the causes of their causes extend back to the First Cause, which is no
Godot with a white beard, but the Pole. And when I mention a system I
am referring as readily to the Sun as I am to Charles Chaplin or to the
River Liffey.

Some Pragmatic Tests

But to get back to some matters of observable fact through which this
entire diagnosis might be tested, we have of course both Entropy and the
arithmetical quantity of 'c'. If Entropy is not slowing down in relation to
the speed of Procession, it follows that we are wrong in our theory that
Observation is proceeding from a Pole of fantastic activity (Lemaître's
Big Bang) to a cosmic Equator, where visual 'happening' (could it exist at
all) is no more. Furthermore, if it can be shown that the quantity of 'c' is
absolute, regardless of the Observer's latitude, we are also fundamentally
wrong in our explanation of what is occurring.

Any practical investigation of such matters is far beyond my capacity, and should be undertaken by qualified persons. All that I would like to repeat is my firm conviction that any cosmic definition or estimate referring to Speed or Time is suspect, except only those concerned with Procession in 5D.

It might also be suggested, as a minor method of disproval, that if it can be shown that the point of reflection of a light signal (i.e. the position of the mirror) is precisely at the half way mark of the sum of the two legs of the extension, then again, the hypothesis is wrong. The outward course of a reflected signal should be the shorter.

Beyond the Equator

The question as to what would happen were Observation to cross the
cosmic Equator is a purely theoretical one. Entropy is engaged in undoing
organisation, and the Observer, being himself a system, would have
experienced this process of dispersal long before his vehicle or its descendants could extend to the Equator.

Speaking theoretically, all that one can say is that, beyond the Equator
lies an anti-Universe through which Procession, were it to continue in the
same direction as before, would observe a rebuilding of dispersal into
organisation, with Entropy operating in reverse.

This is simply an expression of the second phase, originally predicted
by Sandage — that of contraction which follows the terminal crisis of

expansion. Such a Universe would disappear into nothing as soon as the other Pole is reached. In other words, to an Ideal Observer it appears to oscillate. But it would amount to a grave misdescription of what is happening if one were to say that the Universe is blowing up and then deflating. It only seems to be doing so. It is not so violent in its habits.

Deviation beyond the Latitude

There is also another outstanding question that has a bearing upon this matter of logical necessity. When the extension of an observable System deviates from the general direction of our meridian, why should it not occasionally do so beyond the limit of a right angle, and switch beyond what is to us the latitude direction — in other words into the Past? Is such an effect ever known? If not, why not: and if so, what does it look like?

An immediate answer would be that all changes in direction require a cause in order to enable some departure from their basic condition of inertia, and the cause can usually be described as a form of acceleration. My motor car changes its direction in relation to the scenery because of an acceleration imparted by a release of the energy of petroleum. I break my neck because of the fact that Trafalgar Square violently restores my 4D direction soon after I have fallen off the top of the Nelson Monument. But the amount of acceleration needed to deviate a system beyond 90° from the Observer's meridian is enough to make it acquire what would appear to the original Observer as absolute Velocity which, strangely enough, is a condition of All-Mass. And All-Mass presumably means No Signals. Apart from the fact that such inspiration could hardly be expected to come from nowhere, it seems unlikely that we would continue to see visually any System developing such Velocity.

The fact remains, however, that in the data provided by Atomic Physics it is possible to register such a phenomenon experimentally. In 1941 Stuckelberg and Feynman examined a particle known as a positron, which emerges miraculously, together with an Electron, from the nothingness of a Gamma Ray. Each then sets off in its own direction, and the peculiar fate of the Positron is that it appears to collide with another Electron, at which moment both the Positron and this second Electron disappear into another Gamma Ray.

This odd effect of apparent creation and disappearance is so much out of line with standard ideas on the nature of Matter that the Physicists have been having some difficulty, not only in providing an explanation, but even in describing what precisely is taking place. There is, however, one hypothesis, advanced by Reichenbach a few years ago, which is based on a view of the problem as an aspect of 4D extension, and which appears to be fully in agreement with what is being suggested here.

Reichenbach proposes that only one electron and no positron is actually involved in this mysterious affair, and some diagrams illustrating the features of his theory will be found in Appendix D. It is true that, as far as one knows, such a situation is only to be found in the realm of atomic behaviour; but the phenomenon itself, and Reichenbach's interpretation, do provide a vivid example of how the Physicists, whenever they are prepared to accept the conception of motion as a spatial extension in a fourth dimension, are able to offer a rational picture of what would otherwise be not only irrational, but quite unscientific behaviour.

DER GEIST DES WIEDERSPRUCHS

ZOPHAR   It seems to me that you are merely answering a number of minor objections that we Scientists are not actually making. You should be aware that phenomena such as Oscillation, Multiple Causation, and even the slowing down of the Universe are widely accepted by many Physicists today. My real quarrel is that you are trying to avoid dealing with our main criticism, which concerns a fallacy that has been the bane of a long string of amateurs before you.

QUERIST   Then tell me what this objection is.

ZOPHAR   You are trying to spatialise Time. This is due to a confusion of thought that was pointed out by Eddington and demolished by old Miss Cleugh of Bedford College long ago.

QUERIST   But I am not spatialising Time. I am spatialising four dimensional extension, which you yourself describe as Space/Time. Maybe I am spatialising Entropy too by calling it Direction. But my point is that Time is neither of these.

ZOPHAR   Then may I enquire what it is?

QUERIST   If it is anything at all, apart from being a byproduct of limited perception, it is something that only applies to the speed of Procession.

ZOPHAR   Ah, then you *do* agree that speed must not be spatialised?

QUERIST   Of course I agree — adding, however, that there is nothing that can be described as unqualified and measurable Speed, except the speed of Procession.

ZOPHAR   An expression invented by yourself.

QUERIST   (*indignantly*) Nothing that I am saying has been invented by myself. I am merely reporting the data that I am being given by people like you.

ZOPHAR   You mean by people like Ouspensky — a character who is recognised by all serious Physicists as being as nutty as a fruit cake.

QUERIST   Nutty or not, you can't load me with Guilt by Association. All that I am taking from Ouspensky is some of his Data.

ZOPHAR   You are just as guilty as Ouspensky if what you accept from him leads you to that old, exploded conclusion that the Past has got as real an existence as the Present.

QUERIST   Excuse me, that is a philosophical opinion. What right have you, as a Scientist, to draw philosophical conclusions from a field in which you are just as much an amateur as I am?

ELIPHAZ   That may be true enough as regards Zophar, but in matters of Philosophy *I* am not an amateur; and I agree that the Past has not got a real existence. *Esse est Percipi.* For you and me, there is only Here and Now.

QUERIST   That sophism is at the root of the trouble. If I may say so, you don't actually consider that anything exists except yourself.

ELIPHAZ   There is no empirical evidence to the contrary. I have none. Have you?

BILDAD   If I may intervene, if anybody is entitled to mention empirical evidence it is I. You are all expressing matters of opinion, and Opinion is entirely irrelevant. I can create Opinion. But where scientific evidence is concerned, I doubt whether any of you could recognise it when you see it. You are all too busy playing at Engine Drivers.

QUERIST   I don't know whether that remark means that you are on my side or not.

BILDAD   I am certainly not on your side, because you are trying to build conclusions upon a delusion that Thought is something more than a purely mental function. Thought is a private matter that can be controlled by conditioning, and the fact that an Observer is himself a system does not mean that he is unable to contemplate himself. The fact that we perform our experiments successfully proves conclusively that the trained mind can regard itself clinically. We do so every day.

QUERIST   If the Behaviourist is able to contemplate himself, this proves my point that there is an element beyond conditioning that operates his mind.

BILDAD   (*with a smile*) I suppose that you are referring to this miasma you call the Elan. But why not go back to the Sunday School where you picked up these ideas, and call it the Soul? Come now, I'll make you a fair offer. If you will bring me a small portion of Soul, I shall undertake to put it in my Box, and give you the results.

QUERIST   (*despairingly*) I see that I am getting nowhere.

ZOPHAR   Oh, I think you are. Back to the Children's Encyclopedia —

ELIPHAZ   — from where we started.

          (*Laughter*)

QUERIST   (*raising his voice*) Is that any worse than into a view of the Cosmos that is more contradictory than Danté's? In the long run what answers have any of you got? 'You don't know :' 'It all depends.'

BILDAD On the contrary. I have some very good answers.

ZOPHAR We are not looking for answers. Our concern is with Facts.

ELIPHAZ I suppose you imagine that *you* have some answers?

QUERIST Regarding the structure of the Universe — Yes. What I don't pretend to know is something further in — something that is none of Man's business.

BILDAD Well, that ties the matter up, doesn't it? What you don't know — you're too damn knowing to enquire about.

(*More laughter*)

QUERIST (*intemperately*) My curse upon the Yards that give you suck — miserable comforters that you are ! My ignorance is something that is within myself, while yours is spread abroad. But no doubt you are all mortal, and your follies shall die with you.

BILDAD (*after an uncomfortable pause*) I think that this fellow must be pining for a pyre.

ELIPHAZ We are wasting our time, and had better so report.

ZOPHAR We may be having a little trouble with our students, but we should have no difficulty at all in fixing him.

VIII   THERE'S A HORSE
ON THIS TRAM!

Et gladius signo domini agnoscatur
ita verbo orator.

The Green Bay Tree

THIS conception of a time-deleted Cosmos that has been offered as a possible aid to an understanding of some of the paradoxes of Physics is no new thing. Yet it has been relegated to Limbo very consistently by both the Scientists and the Theologians whenever it has reappeared in the pages of Dunne, of Ouspensky, or by implication in the thinking of Parmenides and the Stoics. The fundamental objection is that it seems to be an expression of absolute Determinism — a conclusion that is worse than death in the eyes of those who, very properly, desire a purpose in life. Indeed, my early mentor, Miss Cleugh, refers to it rather petulantly as flourishing in the pages of Dunne 'like a green bay tree'.

It may fairly be asked why we should have all those agonies of indecision if the course that we are to take is inevitably fixed already? Were we to sit back and decide nothing, would the results still be the same? Indeed, what is Thought at all if it is not something more significant than a product of Bildad's Box? Surely to some extent it must be a director of conduct? It would be a grim prospect to find that we are trapped in a single, absolute continuum, with nothing to dwell with except our sins, and still worse if — as some would have it — the only purpose of life is to commit them again and again.

There are, however, those who take the view that the exercise of a function of common experience is not necessarily a form of delusional insanity. The well-loved Limerick that goes:

> There was a young man who said "Damn!
> I've discovered at last what I am.
> I'm a being that moves
> In determinate grooves.
> Not even a bus, but a tram!"

is not sufficiently convincing to make us abandon some feeling of responsibility for what we are doing. Those who advance such formulae are flat continuum men, and descendants of our two sea captains.

I am aware that Free Will is under heavy assault today from many Thinkers about Thought, but thanks to a further element that springs from 4D curvature, I am here suggesting that we are actually as much at liberty as our first parents were, once those gates of Eden ponderously closed behind them, and they found themselves face to face with the business of living.

I do not recollect where I first heard the word 'Alternation', but it

probably originated in those academic circles where, some years ago, the facetious image was being bandied about of a traveller on a tram, who brought a horse along with him. This private, scholarly wisecrack may seem out of place on the lips of Oxbridge philosophers, but it was probably invented to suggest that there might be a welcome escape route from the boredom of trams.

We have seen how the sensation of movement in the three-dimensional field presents itself to us as Observers. Without the faculty of movement that is conferred upon the body by its legs, we would have great difficulty in comprehending the real nature of extension in the world around us. Legs enable the performer to move about in the 3D field, so giving him an appreciation of the meaning of distance and size, and making it possible for him to contribute to the Happenings of that world. This ability endows the animal kingdom with one of the prizes of Evolution, not enjoyed by less advanced forms of life that can only experience the passage of Time, but not the alternative localities that it is possible to visit.

Similarly, the fact that Man's ability to get around is volitional and is usually the result of Thought, is an expression of a further gift — that of being able to control (but not to create) the future. In other words, he finds himself capable of exploiting the alternatives that lie in a deeper dimension than can be perceived by static forms of life. This exercise of personal choice is the faculty that initiates 4D movement, and any insistence upon a single, determined Future merely shows an inability to appreciate what we are doing whenever, for good or ill, we make a decision.

It should be emphasized, however, that the practice of 4D movement is not one of bodily tourism. It is not something that the flesh goes in for— popping about from continuum to continuum — a pointless performance, seeing that the flesh, like the other systems of which it is a part, has its own extension in 5D already. It is the Observer who is capable of focusing attention on the continuum of his choice — a feat that is no more open to all forms of life than is the use of legs. Thanks to an awareness of Alternation, the human Observer can take advantage of the fact that he has more than one predetermined world line from which to select.

This movement in 4D appears as angle in 5D (following the model already applied to the lower dimensions). And I suggest that if we try to follow any other interpretation of the process of voluntary selection, we merely find ourselves back amidst the clatter of the mechanical sciences.

Heisenberg says No !

To summarise the quandary in which we are entangled, both logic and an objective consideration of our Past, together with most of the signposts of contemporary science, all confirm the Behaviourists' determined Future. Yet it cannot be determined, because of the fact demonstrated by Heisenberg, that it is not predictable. What follows from this is even more significant; if it is not predictable, it is probably avoidable. On the other hand, if the future is not determined, are we to concur in the rather pompous conclusion that we are its creators, whether individually or collectively? This is the pretentious, but not uncommon notion that was satirised by Goethe in a celebrated speech of one of the graduate companions of Dr. Faust:

During World War 2 Heisenberg was one of Hitler's most valued scientists, and it is fortunate for us all that his search for the secret of an atomic weapon was too indeterminate to forestall Szilard's work in Roosevelt's camp.

Here is the ringing word of Youth :
This Earth was nothing till I called it forth.
I drew the Sun out of the sea.
With *me* began the Universe in all its splendour.
Day sprang to light my way.
The soil brought forth its blossoms
And grew green at my approach.
At the blinking of my eyelid in that primaeval gloom
The stars shone out.
Like the Great Thoughts set free by my arrival,
My Spirit, breaking forth in joy
From chains of ignorance and cant,
Ranges after an inner light that is from *me* —
And from none other.

Fan-shaped Destiny

In the preface to *Kandelman's Krim* my friend, Dr. Synge, discusses the steps by which a distinguished relative, the eighteenth-century mathematician and clergyman, Hugh Hamilton, attempted to prove the existence of God by means of three propositions. The first of these is the only one that need concern us here. It is described as an Axiom, and runs as follows:

> Whatever is contingent, or might possibly have been otherwise than it is, must have some cause which determined it to be what it is. Or in other words, if two different or contrary things were each of them possible, whichever of them took place, or came to pass, it must have done so in consequence of some cause which determined that *it* and *not the other*, should take place.

This type of statement is easy to laugh at today, on the ground that it argues from data that is self-contradictory. For how — we hear them say — can there be two conflicting outcomes, 'each of them possible', if, for causal reasons, only one of them actually occurs?

The proposition is clearly absurd, unless we are prepared to look upon it dimensionally. Suppose Hamilton is right — not for a reason to which he would probably have subscribed, but because *both* outcomes 'occur' (although we are only equipped to be aware of one of them *per continuum*). This is what makes both of them 'possible'. There is something here that has been referred to by another Physicist, Dudley Towne, under the description of 'fan-shaped Destiny', which may indicate that Hamilton is not so absurd after all.

There is a multiple — though a limited — number of routes by which it is possible for me to travel from Dublin to Galway. Some of these routes are more likely to be taken than others, and if we intend to make the journey, Probability will predict that we will go by way of Athlone rather than through the City of Kilkenny. But both highways have an actual existence, and neither of them is created by the exercise of our choice.

Now, here is where Heisenberg comes in. Even if we are fully informed about the comparative attractions in Athlone and Kilkenny and are properly briefed about the condition of the two roads, nobody — not even Heisenberg or ourselves — can predict with absolute certainty what is going to happen, until it is clear which continuum of the journey is under observation. So far as the physical implement is concerned, it may perhaps be regarded as making the trip potentially by both routes.

It may transpire, as between one continuum and another, that there are no significant differences to be noticed. It may also turn out that, for some reason or other, certain imaginable contingencies are not valid possibilities at all; in which case the alternatives are reduced in number.

But so long as we do not know what limitations there are of this kind, and have not irrevocably set forth in a particular continuum, prediction is impossible, however much factual information we may have. This applies to our observation of the behaviour of inanimate objects as readily as it does to matters where human selection is involved. It is not anything in the behaviour of Matter that is at issue, but the view taken by the Observer: and in both cases, contradictory happenings may occur simultaneously.

So here we are back again with something not unlike the old Platonic conception of a number of parallel Universes, in which all valid possibilities have a real existence, although it may be more likely that we will experience one rather than the other.

This immediately raises the question: Where do these alternatives exist? In answering this we find ourselves answering another outstanding question, already raised on page 77: Of what does the 'thickness' of 5D Cosmos consist? It consists of other Continua in which World Lines, including the Observer's, may extend in depth. Thus each individual's life span (which we reluctantly agree is determined, although in multiple form) may have an unknown number of alternative states in 5D that are capable of contradicting purely 4D Determinism.

We have already used the model of a strip of cinematograph film as an example of a series of linear states that resembles the extension of world lines in 4D. To illustrate in a similar way this more subtle extension in 5D, we might take a number of photographs of varying aspects of a static situation, all taken at the same Now, and placed, not in length as in the case of 4D extension, but one on top of the other — although here again, I do not believe that there is any division between the features of one continuum and those of its neighbour, as the model suggests.

See
Appendix
G

I freely admit that it is almost impossible for us to devise any adequate diagram for such an extension, or to visualise the appearance of a series of parallel continua, each conditioning its neighbour, and all of them presenting the apparent quality of a 4D surface, just as

Perhaps a helpful analogy may be found in the development of the text of this book. There are now about seventy copies at large since it was first printed, none of which are identical. Each might be related to a cross-section of a 4D progression in format each cross section of a cube may take on the aspect of a 2D square.

But it is not beyond the power of the human mind to contemplate it intellectually. We have long been acquainted with the idea of at least one 'other world'. Although there is nothing either ghostly or ideal about these ones, and verbiage in the general direction (it is hoped) of greater precision. Thus the book may be said to have an Entropy, under the arrow of which earlier numbered copies usually disclose no 'memory' of later additions and corrections. Yet each copy has presumably a continuing existence, and presents a 'surface' that may be studied without reference to any other state of the text, earlier or later.

they do seem to provide us with an answer to the glaring paradox that we exist in a determined Universe — limited yet unbounded — in which a power of voluntary selection is nevertheless possible, and is indeed exercised. Yet it is not a power that makes mortal man a divine creator of his Future — turning as it were by magic, the winds of an undetermined Hope into the solid earth of an irrevocable Past, as he proceeds on his selected way.

How curious that an answer to such a problem should be offered to us by the dictates of Mathematics! While egocentricity is a natural, and indeed a necessary feature of human perception, we may relax pleasantly in the knowledge that it is of minor importance that you and I happen to be the Toms who are doing the peeping, and that however much we may be the authors of our own experiences, we have no responsibility whatever for keeping the Universe in existence by our attention.

Back to the Brenner

So, going back to those early morning hours of 4 May 1945, it may be said that the divergence of the two versions of the story took place at the moment when I stood before that neo-Pieta, and heard in the distance the revving-up of Youell's trucks. Did I decide then to go in and speak to her, or did I hurry away? Or did any decision in the matter come earlier, at or before the time when I woke up in the Rathaus?

Such a question is difficult to decide. When one leaves New Haven in a train and proceeds eastward, it is impossible from visual observation to tell for a while whether one is going to finish up in Boston or in Hartford. Both tracks lie in parallel, but it may be argued that the actual track that one is on has already predetermined the destination — in so far as anything can be regarded as predetermined on the New Haven Railroad.

Looking backwards over the two stories as I recorded them, I notice that in Take Two a shower of rain is mentioned, and it was to this that I attributed the fact that I went inside. Whether or not there was a similar shower at the same moment in Take One, I do not remember. But if I were to interpret the situation in some sort of religious vein — which I have no intention of doing — I would probably say that God sent his rain to save my life, and I would presumably go on from this to associate the matter in some esoteric way with the working of divine Grace. Nothing could be more flattering to the Ego than the idea that Heaven was so concerned about my personal affairs that suitable weather was provided in order to ensure my survival.

On the other hand, it would be equally fallacious — though more amusing — to approach the problem scientifically, and apply the Stuckel-berg Effect. There is a double-Now in 4D and an overlap in Time to be explained. Why not take a leaf out of Reichenbach's book and resolve the matter by saying that, somehow or other, I managed to accelerate myself beyond an angle of 90°, and so went back five or six hours to wake up in the Rathaus for a second time, and at a previous Now?

Unfortunately I am not a type that would appreciate any such un-settling haste — much less invite it. Whatever may be possible in the case of an Electron, I am a system, and I would cease to exist as such long before reaching any velocity of that kind. Moreover, Reichenbach's material is giving its performance entirely in one continuum, which is the feature that makes the effect so peculiar. Alternation, on the other hand, is much less spectacular than this, since it does not insist on two Nows in the same continuum.

This present *corpus indelictum* of mine is in a common continuum with the Reader. It never met Otto Suder, and that is why I cannot remember what he looked like, although I am aware, in ways other than by means of memory, of what took place at a meeting, more Elsewhere than is commonly accepted.

This conclusion throws a vivid light upon the meaning — perhaps subconscious on the part of the author — behind a peculiar passage in one of Yeats's later poems that has greatly puzzled me. In this the poet remarked:

> . . . there's another knowledge that my heart destroys
> As the fox in the old fable destroys the Spartan boy's,
> Because it proves that things both can, and cannot be. . . .

Awareness distinguished from Memory

There are two ways in which we can contemplate events that are in a cosmic latitude above our own (in other words, in the Past). The first is the visual method of looking through a telescope at a distant object in the Heavens, or by examining its signals optically in some other way. These signals convey a condition of affairs at an earlier stage of Entropy, and the date depends upon the distance of the object being examined.

The other method has already been described as a reading Here and Now of certain storage cells or brain traces in the physical cranium — an act of the mind called Memory, that closely resembles the studying of the pages of a diary. And as regards date, this *is* a matter of choice, depending not upon distance, but upon the page selected.

Awareness, on the other hand, has nothing to do with Memory, but is part of a faculty that is another acquisition of Evolution, and which, I suppose, may be associated with a sensation common to many that 'I have been here before' or 'I know already what is going to happen'. A good deal of this sort of perception is entangled with mysticism, fortune telling and psychic charlatanry, but this does not contradict its validity, however imprecise and unreliable our faculties may be. As Dunne points out, it seems possible that there is much of what he calls Prevision in our dreams. The dream experience is nonsense but its material may be drawn from the future as well as from the past.

I would go even further and suggest that in sleep the brain, untrammelled by the control of the conscious mind, is not only indifferent to the significance of Past and Future, but is also in close touch with the features of its own 5D extension in the neighbourhood. In short, the material of our dreams may be conditioned by more than one Continuum.

But even when awake, an awareness of Alternation is not an unknown experience, whether intuitively or subconsciously. Man in his present state of evolution has

The biochemists are at present telling us that the machinery of memory is still largely a subject for speculation, but that it is in some way bound up with the manufacture of proteins within the brain. While it is not yet certain that the storage cells of memory can be transplanted from one brain to another (a sinister prospect) it is generally agreed that the material that constitutes recollection is stored in a physical form that is as tangible as the pages of a diary, and can be referred to and read in substantially the same way.

A distinction, however, is made by the scientists between short term memory and what they describe as the permanent storage of long term material. This might well be an aspect of the distinction between what one remembers within the bounds of a a wider familiarity with areas of reality that lie beyond the physical length, breadth and thickness of this simian world, than he is usually prepared to admit.

So Memory is a deceptive element in our sense of the continuity of our lives. Because of the fact that it is obsessed with Entropy, it gives us a depressing sensation, already referred to, that we are drifting helplessly from a condition of affairs that regrettably has disappeared, towards a state of final extinction. But this is not the case.

single Take, and what one recalls of the events of yesterday, or of any other period of one's past history. That there is such a difference seems reasonably clear. For one thing, immediate events are recalled with a sense of continuity. In the other case there need be no continuity at all. We can deliberately contemplate the events of other days in any kind of order, just as we can turn to any page of a book at will. Indeed, the actual sequence of past experiences is often hard to be sure about with the aid of memory alone. But the events of the last hour or two are inextricably bound up with a sense of their temporal order. They are still News, rather than History.

Man's knowledge of both future and past cannot be attributed wholly to the conditioning of earlier experience in one continuum only. Nor does it mean that he has been endowed with some supernatural gift of prophecy. All that it amounts to is the fact that his faculties have grown sufficiently sophisticated to make him occasionally aware that certain things are liable to happen because, somewhere or other, they are already in existence.

Elsewhere I have described how a symbolic voice once spoke into my ear by the headwaters of the Dead Sea, warning me that if I ever carried a gun I would die by what I carried. But it was no voice. More accurately it was an awareness of Alternation — a true awareness because, although it did not happen here, it is probable that it did happen in another neighbourhood. It was inevitable, and yet it was avoidable — which is the most striking gift of Alternation. Indeed, the only surprising thing about the situation is the fact that here, in Take Two, I am so keenly aware of a happening in another continuum that ought to have faded away long ago, together with that doppelganger who did meet Otto Suder and who terminated as a system on that morning in May, 1945. Yet, ended or not, he has had his causal effect, both past and future, on the multiple personality of which he is a part, one instance of which is this book.

Actually, after a little consideration, it may turn out to be not so surprising after all, if one calls to mind other, perhaps less memorable incidents in our separate experiences, that we may have dismissed at the time as dreams. Herein we should find an intelligible model for Wheelwright's Open Past, from which we can appreciate that whatever is present Here and Now is the consequence of cumulative, multiple causes in the past, that are not all in the same continuum, and — leaving aside any mumbo-jumbo in the realm of table-turning and spiritualism — may include facts and events that are contemporaneous and yet contradictory.

We tend to look back upon past events, and say with a shrug: 'I see now that it had to be so', forgetting how convinced we may have previously been that everything depended upon a course yet to be decided upon by ourselves.

In this we do ourselves little justice. We may not have created the situation that followed, but we certainly selected our awareness of it. In this way our decisions can be of the utmost importance — to ourselves at any rate. By the exercise of Free Choice we do not create the Future but selectively discover it. For the Elan, Life itself may be said to amount to a voyage of selective discovery.

The Focus of a Saltire

Here and Now is the focus of a saltire, or perhaps more accurately, of a double cone, as Yeats depicted in his book, *A Vision*, and which opens out from the Observer in both directions — towards Past and towards Future. Whether Yeats was any more aware of the full implications of his symbol than Eliot was when he wrote *Four Quartets*, is a matter of minor importance. I was hardly aware myself of what was involved when I endangered a soberly factual War book by insisting on giving it a double ending, not because the idea seemed cute, but because for me, it happened to be part of the story.

One tries to act rationally, but it does not always sound like that. Yet, curiously enough, it was Science that got me into this, and neither magic, nor poetry.

But we have finished with Science now, so far as this despatch is concerned, and the final word of that Discipline may be taken to be that the implement we know as Man is everlasting, but not immortal; while the bringer of his Verbs has nothing to do with mortality, and is not even a continuous or everlasting visitor, but an occasional one. As illustrated by our multiple genealogy, the flesh sheds and recreates. It has got here by several routes, and — if we choose to do our duty — it will go on by just as many.

So, having thus cast a few bricks — it is to be hoped — at the illusion

of one short life and a miserable one, let us move on to consider some of
the moral consequences that follow from our ability to feel our way —

> . . . down the passage that we did not take,
> Through the door we never opened,
> Into the Rose Garden.

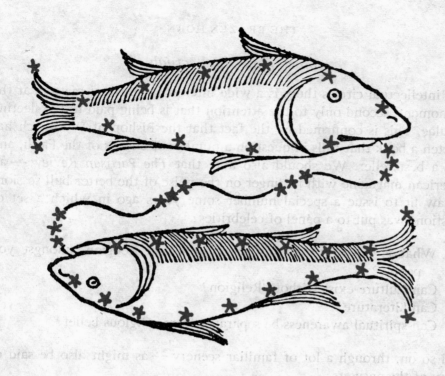

IX   THROUGH
THE DAMASCUS GATE

Ergo cum ignoscentia est
— sicut vermis sectus aratro
et ferrarius malleo ignoscit —

Meet some Intellectuals

IN intellectual circles there is a wide interest in spiritual matters at the moment, second only to the attention that is being paid to the fleeting nebulae. This is confirmed by the fact that the Bishop of Woolwich has written a book that calls in question a number of clichés of the Faith, and was a best seller. We should also note that *The Partisan Review* — an American magazine with its finger on the pulse of the better bull sessions — saw fit to issue a special number some years ago in which a set of questions was put to a panel of celebrities:

> What is the *cause* of this new interest in Religion amongst you people?
> Can Culture exist without Religion?
> Can Literature?
> Can spiritual awareness be separated from religious belief?

And so on, through a lot of familiar scenery — as might also be said of many of the answers:

> Is it 'new'? The term is inappropriate.
> If we can swallow penis-envy, why not Transubstantiation?
> It is easier for an artist to see the inadequacies of naturalism because in his professional work he is occupied with the personal and the existential which are his subject matter. (Auden)
> What they obtain from religion is not an answer — but only a fallacious assurance that there is an answer. (Ayer)

On the other wing of the enquiry, a series of meetings was being held in my native town by one of our religious task forces, in which the answers of the Catholic Faith to current theological conundrums were supposedly explained to the Separated Brethren. There turned out to be an element of disappointment in both these exercises that was not wholly unexpected. *The Partisan Review* selected an interesting panel, but failed to ply it with any significant problems. The Church, on the other hand, went to considerable trouble to make sure that no questions would be raised unless submitted beforehand in writing, so that they could be selected, amended and even invented by the organisers themselves. And even with these advance precautions, it was laid down that there must be no public discussion on the replies.

In all of this, the *Review* disclosed a depressing unawareness of the real issues, while the Hierarchy showed a serious lack of confidence in the ability of its spokesman to stand up to any controversy whatsoever. The spectacle of the clergy being answered back was not to be risked.

This is all very typical of the course that contemporary religious discussion usually takes. On the one hand, we have the familiar reply to any question about the Deity: God is Love. This statement has the happy quality of combining sentimentality, manifest falsity, and an end to any further discussion, which accounts for its unfailing popularity.

At the other end of the spectrum we have those who, in pursuit of the worst of everything, are engaged in the dreary task of constructing a Religion without God; while somewhere in the middle we find the honest Bishop of Woolwich attempting to follow Bonhoeffer in probing the possibility of having a God without Religion. If we are not going to be allowed to have both — says the Bishop — let us at any rate have God.

See Appendix H

The significance of Religion

We had better recognise the fact that some sort of a religion is as necessary for most normal adults as a constitution is for the State, or a charter for a Corporation. Without some rule of life — whether or not we are always able to obey it — we are driven inevitably to the Sartrean conclusion that we have nothing but ourselves, and are damn bad company at that. But a religion is no good unless it can provide us with an intelligible frame of reference, and a sense of purpose that conforms to the promptings of experience and of common sense. It should be of some help in assuring us that the universe is not a crazy ship that is being navigated by a demon — as Saint Thomas Aquinas implies, arguing with the perfect logic of the Church from untenable premises to a horrifying set of conclusions. Nor is it being run by an amateur who is doing his best, poor fellow, as Saint Bernard of Ayot St. Lawrence would have had us agree. Nor, worst of all, is there only a corpse on the bridge, as appears

To this extent Sartre and the Existentialists are perfectly right in insisting that Man is nothing, apart from what he *does* — that our lives are all that we have and are our own responsibility. But in this connection Sartre is not really talking about the Flesh — which *is* — but about the Elan, which *does*, within the limits of five-dimensional possibility. Thus, we see again another example of the prevailing confusion of the Noun with the Verb, which is an aspect of the Heresy of Patripassianism, a Gospel of Pessimism and Despair. With the passage of Time, the Flesh is not destroyed. It merely passes beyond the focus of our present attention.

to be the present conclusion of California — unoriginal as usual. Nor need we accept the common formula that a lot of manifest nonsense presented as fact is all right, because it is 'true in a spiritual sense'. It must be True without any rider to the effect that — between ourselves — it is not true at all.

If any experiments are being tried, they are our own experiments — the voluntary investigations of the Elan that are expressions of the Free Will that we demand. However inept — and even painful — the results may turn out to be, there is no need for them to be regarded as fatal. And if sorrow comes our way, whether unescapably or by invitation, it is something that has been accepted by the Elan in entering on the present Take in the superhuman knowledge that, if joy is fleeting, so too is misery, and that we cannot possibly have one without the other.

As for Death — this is a matter of no significance at all once we recognise the fact that it destroys nothing — that it is not some infernal payment for all our efforts, but a boundary to them — not an objective to strive after, as the Enemy would have it, but a relaxing blast on a whistle at which the cheering temporarily stops.

If any man's framework of belief satisfies him on any of these points, let him stick to it, for he has all that he needs. But for some of us today there are no established creeds that offer us more than double-talk, or a set of insoluble paradoxes to brood upon on the shady side of a Bo Tree.

Is nobody going to be allowed to tell us that we can go as safely to the grave as we can go to sleep, with perfect dignity in the assurance that we are on our way to the least menacing condition in all creation — that the gracious hands in which we lay before we came to Be, are no further off or less friendly at this, the other end of our mortal extension? Do we have to gaze upon a gibbet in order to win confirmation of such a sense of absolute faith?

If anybody feels so disposed, let him gaze upon his gibbet by all means — and send for Extreme Unction too. Heaven will not be offended. But do not let us call it faith, when it is exactly the opposite.

They tell us that Christ came to call the sinner to repentance. Repentance for what? For the sin of being born? If we feel impelled to implore Salvation from some monstrous peril that is felt to be embedded in the facts of life, it is probably just as well for us to remain in our state of terror. The enormous liberty that follows an escape from Salvationism can be exceedingly dangerous in the hands of those who do not also appreciate its responsibilities.

This Sin Business

What I am suggesting is that there are paradoxes in our knowledge of what we think of as God that are as baffling as any that beset us in the snake-pit of Science, and that are all the harder for being hoarier. We do not abolish them by clasping to our bosoms a gorgeous burden of guilt, which we propose to shed by magical means before it is too late; or alternatively by saying that there is no such thing as Sin at all.

There is Good and Evil in this world, whether or not we are always able to distinguish which is which. And for all our pragmatism, nobody has been able to improve much on the Ten Commandments as a basis for a moral law. Why then do we inevitably have to break them — as we all do on our own responsibility, knowing full well the consequences that are liable to follow?

Coarb of Columba

The Reverend Sir George Macleod — to call him by his earlier titles which combine both sanctity and social eminence — is the founder of that admirable group, the Iona Community, and as such may be regarded as Coarb of Saint Columba. Dedicated as he is to a way of life that is outlined in the Sermon on the Mount, he was speculating in public one evening on some of the problems presented to a practising Christian Minister by the Second World War. He had very properly been reluctant to take any personal part in the bloodletting involved in the removal of Hitler, and had sat out a considerable part of that holocaust amid the hazards of the air raids on Glasgow.

Having commented on this experience without much enthusiasm, he then indicated another clergyman — a member of the same Community — who, like himself, had agreed that it would be unseemly for an ordained Minister of an Established Church to shoot and bomb his fellow men in Central Europe. So what this Pastor had done was to take off his Roman collar for the duration, and obtain a job as a tail gunner in the Royal Air Force. Hitler being disposed of, he was back once again in his appropriate cloth, giving voice as before to the Gospel.

How was it, mused Sir George, that although personally convinced that he, himself, had adopted the correct attitude of a clergyman towards the War, he sometimes felt a touch of envious admiration for this delinquent member of his flock who had been prepared quite frankly to place the Beatitudes in suspension for the duration?

Did this mean that there was something radically wrong with the Sermon on the Mount whenever anything serious had to be undertaken? Or was this less prominent shepherd guilty of having let down the side? If there was anything in the first point, might it not mean that the accolade of knighthood had been bestowed upon the wrong shoulders? In short, which presented the more inspiring picture — this temporarily unfrocked Pastor, knocking down Messerschmitts from the rumble seat of a Liberator, or those Air Force Padres whom we used to see waiting in the Anterooms to give spiritual comfort to the Aircrews about to spray hell over Hamburg, and not as a rule being made any use of by the customers?

Has Saint Columba any business to be in an Air Raid Shelter when Evil is abroad, demanding to be met by Evil — or is this an unfair question? The fact that Macleod was himself the person to start this speculation, puts his realism and courage beyond the realm of argument. But what about his qualifications as the Coarb of a sinning Saint — the particular distinction of Columba?

One was strongly tempted to put yet another question to Sir George, that might have led him into even deeper water. What is Man without his Sins? As dead to the business for which he is on this Earth — both sanctified and dirty — as Adam was before he got out of that garden.

MacLeish's Objection to God

We have from another quarter an American comment on the character and requirements of the supposed Almighty, that goes even further than either Shelley or Shaw did in their very undivine pictures. Indeed, it gives expression to an objection to 'God' that is quite as serious as any disgust that Heaven may feel for us.

> If God is God he is not good.
> If God is good he is not God.

This pertinent protest comes from Archibald MacLeish through the lips of his bewildered contemporary Job, and it gives succinct expression to the half-concealed distaste that many sensitive and believing Christians must have for the kind of God who has supposedly placed his beloved children on a tightrope over a pit of flame, and now proposes to save some selected favourites through a sacrifice of himself to himself, which in some way is said to appease his own anger about the position.

Moreover, we are also told that this peculiar dispensation has been implemented by the alleged seduction of the fiancée of a carpenter in Palestine — an aspect of the situation about which the Deity has to be reminded daily by a qualified official in a special costume.

Such a God, if he existed, could hardly be regarded as friendly, and even less as an expression of the divine love that we are told about. Indeed, it would seem that he is not only very forgetful and arbitrary in his habits, but is also a very poor example of the qualities urged upon the human race in the Sermon on the Mount. Not much love of our friends here, not to speak of our enemies.

If such a description of the fundamental myth of Christianity appears to be in bad taste, I can only say that such is my intention. The story itself is in bad taste, and if any feelings are hurt in the process of saying that it is wholly blasphemous, it is high time that they were hurt.

But it is not about the sludge from Middle-Eastern theology that Mac-Leish and his kind are really concerned. They believe in its factuality no more than you and I do. It is over this quandary of the existence of Evil that we are hard put to it to find an answer.

I am not merely referring to pain, which is not so difficult to account for. But why Evil? And who or what is responsible for it? We used to be told that it is the work of a Devil — to God's great grief. But if we are too worldly-wise to believe in Devils any longer, or if we are disposed to ask why any Almighty, sincerely upset about such a nuisance, does not put a stop to it himself, and keep his own delinquents in order, an alternative proposition is usually advanced: that Evil is brought by Man's own misbehaviour in deliberately falling from a state of innocence in which he was created.

This is in a sense true, in so far as Sin and its punishment is a consequence of Man's deliberate departure from a state of Innocence, into a state of Experience. But this is not a 'Fall' from any pristine state of perfection. On the contrary, in his efforts to struggle into an upright position, Man has hardly been off his knees as yet — his

A valid argument is sometimes heard that it is contrary to reason and fair dealing to disbelieve in the Devil without at the same time repudiating the idea of God. 'No Devil — No God!' conveys a perfectly good point that a future resort of everlasting bliss is meaningless without the opposite conception of a place of everlasting torment. It is altogether too smart to demand one without the other, as is a common practice of the day. This is a reasonable comment, if we insist upon a God who is the embodiment only of good, and is not also the author of evil. Such a half-hearted, summer-time God is as childish as the adolescent's dream of the Ideal husband or wife. It is not the picture that is being offered here.

foetal position for prayer. (He might show his age by standing up to pray.)

Whether or not any blame is to be attached to our first parents for giving up a permanent vacation in favour of spadework is a question that will be discussed shortly, but it is clear that most of us have preferred to make the same choice ever since.

Beyond the Damascus Gate

Those who visit the City of Jerusalem in the hope of viewing the place of the Crucifixion are often disappointed on being informed that the sites of both the Hill of Calvary and of the Garden Tomb are now within the confines of that epitome of religious vulgarity, the Church of the Holy Sepulchre. As no visible signs of either are to be seen in that locality, this discovery sometimes arouses scepticism about the whole business — for business it clearly is, if one is to judge by the number of money boxes. Yet, not far outside the Damascus Gate there can be seen for free an alternative site, known as Gordon's Calvary, that is abusively dismissed as ridiculous and indeed fraudulent, by the lobbyists for the official resort.   See
Appendix
J

Similarly, there are a number of neglected passages to be found in our Anthology of Experience that throw considerable light upon this vexed question of the authorship and purpose of Evil. For example, there is that verse in the 45th chapter of the Book of Isaiah in which God openly proclaims his own responsibility — a statement upon which it is difficult to find much coherent ecclesiastical comment, and which was treated with a similar silence when I ventured to quote it in the Clio chapter of my earlier book.

Nevertheless, if treated seriously, it is one of the most profoundly interesting passages in Holy Scripture.

> I am the Lord, and there is none else. . . .
> I make Peace and create Evil.

For some centuries before a line of the New Testament was penned, this downright statement has been there for all to read; and the two operative words of the earliest known proprietors of the text were *Shalom* and *Rau*.

Sanctified by inclusion in the Mazoretic version, translated in the accusative case by Saint Jerome as *Pacem* and *Malum*, and enshrined as such in the Vulgate of the Latin Church, they again appear in the plain language of the Anglican Authorised Version as Peace and Evil. Whether they should now be distilled into Weal and Woe, or (as more recently in the New English Bible) into 'Prosperity' and 'Trouble' is a matter of taste, if not strictly one of translation, since most of us know what *Malus* means, even if *Rau* may be a little beyond us.

My own suggestion is that such juggling with words is, in this case, just another of those attempts to excuse the Almighty for the existence of Evil by calling him an incompetent creator, or alternatively by suggesting that he is not almighty. Even that honest man, Blake, when contemplating the Tiger could not bring himself to answer his own question: Did he who made the Lamb make thee? The answer is, Yes.

But whatever accusations may be levelled against Jahveh on this score, 'X' makes no appeal for any excuses to be offered on its behalf for the facts of Life. So a further gloss may be added to the answer requested by Blake. If 'X' is not to be whitewashed with that worn-out cliché, God is Love, neither is it Hate, nor outraged Vanity, nor even a member of some celestial Police Department who is gravely upset about our misbehaviour. (According to the late Cardinal Newman, our conduct is giving Him Hell all the time.) What we are confronted with here is none of these Gods, but something of which the Christian only wants half — the Peace-in-our-Time Department.

What is Evil?

What then is this element that the Ultimate in its wisdom does not merely permit, but has deliberately decreed? This is a question that I propose to treat pragmatically, because there are limits to self-repetition, and I have already discussed the subject sufficiently in the final chapter of that other book.

It is to a Catholic priest that I am most deeply indebted for the best answer that I have heard to this tortuous query. He described Evil as a disease of the soul, with the characteristics of many of the See the Sangro section of *Nine Rivers from Jordan*.

By a 'disease of the Soul', this Priest, in context, was referring to the Social Soul of a community rather than to any individual distemper.

more mundane bodily complaints — for one, that it is infectious. What he meant by this was that there usually appears to be no practical way of resisting Evil except by adopting it, a paradox that gives the inevitability to Original Sin, which in its turn is one of the facts of life that seems to be manifestly unfair.

Evil, like atomic fission, creates a chain reaction that is almost impossible to halt before it destroys us, or we destroy ourselves. Aeschylus was aware of this human quandary as long ago as the composition of the Orestean Trilogy, and Oscar Wilde may perhaps have been thinking about the same subject when he complained that each man kills the thing he loves. Possibly an even more disturbing amendment to Wilde's celebrated aphorism might be that every man tends to become the thing he kills, and may die by the weapon that he chooses to assume.

An example of this may be found at that moment when, faced with Buchenwald, I abandoned my previous pose of holier-than-thou neutrality, and took possession of a gun. The men who had just broken open that monstrous place were carrying guns, but for which the gates would have remained shut. Why then should I presume to remain in the category of the unarmed? There on the prison door was that sinister slogan: TO EACH WHAT IS COMING TO HIM. If this was intended to apply to the prisoners, why not also to Neutrals? What had come to *me* was a Luger, forbidden, it is true, by my *geas*. But as it now appeared necessary to take a personal part in this bloody business — well then, to Hell with my *geas*.

For 'geas' see page 186

The Dead Sea Covenant

The trouble with that pre-War world had been too many hectoring armed men, all of whom were in the wrong. Neither I nor my City seemed to have been responsible for this situation, so — having found myself up to my neck in it, quite unintentionally — it appeared not unreasonable that I should remain strictly in my professional role as an Observer, and refrain from becoming yet another armed man, if I hoped to come through the upheaval in safety.

This, I suppose, was the substance of a sort of bargain with Providence entered into at the headwaters of the Dead Sea, while brooding upon the question of what the devil was I doing there at all? And although it was obviously a mere piece of symbolism to describe my choice as a 'bargain', it had nevertheless formed the basis of a perfectly definite foreknowledge that, come what may, I was not going to be killed, so long as I stuck to it — a conviction that lasted until that day in Thuringia, and which was at the back of any apparent 'bravery under fire' on my part. In fact, it was not bravery at all, in the circumstances.

But after passing through those gates under the black flag of the SS and seeing what was inside, I knew that this attitude of detachment was no longer tolerable. In the light of that fantastic expression of the de-humanisation of Man, it was shameful to pretend any longer that the issues at stake had nothing to do with me, whether or not there was still a lot that might be said against the motives and behaviour of both sides. The outward and visible sign of that change of heart was, I suppose, the taking of that Luger. The weapon itself was just another symbol. I was not proposing to go roaring through the streets of a prostrate Germany, loosing it off in all directions as an expression of a distaste for Hitler. It was no more than a tangible reminder that I was no longer a 'neutral', and that I was deeply embarrassed by the fact that I had ever been one. But, however inchoate my intention may have been, it was the possession of that very symbol that led directly to the conclusion of Take One — a denouement that was inexorably entangled with a new and perilous frame of mind.

Such a change of heart was entirely justified by the circumstances, and it gets no apologies from me. Yet this does not alter the fact that, from my own angle, it was lethal. A bargain had been broken at my own choice, and if any unfortunate consequences were to follow they were intrinsic in the set-up, and were in no way forced upon me by either Heaven or Hell. So, no question of 'fairness' or 'unfairness' arose. From which one may conclude that since a man's breaches of the Law — when not involuntary — are his own concern and, as such, are an expression of his right to personal discovery, any 'punishment' is, in effect, part of his experience, and may well serve to invest his act with a degree of significance that it might not otherwise have. Provided, of course, that he is prepared to accept it without resent- See Appendix L ment or alibi as part of the deal. and side note on p. 169.

The Acceptance of Evil

But however this illustration may serve to show the workings of the chain reaction already referred to, it still does not answer the question as to why Evil should exist at all. What is it all about — if it only serves to confront us with quandaries of this sort? It is here that the analogy to a disease is a good one.

The ills of the physical body have already been described as part of a scavenging process connected with the blessings of decay. Disease presents a constant challenge by which the flesh is being periodically pruned, discarded and readapted for a later stage of Entropy — a fact that need not be regarded with any particular horror once the benefits of death are understood, and we cease to look on this feature of existence as an individual and final disaster. Indeed, we would have every reason to feel nervous about our future prospects as an acceptable species were we to discover some day that the process had stopped.

So, too, it is suggested that Evil is a disease that tempers the psychological and moral fibre of Man, and exercises his powers of resistance to the winter of Experience. And here, also, Man is not left alone and unassisted in his struggle to survive — if he is willing to survive.

In this case the fairy godmother is not a white phagocyte in the blood, but a measure of divine intervention between Man and the consequences of any moral distemper or misbehaviour. There is an escape route from the dictates of the Law that is described by the Christian as Redemption, but for which there is a much better word in the vocabulary of Theology — a word that has nothing to do with Atonement, or with any arbitrary 'pardons' for being what he is.

A Diet of Fruit

Having come face to face with the reality of Evil — having tasted the fruit of the Tree of Knowledge, and found it to be informative but poisonous — there is something that enables the untired soul to spit it out before the implement is destroyed. This escape route may be available even to a malcontent who has roundly abused his God for having permitted the situation, and has even taken a fatuous pot-shot at the Heavens as an expression of his disapproval of this evidently diabolical Deity. Herein lies a heavenly Equity, which may contradict the Law. The final denouement will still be death; but not a death too soon — before its functional date, and probably without hope of Alternation.

Having savoured the heady knowledge of Good and Evil, it will be discovered that it is the 'knowledge' that is our peril in this life, rather than the tasting. (The same may be said of alcohol.) As it was with our first parents, it is difficult not to taste, if for no other reason than that the apparent invitation is there. But, having bitten the fruit and found it poisonous, it is open to us, not by Atonement but by Grace, to spit it out and insulate this lethal knowledge, if we are still to be of any continuing use to Heaven and to ourselves. In short, we can escape addiction, and may know more the next time.

While this mysterious thing — Grace — remains available it is as much the benefaction of a friendly creator as is the fact that those who do not want it — who find life intolerable and desire no more of it — need not have it. There is no demon here — no unreasonable Nobodaddy demanding that we, his implements, must be governed by rules that he does not follow himself, or accept burdens that we are not equipped to carry.

Let me put it in this way — through an ability to accept Grace, Man may be enabled to circumvent the chain reaction, and thus escape the more proximate termination that Evil is intended to provide in that particular Continuum. Such a man might possibly be described as one of the Elect, were it not for the fact that such an expression connotes an old-fashioned pomposity and exclusiveness that is not to our taste any longer. So perhaps 'one of the fit' might better define that fortunate position. Better still would be to refuse to define it at all.

In any event, it should be noted that we are now back again with something that the more perceptive Theologians have been pointing at for centuries, although generally in more circumspect language.

X THE OXEN
OF THE PENTAGONS

Ita fructum arboris vetiti
exspuo
et simul timorem dolorem-
que peccati
et mala mortifera
quae malo procreata sunt.

Szilard's Bomb

DURING the 'thirties I had occasion to cross the Atlantic several times, and by a coincidence I had twice as my table companion an entertaining Hungarian with vivid, darting brown eyes, and a name — Leo Szilard — that I made use of in a play, much to his amusement. He was a very accomplished Physicist, and what I specially remember about him is the scientific twist that his humorous mind could give to almost any topic of conversation. If, for example, it was remarked that only about half of our fellow passengers liked the other half, Szilard would resolve this generalisation statistically into a figure that he would describe as our Coefficient of Cohesion, which in the case in point he would place at 50.

But best of all he had a chess-board formula with which he alleged that all conversations with a bore could be terminated.

'Are you married?' was the opening gambit.

If the answer was No, then the next question — 'Have you any children?' — was calculated to end the exchange. If, on the other hand, the reply was Yes, the next move again was 'Have you any children?' If the answer to this was Yes, the conversation could be ended by the further query, 'By whom?' If, however, the reply was No, the same effect could probably be reached through the final remark, 'How do you manage it?'

Many years later I discovered the reason for the peregrinations of this ingenious little man. He was engaged in peddling his ideas on nuclear fission, and was actually one of the first to be employed by Franklin D. Roosevelt on the job of inventing the Bomb. I cannot say whether Bronowski knew him or not. In the description of these momentous discussions that is given by the latter, the more celebrated name of Einstein is the one that appears. But Szilard seems to have been ahead of Einstein in any dealings with Roosevelt, and he was not only one of the first to initiate the American experiments, but was also one of the earliest to get out as soon as the wider implications about its use became apparent.

Teller remarks:

> In some sort of crude sense which no vulgarity, no humour or overstatement can quite extinguish, the Physicists have known sin, and this is a knowledge which they cannot lose.

In describing the dilemma of these neo-Adams, Bronowski puts up a spirited defence on behalf of Scientists as a class. He favourably compares their integrity, their acceptance of dissent, and their vigorous pursuit of truth through the application of disinterested intelligence, with that of other professions and professional men. He is loud in his scorn for what might be described as the democratic process — in other words, compliance with directives from the herd. He is extremely sceptical about the finality of all experiments, and is quite delightful in his insistence that any statement that contains the word 'ought' is no statement at all.

But when he comes to discuss the question of current scientific Guilt, as touched upon by Teller, he takes a very peculiar line, which may or may not be due to the atmosphere of a garden at Ayot St. Lawrence where I met him on my one and only encounter.

Should it be incumbent upon Einstein—or more accurately upon Szilard — to refuse to divulge to the President of the United States any information about the possible uses of atomic fission, in deference to the future prospects of the human race?

In discussing this important question, it is interesting to note that Bronowski does not put forward the practical argument that it is quite impossible to withhold any saleable know-how for an indefinite period, and that if Szilard had not come through with the bad news when he did, somebody else would undoubtedly have done so, sooner or later. It might even have been conveyed to Hitler by some other Hungarian — perhaps under torture. Nor does he make the point that, after all, Roosevelt was one of the good American Presidents who was probably better informed about the nuances of the international situation than either Einstein or Szilard. Bronowski uses instead the questionable argument of Established Authority that was flung at the head of Saint Joan of Arc (about whom he probably got his ideas in the garden at Ayot St. Lawrence): Who is Einstein to set up his individual judgment in such matters against that of the elected representative of a great democratic Republic?

Now with all respect to President Roosevelt, who seeems to have been an executive of unusual qualities, anybody who knows how a President of the United States is selected and placed in office must have grave doubts as to whether it would be wise to entrust the continuance of human existence in the hands of such an official rather than in those of Doctor Einstein. For myself, I would certainly have voted for the latter, had I ever been given the choice.

It is clear that democracy, as a means of selecting and disposing of our civil administrators, is more likely to work than any other known machinery, but it provides no guarantees that those who are placed in temporary control of our destinies are those who know best. Indeed, it might be argued that it is a method of making sure that they are *not* antipolitical menaces of the type that really does know best. The Golden Mean may point the way to convenient decisions calculated to avoid trouble at the moment, but it is seldom right about the future, and a dictatorship of fifty-one per cent is no more endowed with divine right than is a Monarch. A set of social manipulators elected by the majority may be the easiest form of government to throw out, but nobody knows better than Professor Bronowski that Wisdom is no more a matter of popular vote than it was in Noah's day.

Therefore I am suggesting that whatever justification Einstein and Szilard may have had for presenting Roosevelt (or that nice Mr. Truman, as it turned out) with the Final Weapon, they cannot avoid their responsibilities by saying, Who am I to say Yes or No in such matters?

Indeed, it is the worst possible escape route for people who have just been highly praised for their integrity, their pragmatism, and their fortitude under pressure from the herd.

Teller is quite right. These Physicists are guilty men and they cannot get away from it — as guilty as Eden's gardener was in introducing this lethal commodity, Knowledge, in the first place — as guilty as I am, myself, for offering a possible escape from the salutary fear of Death to some who, without it, might adopt an irresponsible attitude towards murder. We are all guilty — and in circumstances which seem impossible to avoid. So what are we going to do about it?

The Question of Survival

At the moment, the prospect of survival for the human species is more problematical than at any time since the Flood. Let us face it — before long, not only five or six fairly responsible Powers are going to have the means of atomic self-expression, but also every Tom, Fidel and Abdul with something on his mind. If the Thing does not go off by accident, thanks to the well-known incompetence of military men, it will be let loose by somebody who is simply tired of life, or dissatisfied with the attitude of other people towards his pigmentation or his habits.

It is almost inevitable that the spread of majority rule — against which I do not dare to utter as much as a twitter — means an increasing number of public enemies in public office, who can only stay there by buying the votes of the Many by making life increasingly intolerable for the Few. And when from time to time the Few happen to be the more competent, and take it upon themselves to put an end to too many crooked or lazy officials issuing threats from offices, and too many minor bullies flourishing weapons that are not of their own manufacture, the consequences are liable to be dangerous to a degree never before experienced. The Few are quite capable of abating these nuisances when driven too far — and who can blame them? But this makes our present position acute. Vico's Democracy naturally leads to Vico's Chaos, and given the means to exterminate themselves in bulk, it is more than likely that some inadequate and despairing sections of humanity will try to do so sooner or later. The question, then, before us will be whether there are Enough of a different mind to exercise some faculties of survival?

Trevor-Roper has pointed out that the most dangerous revolutions are not occasioned by the conflict of Classes or even of Races, but of the harassed Public against entrenched and intolerable Bureaucracies.

Such a miracle, of course, has happened before. There have been breeds of men who have successfully avoided following the Brontosaurus into extinction while others did not — although their exit was not so spectacular as that with which we are threatened today.

And what was it that saved Homo Sapiens from the fate of his Neanderthal cousins? It was an element of intelligence that showed itself in a superior use of his faculties, and which he applied to a firm determination to continue.

It may be that there are enough today to organise an escape from race suicide, when it faces us through an unholy union of technical know-how with a knowledge of Evil. Maybe it will require some degree of Mutation. But what of it? There is actually some evidence to show that this process is already under way. Certainly, there is abroad today a full measure of the challenge that has always been needed in the past to bring about Mutation.

There may already be enough in possession of the wider degree of perceptivity that the need for survival demands. With this, Man may be said to have a chance. Without it, he would seem to have very little — the way things are going. If, on the whole, we are no longer interested in an existence that we have come to hate, we will inevitably join the Lemmings on their trek to the seaside. And, curiously enough, some sections of the species will go willingly on their way out. There will be few complaints or hard feelings over this. . .

Identifying the Enemy

. . . except on the part of those of us who are not inclined to regard ourselves as ready for disposal, and have not yet concluded our functional task as performers in the art of being alive.

What should be the immediate concern of such parties is to effect an early recognition of the difference between the Enemy, and those who are merely our Opponents. The latter are those who only want more for themselves, which after all is not an expression of any Death Wish, but rather of a longing for a better and bigger life.

These we willingly fight with what the Sermon on the Mount calls 'love'. We may be indignant with them, but what they are after is only more than enough of what we are all after, and there is no real danger to the Species in this, even if they get it. They are, in a very real sense, ourselves in a different uniform.

The others, on the contrary, are out of concert with Man as a creature, and are ready to dehumanise him if they get the chance. The Enemy belongs to no particular race, sex, creed, or even level of culture. He is usually difficult to identify at first, but he is everywhere, and — as representing Man on the way out — Un-Man — he is as much against the species as a whole as he is against himself. These we do not propose to have any part in. They can go their own sweet way into the Limbo that they perhaps only subconsciously desire. But if they try to bring us along with them, we must be quite prepared to give them an unfriendly push.

If this is sinful, then that is just what it is. And, like the Rev. Sir George's henchman, we will take off our Roman collars till the nasty job is over, knowing that we can still spit out our diet of fruit in time, and graduate to another and better innocence that lies beyond Knowledge, if our Command Post is satisfied with our intentions.

But to do this with the integrity that honest sin demands, we must be prepared to pay the price in danger, and indeed in punishment, and refrain from blaming Heaven for it. How else can our transgressions be regarded as of any significance — any more than those of Peer Gynt? Is there any more satisfaction for the good Partisan in Free Sin than in Free Love?

It was Jonathan Swift who put into God's mouth the following lines which that reverend Dean expects to hear on the Day of Judgment:

> You who in different Sects have shamm'd
> And come to see each other damn'd;
> (So some folks told you, but they know
> No more of Jove's designs than you)
> The World's mad business now is o'er,
> And I resent these pranks no more.

What could be fairer than this? And how important it is that we should follow the example of Providence in its attitude towards Evil, and allow it, under control, to get on with its natural scavenging process. There is undoubtedly a peril involved in having any truck with Evil: but there is also Grace, and there is also that enigmatic quantity described as 'Charity' — one of the most moving words in the language, which should not be mistranslated. As for the peril — this should be sufficient to warn off those who are silly enough to imagine that they can make a fool of Heaven with fraudulent transgressions and phony intentions.

In introducing this peculiar expression — 'fraudulent transgressions' — I am trying to point to an element that is one of the most exciting aspects of the whole mystery. There is no compulsion whatever to incur the responsibilities that breaches of the law demand. We can retire from the problems of life, either to the grave or into some enclosed community, if we are so inclined. But if we are not so inclined, we must recognise the danger, and accept its implications when we choose to misbehave. And in the forefront of these responsibilities is that of being right. This is the nub of the test that Evil presents to Man. In the steps that he takes, Man has got to be right — and in an even more pertinent sense today, he must believe that it is possible to be right. And a very fair test this is of his eligibility for survival.

A striking example of the significance of punishment was recently brought out in the words of Dean Griswold, then one of the top legal advisers of the American Government. Accepting the natural right of the citizen to protest, even to the extent of violence, where matters of conscience and human rights are at stake, he then went on to add that those who propose to break the law, whether justifiably or not, should also be prepared to go to jail in proof of their sincerity. If the law is at fault, this is one of the best ways of changing it, a sentiment that sounds much more Irish than German.

Grace is not a prize for Piety or for Agenbite of Inwit. It can be better described as a graduation certificate for those who prefer danger to boredom, and who in making this choice can also manage to be right, or accept the consequences if they are not.

What is more, it demands as a preliminary, quite a different sort of rite, which, oddly enough, as an expression of our good will towards Heaven, takes the form of an Act of Absolution in reverse.

Inspired by a very understandable disgust for those very pranks — for our manifest shortcomings and failures — we begin our devotions in the Mass by asking forgiveness for ourselves, while still cherishing in the secret places of the heart a deeply rooted, but usually unspoken resentment for what appears to be the unfairness and cruelty of life. There is a close resemblance here to the contemporary hatred of the Pantheon on the part of sophisticated Greeks at the time of Euripides, which is given expression to in his savage play, *The Bacchae*.

But whatever unfairness there may appear to be in the workings of Providence, it is nothing to the unfairness of modern man towards his God, as embodied in the Christian myth. Evil is not here to trap us — as the Christian assumes — but to spare us, and any punishment that we may incur in fighting it is as natural as Fever, or as the weals on the hands of our admirable first father as he digs and prepares to die outside the gates of Eden. And through these gates he would not choose to go back, even if they were carelessly left open by that Angel What'shisname — not Gabriel, but Entropy.

Once a man can recognise the majesty of this mystery, and can cease to fling around cosmic Blame, is it not to be expected that his own paltry contribution of mini-evil to the situation will be regarded by Heaven in precisely the way predicted by Swift?

In short, once we can manage to extend to our Command Post the measure of Absolution that we hope for and demand for ourselves, we will go on to discover that Forgiveness, once it reaches the Stratosphere, becomes as meaningless and as irrelevant as those two second grade commodities, Justice and Gratitude. These are things that we should certainly offer freely to the poor in spirit who shout for them — and indeed to all who honestly require them. But no man or woman of quality (to make use of an excellent but out-of-date expression) should deign to demand either of them for himself, except in matters of no real importance.

Nobody is insisting that we should be so masochistic as to enjoy Evil — licking our wounds with relish. But in refusing to acknowledge its authorship and its wisdom, we display the imperception of the Christian message, which treats the night as an aspect of creation about which the less that is said the better. The tight-lipped disapproval with which the Orthodox regard the miseries of being alive, not to mention the plain sordidity of many of our natural necessities, is really an attitude of great impertinence. It is not unlike the disappointment in Celia expressed by Swift because of the fact that she shits, and the aversion of the Fathers to procreation in so far as it is 'inspired by the lusts of the flesh'. (It was so nice of that fastidious B.V.M. to conceive without any

I remember listening in on an after-dark theological discussion in the dormitory of my Scottish boarding school as to whether Swift's objection to Celia could also be directed against Jesus. Did he have any human functions of the same nature, and if so coarse copulation.)

As for Justice — this is surely something that mainly concerns brokers, chafferers and pimps, which I am sure we are all capable of being at appropriate moments. But Justice has no relevance in our dealings with the Ultimate, not because the Ultimate will have none of it, but because the word ceases to have any meaning in such an environment — like Time in the sixth dimension.

would his detritus qualify as a holy relic? The reluctant consensus was that it must. But an authoritative voice from the Macduff of Macduff (of the 1st XV) concluded the debate with an interesting gloss on the Gospels. In his view, such an object of respect would not have been placed in a Reliquary, but would have been reverently buried in Gethsemane, where in the course of time an unwithered fig tree would spring from the fertilised soil to give shade and nourishment to the faithful. Thus the heresy of Sabellianism was ingeniously avoided, and the real humanity of Christ was upheld without any embarrassment.

Pity is Unjust

It is unjust that we should be forced to feel the agonies of Compassion for those things that we have to wound. It is unjust to know that in injuring them we are probably injuring ourselves — and worse still that we run the risk of becoming some monster that we have had to kill. Pity has become rather a dirty word in the current verbiage of the day, not because it is painful, and indeed quite dangerous at times, but for the specious reason given by some sections of the Insulted and Bothered, that it implies an element of condescension. That some should consider it patronising to experience the pains of others is, I am sure, one of the pointers by which we may recognise the Enemy. So to hell with such people, I say; for if we cast out Pity, then Guilt will take its place sooner or later, unless we are as stupid as the Bull, which — hopefully — we are ceasing to be.

Compassion — like worry — is one of the penalties of growing up. In many ways it is preferable to remain stupid. Nevertheless, as an expression of the universality and oneness of the Elan, and — best of all — as the ultimate justification of the Partisan, Compassion must not be given up, however illogical it may seem, unless we are also prepared to give up Conflict.

The liberal thinker of the day is well aware of the dilemma caused by the necessity of conflict. But instead of cheering Man up in this predicament, he prefers to qualify the Fifth Commandment. This is our principal quarrel with him. In trying to adopt an intelligible attitude towards the problem of Evil, he falls into the Pelagianism of doubting its existence. Yet, apart from some temporal suffering that it undoubtedly causes, Evil can do us no more permanent harm than can Injustice, provided we do not feel impelled to make the worst of it.

We are not existentialist peaks of solitude mulling over our guilt in a malignant Hell. We may have our difficulties in communicating, but if we can manage to look around, we will find that we have plenty of good, uncondescending company in our pains as well as in our pleasures.

The Wages of Sin

Thou shalt not commit Adultery means exactly what it says. It may be that circumstances arise in which it is worse to keep the Law than to break it: in which case, we break it. But this does not alter the Law. I broke that particular Law, and took my share of suffering and danger for having done so. For this offence I am a guilty man; but I am not an apologetic one. Nor do I blame the Lord or the Law for anything that I have been through. And I am pleased to be able to say that what I have been through is over and done with, so far as I am concerned.

This, I maintain, is better theology than to assume a liberal and evasive air, and to say that the law is something that depends. I am quite prepared to agree with any menacing Evangelist who shouts that the wages of Sin are death. I will go even further and support Yeats in his contention that the gravest punishment of the sinner does not lie in a repetition of the offence upon him. This may be education, but it is not punishment. Where real punishment is to be found is in the shattering fact that he himself is probably fated to have to commit his sin again and again and again — surely the Hell of a penalty.

But I would like to add a rider to this expression of an Inferno of Sartrean proportions. There can be an alternative in which he does not have to commit it again. And whatever the wages of sin may be, Death is a matter of little consequence. Curiously enough, if anything depends, it is Death.

A Realist's View of Death

It solves nothing to get rid of our distaste for the idea of Death by fooling ourselves with the notion that it is followed by some sort of continuance of this life of the flesh, in a spiritual sense, in another place that is not a place, and for an unending time that is not Time. Such a prospect does not make sense; nor — if it did — would it be even desirable.

We may deduce from the accumulating data of the Scientists, and from the ways of thinking which these new facts demand, that, in the words of Yeats

> Many times Man lives and dies
> Between his two eternities —

This is taken from his last legacy to humanity — the poem *Under Ben Bulben*. And there is evidence to support his statement, both scientifically and in the light of common sense. To the Existentialist, who regards this life as Hell, such a prospect must seem extremely depressing; but if Sartre does not wish to repeat his distasteful experiences for an indefinite period, there is no reason to suppose that he will be so compelled.

It might indeed be boring and oppressive to keep on living the same life over and over again, were it not for the further element that has presented itself — Alternation. Whenever we are faced with the opportunity of choice, we can decide for ourselves which way we shall go: and these divergent possibilities are not imaginary. In making our selections from Now to Now, no two experiences of life are quite the same. The conclusions, sometimes, but not the routes, and this is what was meant when it was suggested a few paragraphs back that, although our offences are everlasting, they are not unescapable, since — thanks to Alternation — there may well be another Continuum in which we *need* not commit them again. Hence the impossibility of a firm prediction, except on a probability basis. It cannot be said which alternative will be experienced, until the Continuum has been selected.

In the emerging shape of our new Cosmos, this conception of multiple alternatives is much more sensible and straightforward than are any of the other propositions that are to be found in the tangle of confused thinking in which we have been thrashing around. To begin with, all we need is a welcome Bill of Divorcement between our Nouns and our Verbs — or if you prefer it, an escape from the error of Patripassianism, an ancient heresy, consisting in a confusion of the Father with the Son.

Deeply rooted in the heart of the average man is a conviction that, somehow or other — in some way and in some place — he will meet again with everything that he has lost, to which experience Death will be no barrier. He embodies this in the conception of an after-life in Heaven. But although he is basically right in his objectives, his solution — Heaven — is, like Time, another mirage of our defective senses — (except, of course, in the form that the word has occasionally been used in these pages, as a synonym for the source of our directives).

It is Here, on this Earth, that we can find them again, in their ordinary habitat, but under different conditions that may or may not be more to our taste, according to an exercise of choice that will be our own doing.

So when we are told that the Wages of Sin are Death, we should properly answer that Death is no punishment, but is a prize to which we are entitled already, and that we will be pleased to accept at an appropriate moment on a clear understanding that it may be had not once, but 'many times'. Whether it turns out to be a crown or merely a pleasant, brief relief — depends.

Every Day a new Take

We have already applied the term a 'take' to any period of continuous experience that provides material for observation between two terminal points of consciousness — as, for example between waking and sleeping. In the Studios there may be an indefinite number of retakes, in the course of which the same scene will be re-enacted several times with differences in action and performance that may or may not be significant. The governing feature of a Take, however, is that the action in each is continuous while it lasts, no matter how many Retakes there may be.

This seems to offer an informative model for the working of Alternation. Here, too, there may be several Retakes of the same incident with variations between one and another, but all in temporal parallel in 4D, which gives them the same Now. In other words, as was said before, all actual possibilities are determined, but the selection of the one that we choose to experience is volitional — as it is in the Cutting Room. To pursue this illustration even further, it may be said that the only peculiarity of Death is that it concludes a Take that happens to be the last in sequence. The implement of consciousness ceases to extend any further down the meridian. It is like the shooting of what happens to be the final page of a script.

But although this Take is terminal, we must also recognise the fact that at no stage of our lives are any of these Takes interminable. Consciousness ceases, temporally, along the many extensions of the flesh between sleeping and waking. What reason have we, then, to be any more apprehensive about the ending of a shot that is the last in the script, than about the fact that the others terminate, too? There is, of course, this difference that when we go to sleep we are reasonably certain that there will be the start of another day's work in the morning. But once we have agreed upon the physical endurance of all Takes why should we imagine that our capacity to return for more is arbitrarily taken from us by the act of contemplating a Scene that happens to be the furthest along in the direction of Entropy?

Following this analogy of movie-making, an even more probing question might be asked. A motion picture is not necessarily shot in the temporal order of all the scenes in the script. Indeed it would involve an enormous waste of time and trouble to make it in such a way. So apart from this matter of retakes as a model for the working of Alternation, have we any reason for insisting that the scenes in our lives, as between sleeping and waking, must necessarily be experienced in temporal continuity? Continuity must certainly apply to the successive states of the telescope, but must it also apply to the activities of the Astronomer, which are exercised in 5D, and for that very reason are not under the control of Entropy at all?

When I go to sleep tonight it will be in the full expectation of another Scene. But am I justified in insisting that it must inevitably be in continuity with today's location? Surely this assumption, that there must be temporal order in our experiences, is due solely to the fact that at any particular date the physical tablets of memory contain no more than the record of an earlier stage of Entropy, and cannot be read with any recollection of future conditions. Whatever Scene it may be, it will have the memories of its proper date, and no others. It may have an Awareness that can be attributed to the more comprehensive experiences of the Elan, but no later memories.

I do not know the answer to this, and maybe it is carrying speculation too far. Indeed such secret matters may be taking us into a realm where the mortal mind has no business to be trespassing. We have neither the data nor the equipment. All that might be said on the subject is that there appears to be no reason either in Physics or in Psychology why we should not go on experiencing Scene after Scene while whatever is meant by 'Time' remains, without necessarily sticking to the order of the Calendar. An insistence on Continuity would seem to have as little sense about it as an assumption that we can only reopen a book at the page next after the one at which we laid it down.

As for what happens to the Conscious Mind between scenes—this is also a matter that is open to speculation, although it need not greatly concern the Flesh. The Elan has a home and a dimension of its own to which it owes allegiance, and

Much has been written on this fascinating subject, including a significant remark of Jorge Luis Borges: 'While we are asleep here, we are awake somewhere else.'

to which it must return, since it does not cease to be whenever the glove is empty.

Free Will as Movement in 4D

It seems to be reasonably certain that the exercise of Free Will is an operation, in the course of which a particular level of 4D in its 5D extension is selected. But whether the tiller is turned only in the course of sleep, or whether it is a wide-awake affair, functioning at the moment of decision, is a problem that demands a much longer book than this is going to be.

It is my personal belief, however, that there is no discrete division between the levels of 5D extension any more than there is between the moments of the extension of a world line, or between the inches of a plank of wood. It also seems likely that the great mass of small alternatives through which we steer our way in the course of our living makes no appreciable difference to the general direction of the events that make up our lives. Any major decisions leading to matters of life and death are probably great rarities.

The Gift of Years

As one grows older, and the fact of one's longevity becomes secure — as the days pile up with all the changing possibilities that we imagine we have missed — as we become more and more certain that there is nothing to complain about, quantitatively, in our available years, we have every reason to grow serene in our seniority, if not even a little smug. It is hard to see how this can happen in quite the same way, to a good Christian or to an Agnostic. The ageing Christian may die inadvertently in mortal sin, and must expect to face the consequences in either Hell or Purgatory, according to the line taken by his Catechism.

On the other hand, what could be more depressing than the prospects of the greying Pragmatist, with nothing but a landscape of missed opportunities, of disappointments and of withered hopes, to be followed by extinction? Time has eaten up the years, and all that he has managed to make of himself will become so much dust. He hears the cries of frustration winging from the lips of Shakespeare and Donne, and he feels that they are unanswerable. Time is a highwayman and a cheat.

Years following years steal every day.
At last they steal from us ourselves away.
This sable Thief of Life : this pallid Time,
What will it leave me if it snatch my Rhime?

But Time adds to the treasures of a good life, and steals nothing. The longer I live, the more Elysian fields of Space/Time are mine, in which to wander as I choose.

And although we are indebted to the Scientists for the first signposts that point a way to these conclusions, we owe something to our Poets too. To begin with, there are those lines already quoted from *Burnt Norton*; and whether or not Eliot may have been fully aware of the scope of the invitation that he was so generously offering, he can hardly refuse us permission to accompany him into his Rose Garden, now.

Joyce's Favourite Mother

But there is still another image of this interplay of Change and of Eternity that is offered to us by literature. I am referring to the striking analogy of the river that we find in Joyce's *Finnegans Wake*. The river is born in the hills — it flows down into the plain, gathering volume and distinction on its way, until finally it pours itself into the sea, and is lost in the bosom of its 'great feary father'. A leaf, floating on its surface — having got there from who knows what tributary source — will only be aware (could it be aware at all) of a cross-section of the extension of the entire stream; and here we find a simple image of the procession of the conscious mind. Observation begins — it matures — and it ends.

But what of the river itself? — for here is the most interesting part of the analogy. All of these apparently developing processes that relate to the actual stream have a temporal sequence : yet — four dimensionally — they are all happening Now. The river of life flows, and yet remains. The only question is, at what particular point do we contemplate it? All of it is there — Now — its branchings and its tributaries, its source and its culmination — for our perpetual study.

This is Joyce's picture of Anna Livia Plurabelle — our Mother Liffey — the female element that is given the last word in his major work — 'Yes'. But there is more to the image than this vision of a qualified Eternity. For in a more subtle sense, the river was not always there, nor will it remain throughout all the centuries. There is a deeper change behind the seeming permanence of mortal extension.

It is as if Joyce were saying that Space/Time itself will have an end, when the Elan will be carried onwards to new adventures in a field beyond our present comprehension. And maybe he is right.

The Train to Cambridge

I remember once describing how I opened my eyes in bed and wondered for a while where I was, how old I was, and even perhaps who I was? This was the beginning of a Take, and before long I began to get things straight. I was in a Paris Hospital, and I was — let me see — forty-three, and somebody in the next bed had been saying something about the fact that no objects were flying past the carriage window as the train proceeded from Liverpool Street to Cambridge. It was the train that was on the move. That was the beginning of more than a Travelogue.

See Appendix I

The Gospel of Thomas

In that generally unpopular *Book of Ecclesiastes* which the Jews somehow allowed into the Signal Manual, and which Jerome did not dare to expel (and which nowadays is significantly a Tract for the Time if 'Vanity' means 'the Non-Answer') we find that every activity has got its own proper season. . . .

> And a time to every purpose under the heaven :
> A time to be born, and a time to die;
> A time to plant, and a time to pluck up that which is planted;
> A time to kill, and a time to heal. . . .

The Old Testament has its own exciting way of speaking its mind without any of the inhibitions of the pulpit or the Foreign Office, and we must all have the courage of our instructions. So if a time comes along to play the serpent, by lifting the purposeful fear of Death from the shoulders of some man who might not choose to keep himself alive without it, we should not falter in our role. For even the serpent has got its moments, no less than has that lethal Tree of Knowledge.

But there are other passages that did not gain admission to the Textus — that lovely *Hymn of the Pearl*, to give an example. And the Gospel of the doubter — Saint Thomas — the best of the Fifteen, because of the fact that it was to this particular Apostle that the Lord is said to have confided his most secret message.

In the Apocryphal Gospel of St. Thomas, Jesus is alleged to have asked his disciples who he was like. Peter said that he was like an Angel of

It may be that the virtue of Thomas which merited so great a distinction, lay in the fact that he believed, after having been shown — but not without the showing.

Both of these passages of Scripture were omitted from the New Testament by its copy editors on the specious grounds that they were pseudomorphic, which might also be said of most of the other acceptable items.

Righteousness. Matthew called him a man of great understanding. But Thomas said : Master, I am not able to compare you to anything. To which Jesus replied : Didymus, I am not your Master; and you are intoxicated by the fountain from which you have been drinking. After which, Jesus drew him aside and whispered three words into his ear. When Thomas returned to the others, they asked him what it was that their Lord had said? To this, Thomas answered : If I were to tell you even one of those three words, you would stone me to death, and fire would come from the stones, and burn you all to ashes.

Actually, they were out of line with contemporary taste, which even in those days did not care to venture far beyond the Damascus Gate.

But let us take a look at something else that was offered under the name of this good Saint Thomas — something that was left out in Limbo, whether pseudomorphic or not :

If they tell you : "Look upwards, and you will see in the sky the Palace of our Lord," do not heed them. For if that were so, the birds of the air would be in Heaven before you. And if they continue : "No — look downwards, for it is there in the depths of the sea", cover your ears and turn away. For if such were the case, the fish would be nearer to God than you are. But I say this to you, that the place of that for which you seek is within yourselves. And when you find that this is the answer, you will know that you are the children of the everliving God, and one in each other. But until you can discover these things, you are nothing.

Then the Lord himself spoke and said : "If you can grasp what is meant by this, you will be delivered from the fear of Endings. So do not cease from searching. Yet, remember this; when you find that for which you are looking, you will at first be struck with horror and amazement. But after the horror will come understanding; and in the end you will find yourself to be set apart, and honoured above them all."

XI   LADY IN THE LABYRINTH

Cum haec sit mea affirmatio
credo instrumentum perennis
in ingeniis variis
et cum maculis omnibus
spiritum vitae merere.

Coventry

THE Phoenix of Coventry has risen from its pyre to grace the City of Godiva with a new mode in ecclesiastical architecture. And very handsome too, in spite of some grumbling from quarters that are still regretting the demise of Railway Station Gothic.

It has an exterior of striking simplicity, with tiers of cleverly concealed windows in all the colours of Heaven's rainbow, a western front of superb contemporary glass, orientated to the south in deference to some present doubts about the direction of the New Jerusalem, a spire like an antenna very properly placed to receive directives from up-there, and a gracious side-chapel offering a friendly greeting to other sheep not of this fold.

The ruins of the earlier Cathedral stand close at hand in all their charred and muted dignity, cheek by jowl with this expression of the middle of the twentieth century. And behind the shattered altar of the old building we read the words:

FATHER FORGIVE

Not 'Father forgive them', as it might easily have been, but a dignified comment, not only on Coventry but also on Dresden. Not only on Warsaw but also on Hiroshima. An appropriate colophon to all of these suicidal human crimes.

One feels that this is at it should be at Coventry. Even the little Chapel of Gethsemane, with its stylised image of an Archangel, speaks of a myth, the beauty of which is all the greater through an open recognition of what it is.

A Person with a Beard

But what of Christ himself in these surroundings? How is the Word to be depicted on the tapestry of the Reredos in terms that express the current views of our age? There is indeed a problem here. As representing the sentiments of an earlier period there can be both beauty and relevance in an ikon of Jesus and his Mother. But what happens when we are faced with the question of how to embody our own ideas on the subject in terms of a picture?

To begin with, what do we really want to show up there behind the altar, and dominating the entire interior of the Church — Jesus, a Teacher of Righteousness, or Christ, the Infinite incarnate? For in the minds of many of the customers of this and other Basilicas there is a growing distinction between the two that is not uncanonical. A Galilean carpenter, inspired by a divine message, would be easy enough to illustrate, and would certainly be more in keeping with what is wanted than some fellow in a collar and tie, placed there in pursuance of the current practice of bringing the New Testament up to date.

But this is not what the designers are after. What the situation demands is not a human figure at all, but Christ — a vision of the living Word as existing in the eyes of the century that built the new Cathedral. If the answer to this requirement is a person in some sort of bath robe, with an oval face, a fringe of whiskers, and his feet encased in a box, I venture to suggest that we are advertising nothing, except the fact that the twentieth century has got no image of Christ that is its own, because it does not possess any Christ at all. Any regard for such an object as we see here in Coventry is a pure formality, and is as out of touch with the genuine spiritual needs of the day as is Epstein's fraudulent angel, pinned like a butterfly to an exterior wall while employed upon the job of slaying Evil. Here it has to be supported by a number of very unfraudulent rivets, and even a child could see that Epstein knows as little about angels as he knows about aeronautics.

As for the designer of the tapestry, if he is unable to figure out what Christ looks like to us, he should give up the job as impossible, and taking his cue from the architects, refrain from plagiarising the intoxicated visions of our forefathers.

The Need for Symbols

Yet in spite of some built-in sympathy for the Iconoclasts, one is bound to agree that, without the assistance of some meaningful symbols, it is almost impossible to grasp the features of the Universe around us, once we find ourselves shot off into the high stratosphere of speculation.

A well-known graduate of a little-known Cambridge College — a man noted for his hostility to the use of images of any kind — has gone on record as saying:

> Remove those smiling epithets thick laid
> As varnish on a Harlot's cheek.

The operative word, of course, is Harlot. Nobody is objecting to the use of a few clean cosmetics. The real danger lies in our habit of clinging to prostitute images — a peril that exists not only in the realm of religion and philosophy, but that is just as acute in the field of science. Symbols can become as dilapidated and commercial as tired jokes. In this category we have not only 'Liberty' and the Lamb of God, but also the circling motor cars of the Children's Encyclopedia, and indeed Newton's apple — that other piece of fruit which has served as a pointer to many misconceptions about Gravity. We should not hesitate to throw them out with the other trash.

> Those who sit in a house of which the use is forgotten, are like snakes that lie on mouldering stairs, content in the sunlight.

As with a ritual, the question about a symbol is whether it conveys a valid impression of some aspect of human experience — something that can be more readily comprehended with the aid of a rite than can be grasped in terms of plain speech. To the primitive mind the myth of Persephone performed such a function in explaining the passage of the Seasons, just as the story of Abraham and Isaac liberated mankind from the appalling quandary of human sacrifice, as demanded by a demonic Jahweh.

The widespread Zoroastrian concept that assumes a conflict between Darkness and Light, and is linked to an idea that, while Light is good, Darkness is evil, is a peculiar by-product of the fact that the Earth revolves on its axis so close to a powerful source of illumination that two successive effects are produced and repeated daily. This fortuitous feature of Astronomy creates a rite, which in its turn becomes the basis of a Theology — that Evil is at war with Good. In actual fact there is no conflict of any kind between Light and Darkness, which merely complement each other. Nor, for the matter of that, is there any more of a struggle going on between Hell and Heaven as there is between Winter and Summer.

Another example of the danger inherent in the use of unsuitable symbols is to be found in the easy analogy that tempted the early Fathers to describe Jesus as 'the Son of God'. This expression was the cause of some grave confusion when it became advisable for a later generation to devise a precise definition for the consubstantiality of the three persons of the Trinity. In questioning the accepted wording, Arius never wished to deny the divinity of the Word. He merely insisted that, if Jesus was the Son of God, he must be regarded — like any son — as having been created from the Father. And on this issue, Christendom was rent apart for several centuries.

Note too, in the secular field, how the fact that we happen to have ten fingers has resulted in the enslavement of mankind to an inferior decimal system of arithmetic that ignores the much finer base of twelve that is divisible by three times as many factors.

A medal that is undeserved to the knowledge of the wearer, or that has been given — like so many medals — for the wrong reason, is no more than a piece of vulgarity, and its display is an empty gesture. But a ritual such as the holding of two minutes' silence in memory of the dead is a meaningful ceremony, since it encourages some thought about the actual subject, and expresses its intention in a relevant manner that stops the noise, if only for a blessed moment.

The Eucharist as a love feast is a friendly function that merits repetition, but as a method through which some form of sanctity can be obtained by the eating of instant holiness, it is surely a practice to which right-thinking adults ought not to lend themselves.

When the early Christians refused to throw a pinch of incense on the altar of Jupiter, it was not against the character of a non-existent Zeus that they were demonstrating, but against the implications of the ceremony itself. And we have plenty of opportunities to follow their excellent example at the present day, if we do not mind being told that we are acting in bad taste. To begin with, there is this little matter of saluting flags and of standing up for certain tunes. (I used to maintain that we should only insult these items if somebody of another allegiance would undertake to treat his own tribal totems in a similar manner. But now, in later years, I am not sure that we should wait long enough to have this arranged.)

The Voice from the Dead Sea

I am perfectly well aware that no voice actually spoke to me on the shore of the Dead Sea, or made any specific covenant with me regarding the use of firearms. No dove descended from the sky when I baptised myself above the Allenby Bridge. No angel ever pointed out the way from the salt pillars of Sodom to the skyline of the Golden City. No Presbyterian burning bush burst forth in my undistinguished presence. Not even a common ghost has ever pushed a cold finger into my affairs, notwithstanding one or two evenings hopefully spent in haunted houses.

Yet it is sometimes easier to describe unusual experiences in terms of such phenomena, than to go in for ponderous psychological explanations. For example, take this sensation that most of us must have had of receiving directives to do — or not to do — something. (Captain Jack White of the Citizen Army used to call it his 'liqueur sensation'.) Rationally, this may be self-deception; but it may also be attributed to an awareness that certain matters of conduct — apparently innocuous — had better be observed or avoided for good reasons that may be difficult to define.

The Celt would say that some witch had put a Geas on us — a compulsive bond, not unlike a child's 'I dare you', a much more subtle thing than the common Tabu, because usually the Geas is a positive command rather than a negative one. Blake would probably inform us that he had met an angel with whom he had discussed the matter over breakfast, and the peculiar thing is that, in making such a statement, Blake is much more widely appreciated than are the inspired authors of the tale of Cuchulain — probably because he can be more readily disbelieved.

It must also be admitted that lunatics, too, are receivers of directives — instructions that are not always in line with Public Policy. The late Doctor Buchman — who was far from being a lunatic — used to be in constant touch with the Holy Trinity on every sort of topic, by a hot line. Indeed, the only way to counter most of Doctor Buchman's formidable arguments was to insist that one had got a hot line of one's own, over which quite contrary instructions had been clearly received. This would put an end to any further discussion, without however solving the question of the relative temperatures of the competing lines. There is no way out of this impasse, except by agreeing that Time alone will tell.

Still, the fact remains that there are certain things that most of us know have got to be done, probably because in the depths of our perceptions we are aware that they are done already. This difficult involution, for which an apology is not of much use, implies some degree of knowledge of both Past and Future that cannot be attributed either to memory or to the files of *The Times*, or even to conditioned experience, so dear to the Behaviourists. And if you cannot make out what I mean, never mind.

Crosstianity

However, this sort of topic is more in the category of Applied Psychology than in that of Symbolism, which is our present concern. So perhaps we should go back, for the moment, with Billy Graham to the foot of the Cross, and consider that particular object.

The Cross is a gibbet — rather an odd thing to make use of as a talisman against bad luck, if that is how we regard it. Or is it, instead, a cynical reminder that Virtue usually gets pilloried whenever it makes one of its occasional appearances in this world? Not a very inspiring fact to advertise, unless it is needed to support the argument that, as Jesus was crucified and Mahomet was not, Jesus must be better than Mahomet.

More seriously, it might be treated as an image of the dignity of absolute suffering. It might also be taken as saying that all life is a crucifixion that we accept for its own sake. This last is a difficult idea, and not a very widespread one. But it might be a sufficient reason for accepting the Cross, were it not for the fact that, for most, the Cross represents the sacrifice of the faultless lamb to an irritable landlord to whom mankind is heavily in debt for something or other.

When it is held up, is it not meant to say : Remember — you up there — our Redemption has been purchased and paid for. So don't let us have any cheating!

None of these symbolic purposes, except possibly the third, bears very close examination. But before we take the Cross down from our bedheads, we had better pause for a moment, and look around to see whether there is anything else that might go up in its place. If it is only a talisman, perhaps we like talismen, and in moments of depression and despair we might feel inclined to put it back again.

The Holy Saltire

If some alternative for the Cross is necessary — and nobody is insisting that it is mandatory — what is wrong with the holy Unname itself, as embodied in the saltire of St. Andrew? This simple geometric form suggests not only the name of the unnameable, but also a picture of the Open Past and Open Future that shapes a new protest against Determinism. Do we not all stand at the focus of a genealogical saltire that is itself an example of multiple causation? But more important than this is the statement that Alternation is part of Everyman's inheritance, and that, in spite of the eternal reality of his first cause and of his ultimate destination, he is endowed with a variety of indestructible routes from the one to the other.

This is not a simple idea to grasp, but the Saltire — or even better, the three dimensional Hourglass — is a straightforward symbol that is neither difficult to draw nor hard to understand.

Birds and Cows

The image of the compulsive working of Grace in the form of a bird descending upon the Earth is not a bad symbol. The signal is as graceful and as unpredictable as a bird, and as difficult to order around. But what about the incarnation of the Word in terms of a mixed crowd of cows and characters around a manger, and of a star in the East, seen by some odd gyrations of the compass, from further east?

That there was no room at the Inn for tourists in an advanced state of pregnancy is regrettable, but it is a commonplace state of affairs even today. And it is no more relevant to the coming of a new dispensation than the fact that, for reasons that are only of interest to Jews, it had to take place in Bethlehem.

The Hand on the Wall

Why, therefore, should we prefer these images of superhuman manifestations to what is possibly one of man's earliest efforts at artistic self-expression — a hand placed upon a cave wall, and outlined by a curve drawn around the outstretched fingers?

Does not this primaeval scribble manage to convey a sense of the earthly purpose of the Ultimate, and of the function of the flesh in fulfilling that purpose? The hand of 'X', stretching upwards from the soil — be it right or left — an implement of the Whole, incarnate in a member of Man, and diverging into several distinctive fingers, or Uses?

We have, of course, the Rainbow as a visible promise of doubtful value. It tells us that we will be spared another deluge. But death by water does not concern us so much today as death by fire, to which the undertaking of the rainbow does not apply.

We might prefer one of these rarer things — a reassuring message in the audible and amusing form in which it is offered in Yeats's comedy, *The Player Queen*, where the braying of a donkey is used to announce and to promise the imminence of further instruction, of which we are in much greater need than an Ark. It is not always easy, at the start, to distinguish between the voice of a donkey — a grossly under-rated intelligence — and the sound of vital information. They have much the same wave-length.

The Lamb or the Unicorn?

The Lamb of God is not a very attractive animal, for all its precious blood, in which few of us would actually enjoy being washed. I have always felt that the Church makes unfair discrimination between this stupid, unadventurous quadruped and the much more amusing and companionable goat. As for this washing in blood, surely Mithras is supposed to have been disposed of long ago, somewhere in the neighbourhood of the Bank of England?

If we are to have an animal totem suitable for the time, why not appoint an honestly mythical beast that cannot let us down by any mis-behaviour in the Vestry? We are all familiar with that well-known shop-keeper, the Economic Man, fathered on Plenty by Adam Smith. And we also know his antagonist — the Theological Man, who has no right to be here at all, since Heaven is his proper asylum. Then we have the legal eagles — John Doe, the inheritor of badly devised property: and the Reasonable Man who decides so many of our lawsuits for us, to nobody's satisfaction (there being no such person apart from the unreliable pre-judices of the Jury Box). Finally there is 'the Public', and 'the Man in the Street' — whom nobody really regards as himself.

But what about the only real man — the one of whom we have been writing in these pages — the creature that is born, that grows up and that dies, whose purpose resides in his Verbs, the plaything of Entropy, the hammer of the smith, the performer — so admirable in his intentions and often so deplorable in his performance, but without whom nothing can be done out here in this echo-chamber of conflicting messages? A lonely, contradictory, bemused creature that is difficult to ensnare, except by the bait of an Ideal, and that can turn and rend the Ideal when it proves to be a fraud? Is he alone to have no zoological totem? If he is so entitled, what beast can possibly meet all of these requirements, unless it be the solitary, milk-white Unicorn, which seems custom built for the purpose — a royal brute, and the mythical opponent of that other monarch of heraldry — the Tory Lion?

Wanted — a Code of Conflict

In a society that is changing as rapidly as ours is, constant conflicts of interest are inevitable. In the absence of any disinterested political authority — which is rather more than can be expected at our present level of public unsophistication — self-help is the natural method of forcing a decision in a conflict. But self-help combined with a widespread access to an Endwaffe, creates a very dangerous situation, and this is the problem that provides the greatest political question-mark of our day and age, especially as between organised Societies.

At the moment, we have invented an elaborate international machine, the aim of which is directed, not towards any considered solution of the many outstanding arguments, but to the prevention of any decisions at all, whenever there are likely to be objections. This is based on a general principle that Peace is more important than decisions. It is certainly preferable when the only alternative to Peace is a holocaust. Yet it may also be said that a fight that is not allowed to be fought out to a conclusion has got a way of stinking afterwards, like unremoved garbage.

So it might perhaps be argued — in the absence of anything better — that what humanity has the greatest need of at the moment is a Code of Conflict, and not an enforced armistice, which usually amounts merely to an insistence on some arbitrary Status Quo.

This is not intended as a Nietzschean proposition. Nietzsche may sometimes be hard to answer, but he is very easy to dislike — a fact that indicates the presence of a serious flaw in his view of life. What I am suggesting is that the bullying of the weak by the strong is not actually the most acute issue. Most of us who have still got clear recollections of our schooldays will understand me when I say that the most sinister bullies are not necessarily the strong, but are more frequently the weak — those who are impelled to twist the arms of others in order to assert qualities that they have not got themselves.

What I am trying to point out by means of this tiny analogy is that any authority that is dedicated to the job of preventing the fit from exercising their natural right of do-it-yourself, whether in commercial relations or in international disputes, is liable to promote neither peace nor justice, but the very explosion that one hopes to avoid.

I admit that a remark of this kind is open to misinterpretation, and usually leads to at least two loaded questions: What do you mean by do-it-yourself? and Who are the fit? The first I have no time to go into at the moment, apart from pointing out that we live in an age when it is often advisable not to do what needs to be done, when it does not happen to suit the convenience of the herd — a reason for inactivity that is not good enough.

To the second question I have no reply at all, since it is beyond the competence of the Performers to decide such matters, and probably it is none of our business even to attempt to do so. In the long run, Time (or Entropy) will demonstrate to us who the fit are: meanwhile all that Man can do is to make sure, in the process of finding out, that the Species does not exterminate itself. Whatever the verdict on fitness may be, we should all be perceptive enough to agree that it is only the future of the Species that matters.

In the absence of an honest Judge and an effective Policeman, we must do our best to assure this survival, not by stalling the battle, but by providing a sensible code of Conflict. It is not the fact that we fight that matters, but how we do it, and although — to quote the late Ramsay Macdonald — conflict can be 'as dangerous as it is terrible', a forcible showdown leading to a decision is often preferable to the enforcement of a non-decision that is deliberately designed by a committee of liars and racketeers to settle nothing.

The history of the first half of the present century lends support to the view that it is sometimes smarter to lose a modern war than to win it. A military defeat is usually embarrassing to those in office, but the governed frequently turn out to be better off than the victors, in the long run.

No one is being so impractical as to suggest that the Arab and the Jew, the Indian and the Pakistani (or indeed, the Irish) should be forced to resolve their differences through some sort of championship contest in a conveniently cleared arena. All that we are concerned with here are some generalities about attitude, while paying a proper deference to the truism that a choice between Peace and a Holocaust is not a desirable quandary in which to remain indefinitely, particularly when 'peace' is only a synonym for some Status Quo.

Táin Bó Cuailgne

The finest literary parable that deals with this subject is probably the old Irish account of the battle between Cuchulain and his College chum, Ferdia, at the Ford of Ardee. Circumstances force both of these old friends to fight each other, and they do fight. The significant part of the tale lies in the fact that Cuchulain is in possession of an Ultimate Weapon — known in this case as the *Gae Bolg* — which he eventually makes use of, in breach of the championship code (if I may be allowed to venture a criticism of a hero who is highly thought of at home, although an Ulsterman). This is the point at which the public on both sides ought to have intervened, by disarming both champions — not in any sense as a denial of their right to solve their problems by violence, but as a protest against the fact that the contest was getting out of hand. The endangered onlookers should then have swiftly returned the *Gae Bolg* to the witch who had invented it, with an open invitation for her to use it on herself. In short, it is not the What, but the How that matters.

We do not get around the perpetual problem of the need for viable decisions by prohibiting conflict. Behind all these manifestations of human ambitions and jealousies remains the analogy of the poles of the battery, without which opposition no current can be generated — the Positive and the Negative — the Male and the Female — the Partisan and the Culdee — the Orangeman and the Shinner — the Statement and the Comment, in each of which roles it may be our lot to be cast from time to time, just as the physical Universe may itself appear either as Matter or as Energy. There is a natural conflict here that is coeval with Creation, and that will last until that moment of ultimate dispersal which we will not be here to see. But who cares? — since it will not be the least interesting as a spectacle.

To symbolise this permanent condition of anti-peace, a host of reputable charges are available from existing escutcheons — the valid test, as always, being do they clarify, or do they befog? And in the forefront of these images — flaunting themselves openly upon many public buildings — we find the Lion and Unicorn, whose fight for the crown is everybody's legitimate encounter.

In this connection the Culdee may be regarded as a prototype of the art of quietism and resistance, who wins through endurance and suffering. The Partisan, on the other hand, is the activist who is prepared to do whatever has to be done and to take the consequences. The only thing to do with the super-Partisan is to follow him to the end if he happens to be sane, and to kill him as quickly as possible if he turns out to be crazy. The opposite is true of the Culdee, who is dangerous to kill, particularly if he is wrong.

Let us continue to give them their white bread and their brown, according to taste, postponing for as long as may be that dreary moment when there is no longer any Crown to fight over, and when — with them — we have all been driven out of town.

Men do not invent Myths. They only invent fables, and tell lies. True Myths create themselves, and find their expression in the men who serve their purpose.

XII   A MEADOW
FOR THE MYTH

Et nunc et in saecula redeuntia
Dum temporis haec imago manet.

A Cromlech on Howth

SO now we have arrived at the moment to speak in the evening of our days; not as once from the Dome of the Rock, but in the course of a more leisurely progression to — and from — the Island of the Departed — a haven that is vividly described in the pages of Procopius.

It was a poet called Samuel Ferguson who wrote thus of a cromlech that is still to be seen on another hump in the sea, not unlike the eyot to which I refer:

> What arts of death, what ways of life,
>   What creeds unknown to bard and seer
> Shall round your careless steps be rife
>   Who stand and ponder here;
>
> Or by yon prostrate altar stone
>   Belike shall kneel, and, free from blame,
> Hear holy men with rites unknown
>   New names of God proclaim.
>
> Let change as may the name of awe,
>   Let rites surcease and altar fall.
> The same one God remains the law
>   For ever and for all.

The hundred years that have slipped by since Ferguson wrote those lines may perhaps be regarded as an example of the time-lag between the two elements that were defined by the heretic Marcion (father of the New Testament) as 'Gospel' and 'Apostle' which, incidentally, are embodied in the Christian Liturgy in an unnatural order — and even, perhaps by analogy, between its predecessor and this book. (It has been said that there are two books to be written out of the detritus of every man's experience.)

Gospel is the more important of the two, because without it we are merely playing with fiction. But Epistle offers the greater challenge to the writer, since in this capacity he stands liberated from the crevice of the present, ranging a deeper chasm in search of a meaning to what he has been given.

My own excursion into Data, like the bulk of my war despatches, has long since found its way into a limbo, like that file labelled J. UNUSED that was formerly to be seen on a shelf in the BBC News Room. Whenever I got back to Broadcasting House from foreign fields I used to stare with some distaste at this rubbish heap, and note how it had grown over the months. But in the course of time I also noticed that much of its contents had a way of appearing in the Think Pieces of the military experts, where it would make an unacknowledged contribution to something called the Big Picture. So maybe one is not always so UNUSED as one supposes.

The Approach to an Absolute Statement

In a book such as this, where so much space has been devoted to the search for a few acceptable Absolutes, it is to be expected that in its final pages we should pause for a moment to consider the possibility of an Absolute Statement. By this I mean a statement for which we ought to be prepared to go to *any* length — as has been the case with some earlier pronouncements from more dedicated generations.

Such a round-up of the facts, as we know them today must obviously be a co-operative job, for no solitary man would keep his sanity were he to allow himself to imagine that he could peddle such heady wares on his own. This is why we have got to get together on this project, while at the same time making sure that any definitive result will still be open to personal interpretation.

The proper test of such a statement is not whether it is one for which we ought to be ready to die. If circumstances force us towards any such end, there are of course worse ways in which to finish up. But never let us forget that dying for rubbish is a well-trodden route to undeserved fame by inferior performers. What we are after is something for which we should insist upon living, so long as this much more difficult feat remains decently open — and particularly so if living includes the annoyance of some sort of crucifixion, rather than the comfort of oblivion.

Such a statement, if viable, is bound to some extent to be an expression of the obvious; but we need not be greatly intimidated when Father Eliphaz of Bowdoin describes it as a cliché. The Holy Trinity is a cliché. The Catholic Mass is a cliché, but within its structure we can find a striking image of the co-existence of Free Will and Determinism. It begins with the Introit and it ends with *Ite Missa Est*, but we do not get there by one inevitable route. Within the framework of the Ordinary resides the Proper of the Day. What is even more significant is the fact that the Mass is repeated tomorrow, with variations and in other forms; but it remains the same Mass.

Back to Jerusalem

In attempting to frame any rational view of the facts of life, it is often
helpful to go back and take another look at the old terrain, if only to
correct a faulty picture that may have grown up in the course of the years.
The road into Rome, for example, was fascinating to re-identify in 1958
in terms of that fabulous night drive that took place a few hours before
the City fell. The hedge behind which we lay as the shells from an 88
came whistling through, shearing the telegraph poles in half, is now the
wall of a filling station, and difficult to locate on that account. What I
had come to recall as an ornamental archway opposite the field where, in
the dim dawn light, we had made a rendezvous with General Frederick's
tanks, has turned out merely to be a couple of elaborate gate posts.

So it was a lucky chance that brought me back in the summer of 1947
to one of my most informative whistle-stops, the City of David, at a
moment in its history when it was hourly becoming less and less hospi-
table. Indeed, it may be said that I only got out by the skin of my foreskin.

What brought me there was an amusing job of teaching some Arabs
how to run a broadcasting station — a detail of my autobiography that I
have been at some pains to conceal from many good friends on Broadway.
But I suppose that those few stony acres of man's search for the Ultimate
must have some odd quality of loosening the tongue, for what I found
myself actually beginning was a task of much greater pretensions than
the instruction of Sharq el Adna.

Standing there on Midsummer Day by the Dome of the Rock, staring
at the summit that breaks its way through the floor of the Mosque, and
from which Mahomet is supposed to have mounted to Heaven on the back
of a very remarkable horse, it seemed appropriate for a professional man,
then clearly on his way up middle age, to start professing.

As I remember, no particular attention was paid by my three companions to any sound of labour pains that may have fallen from my lips.
It takes more than some mutterings about fundamentals to interrupt a
British conversation on Moslem architecture. But I do not complain about
any inattention paid to me, since the same may be said of the first few rolls
of the Dead Sea Scrolls that had come to light at almost the same time.
As we know now, they were then being unprofitably toted around, just
down the road, by a junk dealer from Bethlehem. Now, twenty years
later, it seems as if this wild ass will have to bray again in louder tones
if it ever hopes to have its supper. Nevertheless it seems wise to retain a
tentative early draft in its rough Latin shorthand, not only as a better

means of camouflage than inaudibility can ever be, but also because it leaves it open to mistranslation, without which there is no salvation. (It also invites grammatical correction from those who would prefer to change the subject altogether to a discussion of loaves and red herrings.)

Too late to stop me now

Strangely enough, with the passing of the years, I am not at all eager to escape into some bosom upstairs. My present thirst is not for oblivion, but for several more Takes, not in any life hereafter, but in this one — here — like a Writer straining to get back to the pages of his manuscript in order to try some better way of framing several of them. And this is an opportunity that I am reasonably convinced I have in some alternate Continuum — and indeed, that we all have, if we have retained any of that old urge for Being.

So what does it matter if the wicked sometimes appear to die fortunate? How can we tell how fortunate they really are, or even whether, if wicked, they will be here at all the next time? *The Dead Never Return* — a pamphlet said, that used to be dropped on the German enemy in Italy. And then, on the other side: . . . *aber die Gefangenen sehen die Heimat wieder!* (But the prisoners see their home again!) Sooner or later, we will all be numbered amongst the Departed — as indeed has been my own condition for some time in the eyes of the strumpet City that gave me birth. But all who have died are not as dead as some. There are those who cannot be plundered of their store of years. On the other hand there *are* Dead who never return. They are not *Gefangenen*. This, too, depends.

Waiting with Beckett

> Astride of a grave, and a difficult birth.
> Down in the hole, lingeringly,
>   the grave digger puts on the forceps . . .

writes one of the fashioners of contemporary ways of thought. And he knows, better than most, that there is nothing unusual in the receipt of signals, or in the compulsive need to deliver one's correspondence. If the signal that Sam Beckett has received is a directive to wait, that is his business. Others may have had different instructions: but I am certain that our Belacqua agrees, whatever our instructions may be, that we have all got this common denominator — we must one and all keep our appointment.

If some of us feel that we have never been granted an appointment, that is a matter for great regret; for there is no more profound tragedy than that of the warrior who is never called up.

But do not be too ready to despair about such a situation, because the occasion for the summons is another of those decisions that are not for you or me to make. Like Yeats and Eliot, we may not happen to have noticed that we are already serving in the draft.

There are also some further lines of friendly advice to be found in that same Book of Samuel:

> It is not every day that we are needed. Not indeed that we are personally needed. Others would meet the case equally well, if not better. To all mankind they were addressed, those cries for help still ringing in our ears! But at this place, at this moment of time, all mankind is us, whether we like it or not. Let us make the most of it before it is too late!

A significant remark in the light of what we have been discussing, and linked with a timely warning about the Calendar. What is more, it comes from one who — for all his lively condition — has been heard to insist that he, too, died some years ago.

'I am a man,' Beckett is also reported to have remarked, 'whose life has no edges.'

Like the 4D continuum, this seer must be significantly curved. So those who, like him, are waiters, may treat his appointment as their own. As for all of us, whether we are waiters or not, we know that in the course of its fumbling, the hand is often the better of a glove. As that well-informed Saint Thomas once said:

> If Man is here for the service of the Spirit, that is wonderful. If, however, the Spirit is amongst us thanks to Man, that is even more amazing. But what we wonder at most of all is that so great a treasure can make its home in such a slum.

These are no days for any more piety over a Christ without a face. So suppose we try to come of age, for time is getting short, and there is much to be handed on to our dear, delinquent offspring. It was this same Thomas who left us a further account of what happened when some of his fellow disciples importuned their Lord about future prospects, and in particular about how long they might expect to have to wait for their individual crowns. 'When will we see you again?' they asked; to which J. C. Godot replied:

When you can take off your garments without feeling disturbed. When you have come at last to understand that you have been given the keys, but instead of using them you have bundled them away.

Ex Cathedra

Hoc est enim Corpus meum — the consubstantial heir of the Spirit, incarnate in the clay for a modest Take or two. And whether it appears as Man or Woman, as Partisan or Culdee, or most happily of all, as a spell of each in turn as the occasion demands, it becomes each of us to stand up for what we are, remembering always to smite our opponents only in respectable places, for they may easily turn out to be relations.

Our immediate objective must be to prepare for survival, if not in one Continuum, then in another — it matters little which, so long as we can be assured that there *is* another. For the decent Sinner deserves survival — impediments and all.

I suppose that in one way or another I have by now broken every one of the Ten Commandments, but I do not feel as yet that they have broken me. I was born on a Tuesday, and do not believe that Heaven has charged up any more against me than I am in a position to pay. Nor am I, on my part, running any charges against Heaven. Fair enough.

So let forgiveness reign, as the cut worm forgives the plough, and the smith absolves his hammer. It is true that we can all find life a little melancholy at times, but it need seldom be lonely, seeing that the absolute of good company is never very far off — no further, in fact, than the end of the present Take. A brief sojourn in this embattled vehicle, and then another fixture — while this dream of Time remains. Beyond these roundabouts — six of them — there is nothing more that is necessary for us to know, at present.

If this sounds like nonsense, make the most of it; but do not presume to contradict me until I have finished speaking, and you have heard what I have said. For mark this well — never once, when speaking *ex cathedra* have I erred. All that you have to know is when I am speaking *ex cathedra*, and when I am not. And to assist you in coping with this problem, you may take it that whenever I am wrong, I am not so speaking.

The same is true of that other Pope, at present occupying more comfortable quarters. But have no fear — I have no qualifications for such an office, whether speaking *ex cathedra* or not. If there were an Ailech of which for a brief spell I might be Abbot, I would enjoy that, while preaching a unity of Creed but not of Use.

For this cause, deny with your lips, if so inclined, but not with your heart. For the heart knows more than the eye sees, and whatever we may say is always open to correction the next time we call.

Colophon

Therefore put on your strength, and do not omit to keep your appointment. Let your voice be heard, whether or not it is to the taste of every jack-in-office who may be obstructing the traffic. By all means, render unto Caesar that which is Caesar's — but this does not necessarily include everything that he says is his. For the rest, we have all performed before, and will appear again, if we so wish, so long as the lights are kept up in the marquee.

> Et nunc et in saecula redeuntia
> Dum temporis haec imago manet.

AN APPROACH TO
AN ABSOLUTE STATEMENT

(See p. 195)

1. This I acknowledge — a one and nameless Infinite
    Beyond this masquerade of Hour and Place,
    Creator of Light and Darkness,
    Author of Good and Evil,
    Father of the Flowers and of the Frost.

2. Here in this prison of the Senses
    I bind unto myself the gift of Joy,
    The Sorrows that give Happiness its meaning.

3. For these two things I render thanks —
    For the agonies of Increase
    And for the bliss of Rest

4. And I hope for the coming of each in its proper course.

5. Blessed be Desire
    And Love, the Apple of Desire

6. With this — my calling and my chief delight —
    The miracle of Being
    Until the coming of its Crown.

7. Let there be praise for all these things
    And for the wit to be glad in them

8. And let the Weapon wear the blazon of its Lord
    As the Speaker is known by the Word.

9. So, when Forgiveness reigns
    As the cut worm forgives the plough
    And the smith absolves his hammer,

10.   I cast forth from my mouth the fruit of the Tree of Peril
      And with it both Fear and Remorse
      And the mortal Ills that are bred of Evil

11.   Through which ability it is my firm belief
      That this enduring Implement —
      This storied and instructed Flesh —
      Is rendered fit to host Divinity

12.   Now, and for a Now forever returning
      While this dream of Time remains.

APPENDIX A
CONTEMPORARY FIELDBOOK ENTRIES
(See p. 5)

In the verbiage of film making, whenever a scene is reshot for any reason, each performance in front of the cameras is referred to as a Take. Following this useful analogy, the two accounts will here be described as Take One and Take Two. The basic situation is the same in each case, and the action is continuous in both Takes, but — as in the Studios — the actual performance is significantly different.

A Xerox copy of some extracts from my Fieldbooks kept during the War was given some years ago to the Library of Trinity College, Dublin, where it may doubtless be examined by enquirers in search of some further information. The original books are in the possession of the New University of Ulster, but there is also amongst my personal papers a more extended account written in 1956, shortly after the events in the Belfast BBC Studio already mentioned. Some of the relevant passages from this memorandum follow below. I have occasionally corrected the spelling and syntax, and have even put in a few words and sentences here and there to make the meaning clearer. But it is neither censored nor materially amended.

ACCORDING TO TAKE ONE

On waking from a short sleep on a sofa in the Rathaus, I went out to look for the party I had heard was going to try to go up Hafelekar, as soon as an operator for the cable cars had been found. This meant, first of all, going up to Hungerburg, the suburb overlooking Innsbruck from the south. It was a fitful night, and on the way to cross the river, a light in a damaged house attracted my attention, and for some reason I looked inside and saw a woman D.P. in dirty rags bending over the body of a half naked man. Beside them a few pieces of wick, floating in a saucer of oil, provided the only light. I did not go in, because just then I heard the sound of trucks revving up in the streets behind me, and I realised that this probably meant that Youell's column was preparing to move up the Brenner. Shifting my Luger (which was encumbering the pocket of my overcoat) on to my belt, I chased the vehicles on foot as far as the Bahnhof, where I gave up. Here a group of G.I.s was loading a truck with Jerricans, which were stacked in a dump beside the tracks. They were going to follow the column as soon as this was done, and they agreed to give me a ride.

It was a maddeningly slow process. They were in no hurry, and as it began to turn light, I finally moved off by myself, up the hill, and before long found myself in company with one of those marching columns of enemy troops that were a feature of the times. This one was unarmed, but carried haversacks and other personal possessions, and it included a number of young girls marching with the men. They were in their own way an attractive, clean-cut bunch of youngsters, and spurred by some instinct of the moment, I fell in with the rear file and found myself marching with them too. They paid no attention to me whatsoever, after the first initial surprise, but continued to whistle their way up the slope towards a road junction hardly a mile out of Innsbruck.

Here by the roadside was a picket of fully armed Austrian regulars. When they stepped out I thought for a moment they were after me. But this was not so. Their intention was to direct the column down one of the arms of the fork towards where there was a cantonment to receive them. Me, they gravely saluted, and as the column disappeared down the road still whistling, I confirmed the fact that, as I had thought, the other road was the route that led up the Brenner. I was tired, and pulling out a pack of American cigarettes, I handed them round, and we sat there engaged in desolutory conversation until the truck appeared, toiling up the slope from the town. It transpired — in so far as we understood each other — that these regulars were on the look-out for SS men. These would be armed — they said — and might have to be forcibly disarmed and locked up. For, unlike the usual columns of ex-belligerents, the SS was still a menace, and particularly so to co-operative Austrian regulars. It would be rash, in fact, to say that the war was over yet. In this odd twilight period our late enemies were falling into more categories than one. First there were the cheering civilians, who were so delighted that the rough stuff was over that they threw flowers into our jeeps. Then there were the run-of-the-mill Austrian soldiers and Landwehr, disciplined and polite, ready to co-operate with what they hoped would soon be their own native government in implementing a peaceful surrender. Next there were the German regulars, aware that the war was lost, and no longer eager to fight, but still ready to resist if pushed around, hoping, not for surrender, but for an armistice, sitting behind their road-blocks, unshooting unless shot at. Finally there was the SS, still at war, but more viciously with their own people than with us. It was through this conglomeration of varying types that Youell pushed his way to the top of the Brenner, his headlights defiantly flashing up the hill with such an arrogance as to confuse and paralyse all thoughts of further resistance — a brilliant tactic, as the road is difficult, and a few determined men might have blocked it for an indefinite period.

It was a tortuous journey, even in the American truck which I flagged down, as soon as it appeared. We stopped continually, sometimes to talk to stragglers, sometimes to give gas to a stranded vehicle. For a longer period we halted at a place with a name like St. Judas. Just short of the summit, at about 9.30, we caught up with the tail of the column itself — the men eating their chow beside their vehicles. Further on, a striped pole had been dropped across the road at the actual frontier.

Hundreds of silent and rather sullen members of the Wehrmacht were sitting in groups along the margin, disarmed, but not under any apparent restraint. Small parties were setting out to call in their pickets, still in position on the upper slopes, and no doubt peering down at us over the sights of their weapons. I got out, thanked my taximen, and set off up the road to the frontier to get the whole picture and to prepare my story. Where was the U.S. Fifth Army? Was it on its way up from the south? The men at the barrier knew nothing of it, but from them, and from the excited group of D.P.s (halted by the pole) I gathered that somewhere down that slope into Italy the Wehrmacht was still astride the road in an uncooperative mood.

I passed through the block and, fingering the holster on my belt, I stepped into Italy myself, partly for the hell of it, and partly to see what further information could be got from the few cars, trucks and oddments that had evidently come up from that direction and were now parked down the slope. From the south an occasional German squad would come marching up, and small parties of GIs were filtering down the road, ostensibly for the purpose of search, but actually to relieve them of their watches and other valuables — one of the most popular industries of the day.

I am not proposing to repeat the rest of this Take in the words of the entry of 1956. I have never managed to commit it to paper to my satisfaction, probably because I have visual memory to assist me until now, but not after I passed through the road block. This may be explained by the fact that almost everything that occurred up to this point was paralleled to a substantial extent by events in Take Two (although not at quite the same hour of the day) and it may be that what I remember of the appearance of things actually comes from that other Take. The remainder of Take One — which is the story told in *Nine Rivers* — does not have the same aids, and its reconstruction in visual terms, as found in that book, requires the addition of a narrative element that I do not regard as wholly genuine. Yet I do not know how else to describe it.

I am however aware that, a few hundred yards into Italy I found this bleeding Nazi official sitting in a car, tearing up papers as he stared up the road towards the frontier. (Actually I think it was one of the G.I.s who were looting the prisoners who pointed the vehicle out to me.) I got in and talked to him for a while, noting from his papers that his name was Otto Suder and that he apparently came from Mönchen-Gladbach in the Rhineland. I did not report our conversation literally in my book because of the fact that, while his words were in German, my own contribution was in my usual abominable patois that bears little resemblance to the carefully phrased language in which the substance of our discussion finally appeared. At its conclusion he asked for my gun which I gave him for reasons appearing elsewhere. But before using it on himself, as intended, it was first, surprisingly, turned on me. The end of the Take came when I saw his finger close around the trigger.

ACCORDING TO TAKE TWO

When I opened my eyes, it was not with any knowledge of these events. It was like any other morning in those times, when I would wonder for a while where I was, and gradually ascertain not only my location, but also my age and my immediate business. I was in the Rathaus, and what I remembered was only the sequence of events that had brought me there to sleep. I must get up and go up to Hungerburg, otherwise that party bound for the summit would be gone. I had no immediate recollection of Otto Suder or the contemporary Brenner, or of any of the other incidents in Take One. Passing through the empty streets, I saw the light in a house, and paused to look inside, without any awareness of having done so already. But just then a sudden downpour of rain mixed with a little snow sent me indoors for shelter. But for this I would not have noticed another thing that seemed familiar. The tattered shawl and dress of the woman — dirty and stained as it was — the tragic angle of her head as she looked down at the emaciated figure of the man before her, was not just that of a woman D.P.; it was also an image that I had seen in Rome. It was the Pieta. And as with the Pieta, I could see that the man beside her was dead. In the flickering half-light it was difficult to see her face. It may have been that of the Pieta — or of Anneliese. Indeed it would be facile and dramatic to say so. But I will not say so, because this is too serious a moment to trick out with any fanciful trimmings, as the inmates tricked out the ovens of Buchenwald. I do not know what her face was like. But what did strike me with a cold shudder of recognition was the fact that the face of the dead man seemed very like my own.

In that confused international mixture of languages that the D.P.s used we spoke for a little while. In the distance I was aware of the revving up of petrol engines, but I paid no attention to this. I was far more interested in the scene before me. We did not speak so coherently as I have reported elsewhere, but the effect was the same — my revivified fury over this dehumanisation of humanity — her perfect dignity — I cannot call it resignation for her attitude had something about it that put it in a category far above any mere stoicism.

It was Absolute Despair, yet in a sense it was also Absolute Acceptance. She could hardly be said to be grieving, because that which had been taken from her was no longer her man (son — husband — brother — I don't know what he was). He had been changed long before this — as had another prisoner in Perugia been changed by torment. Yet I could no more conceive of her calling for vengeance on whatever thugs had done these things to her and hers, than I could imagine her belching. And when I left, and found my bemused way up to the Nordkettenbahn, it was not a fire against the Nazis that I was breathing, but a fury with the facts of life — a rage against the God who had presented his creatures with such data. This world would never be set right by the slaughter of a few members of the Gestapo. There was something at issue here that was far more serious than that. It was man versus Man's Architect. Maybe it was the face of the dead that made me see myself as him — and like him as one of the dead, far above and beyond all cheap preoccupation with the problem of revenge. I have tried, not very successfully, to simplify the complexity of this revelation in the verse-form of the first part of the Canon in *Nine Rivers*. But the fluid exaggerations — the changing identities of the living and the dead — the voices speaking through the lips of others — the flux of personality and of human relationship that are to be found in the original *Dionysia* — rococo and over-written as they may be — these are far nearer to the truth than anything I have cared to publish. It needs a poet to give adequate expression to its complexities, and I am not a poet. So I dealt with it as well as I could in the *Dionysia*, and placed the text thereof beyond the reach of any tampering at a later date — particularly by myself.

But back to the events. I got to the rope railway and went up — not to the uppermost summit, which is reached by a second lift, but to the terrace of the

Innsbruck, Hungerburg und Nordkettenbahn.

Gasthaus that is at the top of the first long rise. It was not yet dawn, although the sun was close below the skyline to the left as I looked down over Innsbruck. It was extremely cold up there in the snow, and I have never known such a silence. It seemed as if there was not a vestige of sound of any kind in the frosty air, until somewhere in the sky above me I heard the rattle of the second lift as it approached. Were those German signalmen in it, or did they come across from somewhere else on foot? I cannot be sure, for I know I paid very little attention to them. I was going through in my mind what I have embodied in the second part of the Canon — something that perhaps can best be expressed in terms of some sort of a Liturgy. (The Old Testament writers knew better how to report a conversation with Heaven than I do. And an image of these high matters cast in the form of imaginary dialogue is not a bad one. So who am I to try to improve on it?) Why I fired that shot into the sky (as described in Nine Rivers) is another thing the answer to which I am not certain of at this distance. Maybe it was for the lower lift to come up for me again. Maybe it was a protest against the silence. Maybe it was what I say it was in the Canon — an act of defiance of the Almighty and his arrangements. Whatever it was, that shot into the sky was real, the dawn that followed was real, and the answer was real. No thunder-bolt struck me down. On the contrary, a great peace of mind descended upon me — a peace that was at one with the stillness and the God-like calm of those hills — a majesty, in deference to which I flung myself on my knees after taking my silly gun and sending it hurling over the parapet into the snow below.

So when in the course of human events I descended once more in the dangling cradle to Hungerburg far below — this time accompanied by a mixed bag of G.I.s and Wehrmacht of undefined status — I had no longer any Luger.

Nor could I conceive of any valid reason why I should want to carry a Luger, however necessary it may have seemed during the past fabulous month. What I had discovered at Buchenwald was true. It was also dangerous to know, but it could hardly be refused or denied on that account. The point being (as I look back on it now) it was a knowledge which, like the gun itself, could and must be acquired at some point in one's journey, but had better be thrown away before it becomes lethal. One dies by what one carries. So, it may be said that it was in a state of neo-innocence that I went along to the railway station — now in broad daylight — and was picked up somewhere by Abe with his (now) two jeeps. How or where he had got the second jeep and a young American officer as a "guide", he did not explain. Nor did I enquire, because from now on I was beginning this series of disturbing sensations. Somehow or other, all that was happening had already happened in a different way. These experiences started at the Railroad — now littered with rubbish and with K Ration boxes, but empty of any American troops. It rose to a peak when, on our way up the hill, we were confronted by a picket of Austrian regulars. In a panic at seeing that they were fully armed, our Guide reversed back down the hill and passed us. It was I who knew what they were, and that there was no harm in them. It was I who, further up the valley, knew whose tracks had been left in the slush, and insisted on going on in spite of our escort's doubts.

When Abe asked me how I knew they were Yank tracks I said that there had been a K Ration box by the side of the road. But there hadn't been anything of the kind — not here. It was a lie, invented because it was easier to lie than to try to explain that somehow — in some inexplicable way — I had already been there that same morning — although this could not have been the case. This peculiar impression came upon me once again when, near the summit of the Pass, we met another of those whistling columns of enemy troops, swinging down the road, with their girl companions marching in the ranks. In the *Dionysia* I describe how it seemed to me that I was marching with them, and that they were snubbing me. The conqueror was being cold-shouldered by the vanquished. But it was not this column that I had been marching with. It was another one — further down. At the Brenner we found Youell shaving himself in the best Gasthaus, and we talked with him as reported in *Nine Rivers*. A party was being got together to go down into Italy to locate the supposed German roadblock and to find, if it could, the Fifth Army. We asked if we might go with it, and were soon under way, as already described. What I did not describe was a further shock of recognition when we passed the parked car by the side of the road. This was the final experience that led to my awareness of Take One. The details were not present in my mind from the start — they only took shape there by degrees. But the basic fact was now staring me in the face. I had been here before. Or perhaps I was here again at a new "Here and Now".

And so to the memorial by the roadside near Colle Isarco, elsewhere described, where we were not killed by an amiable German officer, who could easily have blown us up, but who came up the road, at some peril to himself, to warn us of the danger we were in.

Returning to the frontier with two American officers whose appearance from the south signalised the junction of the two U.S. Armies, I tried to peer into the parked car as we flashed past, but all that can be said was that there was something there, and I enquired no further. Indeed, when back again behind the roadblock, and some of the P.R. boys excitedly told me that they had heard there was a dead Nazi in a car down the road, I politely declined to go with them back into Italy to investigate — I felt so strange about it all.

"Dead?" I asked. "How did he die?"

"He shot himself when he found the Pass was blocked."

"Shot himself?" I asked in some surprise. "With what?"

"With a gun, I guess. The Priest is the one who knows all about it."

"Was he alone?" I enquired, wondering what the answer would be.

"Yes. He seems to have been quite a high-up Nazi. Trying to get back home, I suppose. Want to come down with us and see?"

"No thanks," I answered cryptically. "If he's dead, that's the end of it."

So I never saw him in Take Two. Of course I should have gone back and looked for the Priest, but as it was I preferred to stay and talk to two American Generals. It was the end of the War in that area — maybe in Europe — and an occasion that cried out for a Press photographer. But, strangely enough, nobody had a camera except Abe Goldberg, in spite of all the looting. So he took a picture — not a very good one. And I still have a copy of it.

The snows of the Brenner — a white scene, no less bleached than were the salt cliffs at the headwaters of the Dead Sea, from which I had set forth upon a lengthy pilgrimage about three years earlier. White — but now considerably colder. A name-dropping picture showing Major General Nuts McAuliffe, Lieutenant General Brooke, Miss M. Higgins's jeep, and your (incidentally gunless) Correspondent — a detail that indicates that the photograph belongs to Take Two.

'From where it is white, to where it will be white again.'

When in the course of writing my *Dionysia*, I found myself approaching the moment when it would be necessary to describe my chase of
Youell's Column up the Brenner, it became increasingly evident that I
would now have to face up to a sixty-four dollar question that I had been
deliberately avoiding for a number of years. Was I alone on my way up,
or was I with Abe Goldberg? Did all of this take place after I had been up
Hafelekar, or was Hafelekar both before and after? Why do I remember
quite clearly the appearance of those Austrian Regulars, and yet have a
mind that is a complete blank on the subject of Suder's physical appearance? And when was I marching with that whistling German column?
This could hardly have been in Take Two, unless it was before I was
picked up by Abe. It was only after the incident in Belfast that I felt
impelled to write down in any detail what I could remember of both Takes
without any inhibitions, and regardless of whether they jointly made
sense or not.

The fact is that I have long ago exhausted the various explanations in
my own mind, and am now bored with the subject of factuality. Dream
interpretations are as phoney as they are in *Alice in Wonderland* and in
The Pilgrim's Progress, and simultaneity seems to be the easiest way out.

Besides, the question arises as to whether one story *could* be real without the other. In certain important particulars, both are incomplete, since
what I knew and did in one had an effect on what I knew and did in the
other. Indeed, I now have some doubts about naming them 'One' and
'Two', since this terminology suggests a sequence in which One precedes
Two. They should probably not have any numerical description at all.

Before the end of Take Two I was aware of the existence of Take One,
but I am not at all sure whether at any point in Take One I was aware of
Take Two. If there is any significant difference between the two Takes it
lies in the fact that the second is more confused with regard to the actual
sequence of events, while the most striking parts of the first are oddly
deficient in what I have already described as the visual qualities of
memory.

If the first Take is a dream — which is, of course, the explanation that
immediately comes to mind — it contains a surprising amount of Dun-
neish pre-vision of a journey that I had not yet taken, and which was the
source of a number of experiences that affected my behaviour on the way
up with Abe in Take Two. Then there is the question as to where the name
'Otto Suder' comes from — a piece of information that does not appear
in the second Take at all. Did any such person from Mönchen-Gladbach

die in the Brenner on the 4th. May and if so, How? For I certainly did not kill him either in my dreams or otherwise, whatever he may have done to me. A prominent Nazi leader is reported as having committed suicide a few hundred yards down the road, and it seems most unlike my habits as a Reporter not to have gone down with the others to take a look — unless indeed, I had somehow seen him already, and had no wish to see him again (or anything else that might have been in that car).

In this impasse, I have not been of any assistance to anybody. I have not been back to the Brenner. I have made no enquiries at Mönchen-Gladbach to ascertain whether there ever was a Nazi by the name of Suder, and if so what happened to him?

In 1966, a Smith graduate, by name Fairinda West, while engaged on writing a doctoral dissertation on my other work, got in touch with the German Red Cross, and asked these people whether they had any record of the death of anybody of the name of Suder from Mönchen-Gladbach. The reply which is translated below is a curious document.

> Esteemed Fraulein West,
> Your letter of the 9th October to the General Secretariat of the German Red Cross in Bonn has been forwarded to us for reference. It does not necessarily follow from this that Otto Suder is dead. Rather, it is a question as to whether your enquiry can be related to a Report of a Missing Person that was lodged with us by the wife of somebody of the name that you mention.
> It is possible that the person about whom you are enquiring was killed in the Brenner, or he may have died in some other way. We would be very grateful if you would give us some more details of the circumstances of his death, if they are recorded in the diary extracts that you mention, or anything else that may give us some indication of the facts surrounding his death. In this way you would be giving us valuable help in our work.
> Even if the facts that you have do not contain any information of a precise nature, which we conclude from the fact of your enquiry to be the case, any piece of information is of help in our work, even if it only gives a clue in some direction. When we receive your reply we shall probably be of more use in fulfilling your wishes.
> With friendly greetings . . .

From this it would seem that an enquiry was in fact made after the War to the Bureau of Missing Persons by the wife or widow of somebody of that name. The German Red Cross appeared to be interested in obtaining further information from Miss West about the case, but seemed reluctant to divulge any details from their own files until the enquirer first came through with hers. As far as I know, Fairinda — having satisfied herself that there was nothing fictitious about Otto Suder — did not pursue the matter any further. So there it rested until the month of October, 1974.

Postscript to Take Two

Laurie Heyhurst arrived on the evening before the formal surrender with our recording gear and the BBC Utility, and he joined us in the hotel up on Hungerburg where we had been billeted. It was next morning—shortly before the surrender ceremony, I believe—that I invited him to come with me when I went up in the cradle once again to Hafelekar. In the snow below the Terrace I sought for and found my Luger. The hand grip on one side of the stock had been broken off in its fall. I gathered it up and brought it down and in due course it arrived in Belfast where — growing tired of Lugers — I left it behind.

So also were left behind for a number of years at least two unanswered questions that still interest me. To begin with, there is the more general one as to whether it is rationally possible for there to be two contradictory conclusions to such a story, and if not, which of them can be accepted without ignoring the other? For it would seem that in a number of details they are mutually dependent.

Secondly, how did Suder die in Take Two, since neither I nor my gun had anything to do with him in the present Continuum? Yet it seems that he died in any event, so that it comes to the same thing in the end. Had he a gun of his own, and if so, why would he want mine? How was he wounded in the first place? And what part did the Priest play?   See Appendix L

Some day I shall perhaps go back in a car of my own, and drive through to Colle Isarco to see whether there is still any 'Dove' on an inscription by the roadside. After which I shall return to the summit, and look for a grave — or maybe two — and enquire for that Priest as well. Not that Priests usually have much of an answer these days.

Later, in October, 1974, in reply to a query from my friend Gerhard Fessler, DRK-Suchdienst, München, replied as follows:

Herrn Otto Suder, geboren am 4.8.1907 in Mönchen-gladbach der aus dem Kriege nicht heimgekehrt ist. Herr Suder war Obersekretär bei der Kriminal-polizei in Luxemburg und im Kriege SS-Oberscharführer beim Chef der Zivil-verwaltung für das Land Luxemburg. Herr Suder befand noch am 1. April 1945 in Blankenburg/Harz und wurde von dort zum Einsatz in Raum Brenner abgestellt.

APPENDIX B
WRIGHT'S WRIST WATCH
(See p. 37)

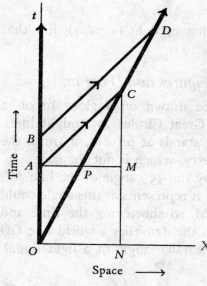

(See diagram.)
OAB is world-line of the earth.
OCD is your world-line.
You travel with velocity v relative to the earth. That means that

$$v = \frac{\text{distance travelled}}{\text{time taken}} = \frac{ON}{NC}$$

At event A, a light signal is sent out from the earth, and reaches you at event C. At event B, a second light signal is sent out from the earth, and reaches you at event D. Then AB is the interval between the emissions as judged by the earth-clock, and CD is the interval between the receptions as judged by your clock. We want to calculate the ratio CD/AB.

By similar triangles, CD/AB = OC/OA.

Draw AM parallel to OX. Then CM = AM = ON (Why?)

(Presumably because on Synge's scale he has set the speed of light as equal to 1, so $OC^2 = CN^2 - ON^2$ ('Yes, minus sign, because this is the geometry of Minkowski, not Euclid.') Thus

$$OC^2 = (CM + MN)^2 - ON^2 = CM^2 + 2\,CM.MN + MN^2 - ON^2$$

$$= ON^2 + 2\,ON.OA + OA^2 - ON^2 = 2\,ON.OA + OA^2$$

So $\dfrac{CD}{AB} = \dfrac{\sqrt{2\,ON.OA + OA^2}}{OA} = \sqrt{1 + \dfrac{2\,ON}{OA}}$ But $v = \dfrac{ON}{NC} = \dfrac{ON}{NM + MC}$

$= \dfrac{ON}{OA + ON}$, $\dfrac{1}{v} = \dfrac{ON + OA}{ON} = 1 + \dfrac{OA}{ON}$ and so $\dfrac{OA}{ON} = \dfrac{1}{v} - 1 = \dfrac{1 - v}{v}$.

Thus $\dfrac{ON}{OA} = \dfrac{v}{1 - v}$, $1 + \dfrac{2\,ON}{OA} = 1 + \dfrac{2v}{1 - v} = \dfrac{1 + v}{1 - v}$.

Consequently the required ratio is

$$\frac{CD}{AB} = \sqrt{\frac{1 + v}{1 - v}}.$$

This is certainly greater than 1, so CD is greater than AB. Hence a Doppler effect — red-shift in the spectrum.

If our speed is nearly that of light, v is nearly equal to 1, and CD/AB becomes very large.

He would not allow our speed to be that of light (v = 1), for 'that would not make sense'.

Some Criticisms of the above Figures and Diagram

First of all, the diagram should either be drawn on a globe or on a Gnomonic projection, showing only the Great Circles as straight lines, and with the co-ordinates as curves. As it stands at present, it treats the whole matter as a problem in plane geometry, which is not the case.

Secondly, the speed of light, as shown by the 45° angle of the line AC, seems to be questionable. The velocity that it represents at this angle could be increased up to the right angle of AM, so shortening the time and distance in arriving at an earlier point on the Traveller's world line OD (at P). AC cannot truly represent the unbeatable angle of a light signal, as AP is obviously shorter than AC.

Nor do we know what is going to happen if the Traveller alters his direction at D, and returns to his original meridian OAt. In other words, are we merely talking about a Doppler Effect in discussing the effect of Velocity upon time reckoning? Or does the situation take us further than this?

Shorter still would be a perpendicular dropped from A on the line OD, but this would be the course of a signal originating in the past, and elsewhere. Otherwise Entropy would be reversed.

Clearly we need a different diagram that will represent a plotting of the exercise as taking place on our Cosmic globe. This should make the nature of the actual problem much clearer, whether or not it provides a final solution. So let us go back to that Base Point already selected on page 115 (Long. Zero; Lat. 50°N.) and suppose that the Traveller's world line diverges here at a 4D angle of about 53° to the Observer's meridian (0°). This is rather more than half the speed of light, and it is selected because, if he holds this direction, he should cross the Fifteenth Meridian at the easily definable level of the Fortieth Parallel. (See the Plan on the next page, which in the absence of a practical globe, is plotted, instead, on the appropriate projection.)

Let us suppose that, having found himself at what the Observer sees as the distance of Long. 15°, he holds up his watch, and that the Observer, thanks to some miraculous telescope, can read it. Of course, the Observer

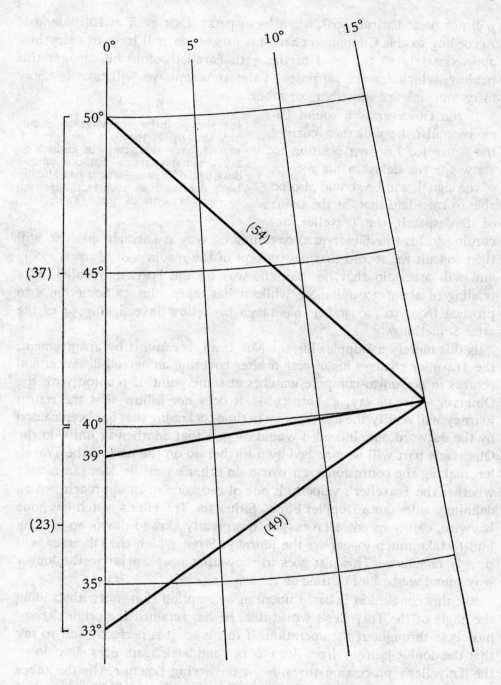

will not be at Latitude 50° when he inspects it, or even at Latitude 40°. According to this Gnomonic chart, his procession will have to carry him approximately to the level of the 39th Parallel before he can get this reading, which for the purposes of the argument we will take to show fiifty-four units of something or other.

If the Observer is a sound Dimensionalist, he will then correct the figure for his own position to allow for the delay in his receipt of the signal, and he should also be able to calculate that, at the point of its despatch, the Traveller, according to his (the Observer's) co-ordinates, was at Latitude 40°. He will then consult the record that he has kept of the readings of his own clock, and will ascertain that he, himself, was on the Fortieth Parallel, at a reading of about 37 units. So, while it has taken him 37 Somethings to proceed from 50° to 40°, it has taken his fellow investigator 54 of the same Somethings.

It makes no difference what these units are, so long as they are consistent. I, myself, have used tenths of an inch on my original chart, a distance unit — defying Eddington — which has already been discussed as a correct approach to measurements of Space/Time.

Is this merely a Doppler Effect? Not at all, because if by arrangement, the Traveller changes his direction after covering an agreed distance, and returns in person to compare watches at some point of reunion with the Observer — let us say, at Lat. 33° — it does not follow that the return journey will rectify the discrepancy in time-reckoning that has been caused by the outward one. Indeed, I would suggest that another 23 units on the Observer's part will be matched by a further 49 on the part of the Traveller, making the confusion even worse. In other words, it does not matter whether the Traveller's velocity is one of recession or of approach, which definitely rules out a Doppler Effect. Either the Traveller's watch has gone haywire, or his speed of Procession has greatly slowed down, so causing him to take much longer on the journey. From which the Observer will smugly conclude: This just goes to show that people who go the longer way round waste a lot of time on the trip.

But this conclusion is based upon an assumption that, notwithstanding the angle of the Traveller's world line, he has retained the original common Pole throughout the operation. If this is so, it is perfectly fair to say that the double-journey from Zero to 15° and back again does slow down the Traveller's procession towards an unvarying Equator. On the other hand, if it may be said that a change of direction of a world line *does* alter the Pole of a travelling Observer, it would be equally legitimate for such a Traveller to insist that at the moment when he held up his watch he was not at Lat. 40° at all, and that his friend's calculation of simultaneity is totally wrong.

This question of whether we alter our Pole with every change of direction seems to be at the root of the matter, and it is discussed further in Appendix E. Although the data is inextricably mixed up with subjective observations, it does not necessarily follow that there is not an answer.

What is actually slowing down? Is it a time reckoning in relation to watches, that has the effect of making them appear to go, not slower, but faster, while Entropy remains constant? Or is it the Traveller's procession? Or is it none of these things?

It seems extremely unlikely that we will be able to send a watch-owner off on such an excursion in the foreseeable future, so that we can examine his turnip after welcoming him back.

APPENDIX C
BLAKE
(See p. 52)

> What is the price of Experience? Do men buy it for a song?

> The man who never alters his opinions is like standing water, and breeds reptiles of the mind.

> A Passion comprehended by Reason ceases to be a Passion and becomes itself Reason.

Blake provides a significant example of the danger of too many symbols, particularly when they are anthropomorphic ones, of which he is especially fond. His vision of Good and Evil and his multi-sensual perception (which he calls 'Imagination') is usually clear without the aid of his images.

It is true that every poet is entitled to his own vocabulary, but when Blake makes use of the word 'imagination' in the sense mentioned above, he invites us to suppose that he is talking about illusions, and expressing a belief in the non-existent, and this confusion does little justice to the great importance of his message.

On the topic of Perception — which greatly concerns us here — he has three aphorisms to offer:

> If the doors of perception were cleansed, everything would appear to man as it is, infinite. For man has closed himself up, till he sees all through narrow chinks of his cavern.

> How do you know, that ev'ry Bird that cuts the aery way, is a common world of delight, clos'd by your senses five?

> . . . seeing, though not with the eye, hearing, though not with the ear, which alone can lead us to the knowledge of the true Man and of the true Universe in which he lives.

Blake's Oothon — a symbolic figure of one who has regained his innocence — says that

> . . . there is that in man which is beyond his knowledge in the sense that he cannot know what it is — But though he cannot know *what* it is, he can know *that* it is.

One sometimes wonders what fantastic names he might have dreamed up for the Gold Standard or for Parkinson's Law if these had ever come his way. But on the subject of Conflict there is little doubt about where he stands:

One Law for the Lion and the Ox is Oppression.
Contraries are Positive. A negation is not a Contrary.
. . . whoever tries to reconcile them seeks to destroy existence.

(So much for the practice of Non-Decisions.) But there is something about the Bunyanesque vulgarity of his personified images that is as irresistibly cockney as Keats, and it makes one wonder whatever possessed Yeats to suggest that Blake was anything other than a Londoner.

When Blake watches the sun rise, he insists that he sees a heavenly choir singing the Hallelujah chorus, and he actually intimidates some of his most perceptive commentators into agreeing that this is an informative view of daybreak. As an Irishman I would not greatly enjoy the Hallelujah chorus at that hour of the morning; and it seems to me that it is a pity to treat the whimsy of a major seer in a way that makes us think that he must either be a fraud or a mental case.

When the British Constitution insists that all power comes from the Crown it is not being fraudulent, however untrue the statement may be today, because the conception forms a useful basis for thought on the subject, so long as it is not put into practice. But I cannot see of what particular use Handel can be to the dawn, even as a formula, and I am quite sure — to reverse one of Blake's best known remarks — that this Poet's heart knows considerably more than his eye sees.

As an example of Blake's imaginative view of Oscillation, see his poem, *The Mental Traveller*, and its treatment by Yeats, as discussed by the poetess Kathleen Raine in a BBC Third Programme broadcast, the text of which is reported in *The Listener* of the 9th October, 1958.

His Proverbs are as prophetic as the Book of Isaiah, and we should be glad at any time to act as Ushers at his Marriage of Heaven and Hell.

APPENDIX D

THE STUCKELBERG EFFECT

(See p. 133)

This peculiar effect was vividly portrayed by living actors in a short British documentary film dealing with the nature of Time. In this picture the explanation offered for the phenomenon was that of Reichenbach. Here we see a problem of Physics presented in terms of a number of actors who appear out of nothing and then disappear in the same mysterious way on meeting each other. It is important to remember that both the film and the diagram given below show movement as 4D extensions in Space/ Time, which must not be confused with the 3D activity portrayed in the actual performance, which is merely a visual cartoon of the 4D effect.

Upwards on the diagram represents the direction of the Observer's Entropy, while right and left depict divergence from the Observer's direction that is imparted by Energy to the world lines of the particles involved. In Diagram 1 we see Electron 'B' extending up through the Continuum at an angle to the Observer's Entropy that indicates considerable apparent speed. Elsewhere a Gamma Ray (a negative expression) on Latitude 'X' apparently creates out of nothing another Electron ('A'), together with a Positron, each of which sets off in its own direction. The newly created Electron 'A' continues up the field indefinitely, but the Positron, on reaching Latitude 'Z' appears to collide with Electron 'B', whereat they both disappear into another intangible Gamma Ray.

According to practically all standard ideas on physical behaviour, this is quite contrary to law. However, Reichenbach explains it convincingly in dimensional terms that are set forth in Diagram 2. Here again, what is seen visually as 3D motion is 4D extension.

Reichenbach says that only one Electron is actually involved in the effect, and no Positron, and what he means is described in Diagram 2. Here, the World line of Electron 'B' extends from Latitude 'X' in the same state of Energy as in Diagram 1. At Latitude 'Z', as a result of even further acceleration, it deviates to an angle greater than the direction of the Observer's Latitude line, which means that its further extension goes down the Plan, past Latitude 'Y', and towards the Observer's Pole. At some point in this progression — here shown as at Latitude 'X' — it decelerates through some further influence, and resumes its previous direction, up the Plan again.

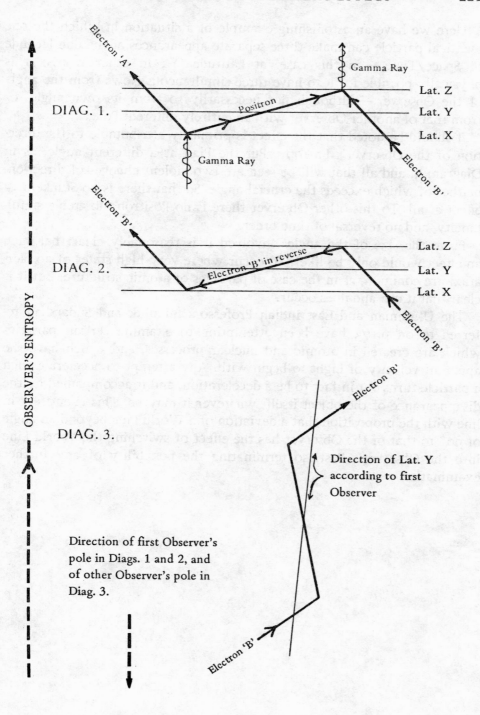

OBSERVER'S ENTROPY

DIAG. 1.

Electron 'A'

Gamma Ray

Positron

Lat. Z

Lat. Y

Lat. X

Gamma Ray

Electron 'B'

DIAG. 2.

Electron 'B'

Electron 'B' in reverse

Lat. Z

Lat. Y

Lat. X

Electron 'B'

DIAG. 3.

Direction of Lat. Y
according to first
Observer

Electron 'B'

Direction of first Observer's
pole in Diags. 1 and 2, and
of other Observer's pole in
Diag. 3.

Electron 'B'

Here we have an astonishing example of a situation in which the one identical particle can make three separate appearances at the one latitude of Space/Time — in this case, at Latitude 'Y'. In other words, it is physically possible for it to have three simultaneous Nows from the angle of the Observer — although not necessarily so from its own angle, or from that of another Observer with an entirely different Pole.

It should be noted that the effect is primarily attributable to the direction of the Observer's Entropy. Put the Plan at a different angle, as in Diagram 3, and all that will be seen are two violent changes of direction, neither of which exceeds the crucial angle. So that there is no Stuckelberg effect at all. To this other Observer there is no Positron, no treble simultaneity, and no reversal of time-order.

From the size of the angles involved it is reasonably clear that such an effect would only be likely to occur where very high states of acceleration are common, as in the case of particles of atomic structure. But it is clear that it can and does occur.

The Ukrainian and East Indian Professors Bilaniuk and Sudarshan referred to on p. 73 have been attempting to examine certain particles which are created in atomic and nuclear processes, and which have the apparent velocity of Light to begin with. Any attempt to accelerate such a particle turns out in fact to be a deceleration, and is accompanied by the disappearance of the object itself, whatever it may be. This is entirely in line with the proposition that a deviation of a World Line beyond an angle of 90° to that of the Observer has the effect of switching the World Line into the Observer's Past, so terminating the possibility of any further examination.

APPENDIX E
GRAVITY AND THE RELATIVITY OF THE POLE
(See p. 121)

The view of Gravity as a signal that is put forward in the text, can be better defined pragmatically as an urge on the part of World Lines — in the absence of interference — to curve in the direction of the source of the strongest signals that are operating in the neighbourhood. This, in effect, is another example of the hankering of Matter after a state of 'Inertia', which in its turn embodies the correct definition of Mass. As with the General Public, Matter — like Man — tends to follow the fashion, and to copy Direction from other systems around it. In our own experience, the overpowering proximity of the mass of Happenings that comprise the bulk of the Earth itself provides the reason why our bodies remain firmly in the global scenery in the absence of any acceleration strong enough to shoot them off into the sky.

Without the effect of Signals, a free moving System should continue to accelerate in a Newtonian unfluctuating orbit through empty Space at the classical increase of 32 feet per second, brooded upon by Leopold Bloom. But this does not really mean that such a body would travel at a greater and greater velocity, since it would be equally true to say that the non-existing surroundings were becoming slower and slower — a piece of nonsense that reinforces the contention that the whole subject is one of pure theory, and is quite unconnected with any situation that actually exists. There is no location where Gravity — that is to say, the causal effect of Signals — can be non-existent. Not even in a Space Rocket in free flight does Mass totally disappear.

So for the sake of clarity let us for the moment drop the familiar expressions, Mass and Energy (which seem fated to be confused with those unwelcome relations, Weight and Velocity), and let us refer instead to Inertia and Acceleration. When a Space Ship takes off, Inertia decreases with an increase in Acceleration — not the reverse. So also a Space Ship is enabled to land through an increasing Inertia brought about by reducing Acceleration. The key to the situation lies in a proper reading of Einstein's formula which does not aver that the product of Mass and Energy is constant, but that Energy balances Mass when the fastest apparent speed of Light (Signals) is added to the equation — in other words by the intrusion of Gravity into the calculations. But this apparent speed ('c') has already been shown to be a variable, dependent upon the Cosmic Latitude of

Observation. Consequently the whole equation is variable, quite apart from the fact that it professes to balance Ergs against Grams multiplied by miles per hour. Yet — as has already been pointed out — it works. And what makes it do so? — unless it is the relation of its unrelatable elements to the only Absolute within sight, namely the Speed of Procession.

Which brings us, of course, to the sixty-four thousand dollar question : Is it possible to calculate this Speed of Procession? At which point, all that can be offered by the present Incumbent is to be found in the final paragraph of the Sagittarius Chapter, on p. 128 above.

The next question that arises is whether the Pole, as we each individually know it, is dependent upon the direction of the World Line of each Observer, or whether it has a universal quality that makes it common to all systems with which we can communicate? If another speculative opinion may be expressed, I would suggest that Gravity, once again, has got a say in the matter.

While driving along a Turnpike at sixty miles an hour I am aware of my speed in relation to the countryside around me, and am conscious of an element of danger inherent in the fact that I am not in a state of rest, and do not so feel. What is more, it is necessary for me to continue to provide energy through the use of my accelerator, if I wish to keep myself in that state of motion. This means — I suggest — that my Pole is still that of the Systems around me, and that I am disregarding the dictates of Inertia at my peril. Were I to be projected into outer space at a velocity so great that it ceased to depend upon any further artificial acceleration to keep me going, I would lose all sense of 'flying', once I had fallen into some appropriate orbit. To this extent, I think that I would have altered my Pole, although the change would probably be an infinitesimal one, in view of the fact that the Earth, which I had left, is itself a part of a wider system to which I still belonged.

So it would seem that I do not alter my Pole however slightly by starting to run. Indeed, Gravity in this connection, may be regarded as a temptation to stop running, and to relapse into an unexhausting conformity with my geography. From which we may perhaps conclude that for all practical purposes that concern Homo Sapiens, the entire appreciable Universe should be looked upon in relation to a common Pole. Which means in turn that we all have what is substantially a universal Norm for 4D Direction. Subjective as this may sound, its subjectivity is the same for everybody with whom we are likely to get into conversation on the matter.

APPENDIX F

THE OPEN PAST
(See pp. 94 and 147)

The expression, 'The Open Past' was first presented to me by the distinguished philosopher, Dr. Wheelwright, at a meeting in New York of Professors of English, before whom I was discussing certain aspects of a controversial motion picture called *Last Year in Marienbad*, and making very heavy weather in the process.

I had pointed out that, unless we are convinced Determinists, we have little difficulty in conceding the existence of real alternatives in the future. Why then do we feel such reluctance to regard the past in the same way? Might it not also have a multiple reality, as was suggested in the picture? Or does the passage of 'Now' solidify Fact in some mystical way as required by Bragg? This proposition was being treated with considerable scepticism by my audience, when Dr. Wheelwright rose to his feet in the body of the hall, and came to my rescue with the statement that there is nothing surprising or philosophically unsound about the idea of an Open Past — as he called it. It was quite a respectable proposition, and should be treated as such. Indeed, it was not unknown to Plato, although not under that name.

For the benefit of those who have not seen the film, perhaps I should say that what story line it possesses concerns the efforts of a Narrator, referred to as 'X', to convince a very beautiful woman, known as 'A', that they met last year at the Victorian Spa mentioned in the title. There they either had, or did not have a love affair. Maybe there was a rape, or perhaps whatever did occur was invited. Both alternatives are there to be seen on the screen. But the response of 'A' goes much further than any acrimony over whether she was, or was not a willing party. She insists not only that she never met 'X' before, but that she has never been in Marienbad.

If this were a mere matter of discussion it would sound suspiciously like an unresolved alibi, the answer to which is that somebody is lying. But here we actually see for ourselves some of these supposedly earlier encounters, presented on several levels of Alternation, and with various clues to help us to determine which Continuum is before us. In the course of these we see both the death and the non-death of the woman. What is more, we are also left in considerable doubt as to which scenes *are* the earlier ones, and which — if any — are intended to relate to some contemporary Now. Indeed, it may be argued that there is no Now to be found in the entire story, or alternatively — as in *Finnegans Wake* — that it is all Now. (All or Nothing are sometimes found to be very like each other.)

This state of apparent confusion is clearly intended by the Director, and it need hardly be said that the question most frequently flung at the head of the author, Robbe-Grillet, by irritated members of his public, has been, 'Did they or did they not meet last year at Marienbad? Kindly give a straight answer to a straight question — Yes or No?' Robbe-Grillet's reply bears some resemblance to the answer given to me by the Astronomers. Like Dr. Synge, he attacks the question itself as being meaningless — maintaining that there is no such place as Marienbad (in which point he is correct as far as geographical nomenclature stands today), and secondly, that there is no such thing as last year (which is more arguable).

My own answer to any question about the existence of either Marienbad or last year would be precisely the opposite. I would say that they both exist, and that this should be regarded as the point of the film. But I can see what Robbe-Grillet is driving at, as it reminds me of the quandary produced by the question, 'Has Abraham Lincoln a beard, or has he not? Kindly give a straight answer — Yes or No?' There is a widespread fallacy in our usual ways of thinking, that encourages us to insist that a thing must be either Be or Not Be. Such is not the case. Abraham Lincoln's beard both Is and Is Not. It depends upon cosmic latitude.

Robbe-Grillet, on the other hand, would presumably react to this Lincoln problem — not by producing a Calendar as an antidote to this Either/Or poison — but by replying that there is no such thing as either Lincoln or his beard. Any answer — he would argue, depends upon memory or the record — something that operates Now, through the exercise of a present faculty. *Now* is all that we have, and whether one is reading a book, or contemplating the disfigurements on the face of the Sphinx, or studying the brain-traces within one's own cranium, we are not going back to anything, or in any sense recreating a Past by thinking about it. We are performing a purely contemporary act, and our conclusions depend strictly upon the evidence, and on the reliability of whatever sections of the record we have reason to select Now. If one authority differs from another, and both interpretations are equally credible, then — for you — the one that you pick is the true one, and it is immaterial that I may select the other one. In short — there is nothing but Now.

In adopting such an attitude, Robbe-Grillet — if I have interpreted him correctly — is behaving very like a lineal descendant of the late Signor Pirandello. But having subsequently had the pleasure of listening to him in person, while discussing some of the ideas that went into the making of this memorable picture, I am not at all certain that there was any deliberate intention on his part to get entangled in the problem of a multiple Past, although this is distinctly suggested by what one sees on the screen.

So probably this 5D element is one of the many original contributions of the Director, Alain Resnais. But in any event it is fairly certain that Robbe-Grillet's ideas on the subject would have had the episcopal *Nihil Obstat* of the Bishop of Cloyne. From another angle they bring to mind one of the prevailing practices of the English Common Law in determining the guilt or innocence of a man arraigned on a criminal charge. If the weight of the evidence points to a verdict of Guilty, then it must be assumed that the offence took place. If later investigations show that it did *not* take place, the verdict is not reversed. The convicted criminal is 'pardoned' — usually to his great irritation.

Following the precedent set by the case of Lincoln's beard, I have heard some philosophical gymnasts attempting to apply this conception of the open Past to the case of Madame Tchaikovski, by arguing that there is no such thing as an Absolute of History, and that consequently it is possible that this lady both Is and Is Not the youngest daughter of the last Tzar of Russia, according to one's view of the matter. However, it seems to me that we are in danger here of carrying the conception of Alternation into the realm of Nonsense.

We must not lose sight of the fact that the reality of 5D alternatives in an open Past is limited to *possible* alternatives, and does not amount to an unrestricted licence to argue that every conceivable contradictory statement may be regarded as true. I would suggest that the case of Anastasia offers an excellent example of how the principle should properly be applied.

It is possible that Jesus Christ was both crucified and not crucified. There might be two contradictory denouements of the story existing in 5D parallel. It is not reasonable, however, for the system at present known to us as Mme. Tchaikovski to have been two different people in the past. This is an alternative beyond the bounds of reason, and as such, the answer of Alternation could not apply to the problem of her identity. It is legitimate in such a case to state didactically that an Historical Absolute exists. Either she is Anastasia or she is not. She cannot be both.

This inescapable fact does not depend upon anybody's opinion — as Pirandello would argue. The rightness or wrongness of our several views on the matter can probably never be determined. But determined or not, our differences of opinion do not affect the existence of an historical truth.

APPENDIX G
EXPANSION AND THE HUBBLE CONSTANT
(See p. 113)

It was evident from a remark dropped by Professor Sandage in answer to a query of my own, that the prevailing picture of the expanding Universe amongst contemporary Scientists is that of the balloon image. In other words, it is not only the 4D continuum of Space/Time that is expanding, but also what is referred to as the 'radius of the Universe'.

Here, again, we are faced with another example of the peculiarities of current explanations. Accepting the picture of Space/Time as a four dimensional extension, and then going on to agree that it is curved — and curved as a balloon is curved with a radius — it naturally follows that, if a balloon is blown up, not only does the surface expand, but also the radius.

Having gone so far in the construction of such a picture, one may reasonably point out that, when you or I inflate a balloon we can relate its expansion to ourselves. Indeed if we wish to be really cute about the matter, we may even put up the argument that it is not the balloon that is getting bigger, but that we, Tiny Alices, are getting tinier. Yet in both cases there is something to which size can be related. But to what may we relate this supposed expansion of the Universe itself, if the Universe is all that there is? To some Atlas, who is no longer a porter, but a pump?

What is even more peculiar is this strange reluctance to agree that the radius of any sphere is in a different dimension from the area of its surface. If we are going to talk about the expansion, not only of the 4D continuum, but also of the radius of its curve, we are admitting the existence of a further dimension, and can hardly go on talking about such a feature as being 'contrary to human experience'. One might fairly ask, who is being Newtonian now?

The conclusion suggested in the text is one that only concerns the Observer. Neither the continuum nor the radius is blowing up, any more than is the world of Zophar's mariners. As has already been pointed out in the case of that world, the measurable Expansion is merely a drawing apart of the Observer's co-ordinates. It would seem at this stage, that if I had ever had the honour of discussing the matter at all with Dr. Sandage, the only point at issue would have been whether Oscillation is a matter of physical fact or merely one of appearance, based on observation from a particular position.

However, he is now reported as having changed his mind under pressure from some of his western colleagues, and has accepted the view that, for reasons connected with Gravity, there can be no end to Expansion. This readiness to alter one's conclusions in the face of apparently unanswerable adverse evidence throws an admirable light on the honesty of the best scientific approach. But it also illustrates the persistence of Newtonian assumptions in our ways of thought, even at the highest level.

If the expansion of the Universe is an actual kinematic performance on the part of inanimate Matter, operating under the aegis of a mysterious force called Gravity, it is perfectly logical to expect that, with an increase in distance, (which is clearly taking place all the time) the power of the Signal (Gravity) must become weaker and weaker until it ceases to have any appreciable effect at all. Hence the 'Big Bang' must be expected to go on for ever, if Gravity is the only force to counteract it. So here we are, face to face once again with the Mathematicians' panacea for all their insoluble situations — Infinity — an impasse that at an earlier stage, must have confronted Students of Flat Earth Geography with a similar headache.

Unfortunately, such a conclusion throws overboard not only Oscillation, but also most of the *bouleversements* in Physics and Astronomy that we have been taught to welcome ever since Michelson and Morley.

The Hubble Constant is Constant

Another of the questions that may have induced Dr. Sandage to call for the assistance of Infinity lay in the difficulty of finding some generally acceptable answer to the question as to why the expansion of the Universe should reverse into contraction at the point where the apparent speed of its recession reaches the figure of 'c', rather than at any other? Is it just a matter of gravitational exhaustion, and if so, why at that significant velocity? The thesis suggested here is that most of the recent discoveries appear to confirm the view that Expansion is not a kinematic phenomenon at all, with Gravity at the helm, but — like the experiences of our two Sea Captains — it is another aspect of the Observer's procession through a curved, five-dimensional field. On this basis, the reversal of Expansion into Contraction is brought about in precisely the same way as the Climate changes from the Arctic to the Tropical and back again, if one travels on the Earth from Pole to Pole. The location in which that reversal takes place is not conditioned by Gravity, but merely by the quantitative size of the Earth. It is similarly suggested that the reversal from Expansion to

Contraction is governed by the size of the Cosmos at the particular 5D level of our Observer's Continuum — an actual fact that cannot be argued about, or that requires any appeal to Infinity. What is more, on the basis of the figures generously supplied by Dr. Sandage himself, it should now be possible for a competent mathematician to calculate the material length of the Radius of the Cosmos at our particular level.

Such a feat would be comparable to that of those early Astronomers who managed to calculate the size of the Earth from observations made in the deserts of the Middle East, without ever leaving home.

The actual route by which the Palomar astronomers arrived at their present conclusions is mathematical rather than logical, and it is of interest to note how some of the difficulties that it still harbours provide us with another example of the dangers embedded in the practice of treating Signals as messengers that travel. What is more, it may well be that the noticeable difference between Sandage's estimate and the figure of between nine and ten thousand million light years that is pointed at by the line on Hubble's Graph, is due to the fact that, while the line appears to be straight in 4D, it actually follows a curve in 5D, preparatory to a complete change of direction, which naturally makes it longer to the point where it arrives at its ultimate level, where acceleration reaches the apparent speed of light. If so, it may be that there is not very much wrong with our estimate of the linear distance of the Pole, as indicated by the direction of the Constant, as we know it hereabouts.

We are only making difficulties for ourselves by arguing that these displacements that are now being observed near to the Cosmic Pole indicate that Hubble's line is not substantially constant whether or not it is straight.

Entropy and Inertia

If the situation is regarded unkinematically — as in the diagram on page 119 — signals originating on distant meridians must extend to the Observer's position from a direction approximating more and more to that of his Meridian. Indeed, a signal from a source on Longitude 90° (which must be at the Pole) will actually coincide with the Observer's Meridian, and will have a Doppler Effect that is so 'tired' as to be no effect at all. In short, the apparent speed of a light signal coming from the direction of the Pole corresponds to that of Entropy, and consequently it cannot be observed.

This is in accord with the further statement that any System lying along the Observer's Meridian must present the appearance of Inertia, which seems to have no velocity. So, paradoxically, it follows that for a System to retain this Inertia, it requires the aspect of total Energy, rather than that of total Mass. Transform part of this Energy into Mass by changing the 4D angle, and the System gains apparent Velocity — a change that actually reduces rather than increases the aspect of Energy, notwithstanding the apparent contradiction of acceleration. This is in line with the finding that Mass increases with apparent 3D Velocity until, at the ultimate divergence of a 4D right angle, the aspect becomes one of absolute Mass, and the 'Speed' amounts to simultaneity.

The Increasing Size of Alternate Continua

As a gloss upon the description of alternate Continua that is to be found on page 142, there arises a further subtle point that should be mentioned. It will be appreciated that a three dimensional cube may be regarded as the sum-total of the successive two-dimensional squares into which it may be sliced. So also a Cosmos in five dimensions may be said to amount to an aggregate of the layers of Alternation in which — like a series of concentric spheres — each presents the aspect of a spherical surface.

It will also be noted that each such Continuum must be relatively larger than its inner neighbour. From this we may also deduce that the quantitative measurement of any Continuum applies only to itself, and that, like Entropy, this progression in size is closed at one end in Zero. See marginal note on p. 124.

What this amounts to is that the further Observation is functioning from the geodesic centre of the Cosmos, the wider is the 4D field that is open to experience. In other words it is not sufficient to state that the Universe appears to expand as Procession carries an Observer away from his Pole. It should also be recognised that a switch of observation from any Continuum to one further 'out', places the Observer in a larger field where more systems can be accommodated than is the case further in.

In short, there is less Data at an inferior level of Alternation than there is at a superior one — a statement that may answer a question that is occasionally raised by critics of the Open Past: What happens to my son, Rory, who has assisted me with the mathematical side of this work, if I am killed in some other and lower Continuum before he is conceived? The answer is that on the 5D level of Take One or lower, Rory does not exist any more than I, myself, exist beyond my own limited extension in 5D. But at the level of Take Two, in which Continuum we are all communicating here and now — and outward for another unknown but limited distance — he exists as of right, as you and I do, too. And very nice it is to have a little more room to breathe and run around in than we had further in, where the Company is sparser, and probably less attractive.

APPENDIX H

BONHOEFFER

(See pp. 53 and 151)

There is not very much to be read from the pen of this anti-Nazi hero, Dietrich Bonhoeffer, but what there is shows him to have been a most endearing and admirable man both in his fortitude and in his readiness to do something tangible for the literal salvation of his community. This courage led directly to his murder in a Concentration Camp shortly before the end of the War.

I am deliberately making use of this loaded word, 'murder', as a counter-blast to the statement — undoubtedly true in the eyes of those who regard the State as a system — that he was a traitor to his country. A 'traitor' is usually one who is not wholly devoted to the particular interests of those who happen to be running the political machinery in the notional area that we call our 'country'. Sometimes the traitor is, in fact, betraying the legitimate needs of his kith and kin — a deplorable thing to do — but as often as not he is merely refusing to commit suicide in order to save the face of an incompetent or criminal Government, and under these circumstances he deserves our congratulation rather than our disgust. This was certainly the case with Bonhoeffer, so I see no reason why the dirty expression 'murder' should not be used on his behalf, if 'traitor' is to be applied to him.

But of greater importance than any of this political mud-slinging was Bonhoeffer's concern over keeping his Church alive under conditions of mounting hostility to what passes for religion. In this, he did not attempt to follow in the footsteps of his predecessor, Bultmann, who took the line only too common amongst theological reformers, of bringing nonsense up-to-date, by arbitrarily throwing out Myth.

Bonhoeffer was not at all keen to enter into any of those arguments about the historicity of the Virgin Birth because, if it was a myth, it was probably all the better for being one. The myth is the loveliest part of the Gospel story, and whenever any question of the factual existence of Jesus turns up, one can hear this contemporary prophet say that something must have sparked off Christianity. Maybe it was one inspired man, and maybe it was a committee. Perhaps it was no man at all, but simply the mysterious workings of the Holy Spirit. But whatever it was, we might as well call it Christ.

Bonhoeffer was very much at grips with the problem of how the conception of any God — spiritual or anthropomorphic — could survive in a world that was steadily growing, not more sceptical about Nobodaddy, but frankly more anti-God. If the Faith to which he was sincerely attached could not manage to keep in step with the ways of thought of the age that it was supposed to serve, it would become — he feared — a mere formula, a windy piece of decor, as meaningless as Samuel Butler's musical Banks. With this, it would inevitably fade away, leaving nothing in its place except an Edenless Adam and Eve, closely resembling Professor Ayer and Miss Laski.

Consequently he took it upon himself to attack, not the Ten Commandments, nor the Beatitudes, nor even the Resurrection, but what he considered to be the Pauline accretions on Christianity — notably Salvationism. Christianity, he maintained, ought to change *this* life, and should not be regarded as providing an Entry Ticket (or so many divine Travellers' Cheques) for use in another life elsewhere. In this he was perfectly right, according to his lights, and before we listen to the obvious retort that the basic Christian message is so entangled with Salvationism that it is now doing more harm than good, and should not be salvaged at all, let us remember that Bonhoeffer was a clergyman, and had no alternative. The vacuum that he feared is precisely what has come upon us all.

But what is the situation of Bonhoeffer when compared to that of the unfortunate Dr. Robinson, Bishop of Woolwich, who was employed by Her Majesty to keep the ark afloat, not merely as a gorgeous idea, but also as an organisation. St. Paul is reported to have said '. . . if Christ be not raised, your faith is in vain.' And if it is of no real importance whether he was actually raised or not, what sense does this make of the episcopal office with a possible seat in the House of Lords? Can a Church that claims to be apostolic and universal maintain that proud position once it agrees that the basis of its message is a matter for individual doubt, rather than an expression of inescapable Truth? For the matter of that, has not the fear of the open vernacular Bible that was expressed by the mediaeval Popes been shown to be fully justified from the angle of the interests of the Vatican? Oh, these intolerable Enthusiasts — as Father Ronald Knox has been heard to complain, when contemplating the people who read and quote it.

It is all very well for me to raise a cheer for Bonhoeffer when he questions Salvationism. To me this is a monstrous idea, invented by Priests with the object of disciplining the laity. But in applauding Bonhoeffer, I am not at the same time claiming to be a Christian. So long as one does so, and claims membership of the fold, one can hardly blame Mother Church for defending herself, any more than one should ask any perceptive and sincere Roman Catholic to abandon what appears to be the perfect logic of his faith in order to become an illogical Protestant. Such a proposition should not be pressed.

But what we *can* all say—without in any way playing false to our upbringing or letting down the side—is that it is high time we were mutually honest with ourselves, and suspended double-think for long enough to meet together in some common congregation—neither in Church, Chapel, Mosque nor Synagogue, but outside all of them — on some Dome of the Rock, in some forcibly unified and unpartitioned Jerusalem.

In those refreshing surroundings it is improbable that we will ever be joined by the Bishop of Woolwich, grateful as we are to him. By virtue of his office he is imprisoned by his Vestrymen behind thirty-nine bars — for it is a peculiarity of the time that it is now usually the laymen who bully the more perceptive Priests, and not the other way round. When Dr. Robinson tries to get within shouting distance of the main questions of the day by saying that there is no God 'up there', some menacing Christer inevitably rises to his feet at the rear of the hall and demands to know, 'Is God a person or is he not?' What can any Bishop reply to such a question except to say, 'Yes, He is a person' — or else keep his mouth shut, and his mitre on his head — as Dr. Robinson did when I heard him confronted by this very situation.

On the other hand, the Bishop's professional colleagues and Brothers in God attempt rather meanly to discredit him in more subtle ways.

'But nobody has believed in a God-up-there for years', is what we hear some of the contemporary Theologians say.

'Dr. Robinson is old-fashioned. As for Hell — that came out of the Articles of Religion in the seventeenth century.'

This last is actually a most uncandid remark, as a glance at the Book of Common Prayer will show, notwithstanding the abandonment of Article 42 of the Anglican Articles of Religion. The Bishop is not old-fashioned. What is remarkable about him is not that he agrees with Bonhoeffer. His major claim to immortality lies in the fact that he has had the fortitude to say so in print.

Since this part of the text was written, Dr. Robinson has resigned his Bishopric, and become Dean of a Cambridge College. Perhaps in this capacity he may be in a position to join us on the Dome of the Rock after all.

Christianity belongs to the Christians

How much better, therefore, to clarify the issues by allowing words to mean what they say. If it then proves to be impossible to call oneself a Christian without getting entangled in Christianity, who are we to steal the term from its rightful owners?

It is a common attitude today on the part of those who wish to be Christians without the nuisance of going to Church, to think of Jesus as a very nice fellow with a charming mother, a clean record, and a message that nobody would listen to at the time, because they were all so much stupider than we are. A good-looking Indo-European beardie, who would have been greatly appreciated by us if we had been privileged to meet him — a fellow with a sound, if somewhat idealistic message that anybody ought to have understood and agreed with after a little quiet thought. He was unfortunate in trying to get it across to all those Jews and Italians.

Whether or not he was actually an agitator from Capernaum, or the Teacher of Righteousness referred to in the Scrolls, or whether he was merely a character in a play, is a matter of opinion. Archdeacon Paley used to insist that he must have been both real and divine because people were ready to die for him, and they would hardly have been prepared to go as far as that if he hadn't greatly impressed them, would they? But people enjoy dying for things. They have been quite willing to die for Cathleen ni Houlihan, whose name it would be difficult to find in the *Eolaí Telefóin* of the *Oifig an Phoist* — and even for Mussolini.

Actually, it has been said of Jesus that what he brought was not anything particularly new in the way of doctrine, but some very good new stories. He has long provided a convenient peg on which to hang such excellent sayings as the Beatitudes, the Lord's Prayer, and some useful extracts from Stoic philosophy, together with a pastiche of many other miscellaneous fragments of human wisdom. Whether there is anything left once these garments are removed and returned to the original owners is a matter of doubt. Albert Schweitzer tells us that nothing is left that could be described as history, and such a conclusion is not a bad corrective to flabby thinking on the subject.

The fact that his tomb was empty a couple of days after his reported demise is vouched for by a lady of the town who went there with a friend (some say, two) in order to anoint the body. In another account there is a further deponent, who is generally regarded as having written under a name that was not his own. And this, together with the fact that some of the disciples were convinced that they saw him afterwards, is the evidence that is the keystone of a world religion. There are many similar stories that tell of celebrated figures having been seen around after death, but in fairness to this particular one, the very confusion in its documentation might be regarded as something in its favour. Besides, we are frankly told that at least one of his intimates who met him afterwards had considerable doubts about his Lord's identity, and had to be assured on this point — an element in the story that suggests that it may not have been wholly fabricated.

For my own part, I am not prepared to go along with some of my Rationalist friends in denying that there could have been even the semblance of a resurrection. It would be quite in line with some of the phenomena that we have been discussing in earlier chapters to say that maybe a Jesus both died and did not die.

Robbe-Grillet, of course, could make a good thing out of this. He might say that some of the witnesses remembered him dying, and that some also remembered meeting him afterwards. Both recollections, according to Robbe-Grillet, being equally real (although contradictory), are equally acceptable. It is only the crucifixion that has no reality, because of the fact that it is not Now.

I do not hold with this sort of argument, but if I were asked for my own views on the matter (which has not been the case) I would approach the subject from quite a different angle. Both of these memories, being as unreliable as memories can be, are of minor importance. But the two statements, that he died and did not die on the cross — although incompatible — are both contemporaneously acceptable, as an expression of the Open Past. There is more than one Continuum in which each historical truth might exist, both of them being alternate.

APPENDIX I

EUDYISM
(See pp. 12 and 38)

One of the principal points raised in this book might be summed up as follows : We usually visualise ourselves as Observers standing upon some fixed and central peak which we regard as "Here and Now" — a good expression to apply to a cross section of Space/Time. Around this, a vista of ceaseless activity is going on in the physical world. Inanimate matter can be seen running about in all directions, from which we naturally conclude that we are in the midst of a kinematic setting in which Events are constantly "taking place", while we stand by and watch them at it. Nature is alive and kicking, and we are its appreciative spectators.

However, as a basis for scientific thought there is something very questionable about such a picture, as Zeno pointed out long ago.

The position is amusingly reminiscent of a poem by a Mrs. Eudy of Louisville, Kentucky, that has been the subject of many late night arguments during the past forty years, and more recently amongst my own students of Freshman English. Mrs. Eudy was a prosperous manufacturer of shirtwaists, with a sideline in versification, which she studied in later life during summer sessions at Columbia University. Her slim volume, *Quarried Crystals*, contains, amongst other pieces, the following rhyme :

> Hope is my candle.
> I set it firm and high.
> Life but casts shadows
> When passing by.

This verse, like our current vision of the scene around us, has the remarkable quality of becoming less intelligible the more we think about it. At first blush, it seems to state quite clearly : Cheer up ! Once our poetess has lit her candle, the dark corners of life will turn out to be mere shadows. (She regards shadows as Bad Things.)

But is this what the poem actually says ? To begin with, there is the problem of Who is passing by What ? Is Mrs. Eudy, herself, the life that is passing by the firm-and-high candle, without the presence of which there would, of course, be no shadow of Mrs. Eudy at all. Next comes the difficulty as to what it is that life is casting the shadows on ? Is it into the dark corners of something else somewhere else, since it obviously cannot be where the candle is ? Or is life passing by both Mrs. Eudy *and* the candle, and casting shadows on her? If so, what is Life if not Mrs. Eudy? And why are these shadows in the plural? If there are more than one, does this mean that several lives are involved in the shadow-casting? If so, how many, and who arranged this?

Again — why "but casts"? Were these Lives previously casting something more lethal than shadows — bricks maybe, or possibly some symbolic petrol bombs from a disturbed area? — something that now has had to be given up in the light of the candle? Or is it just that some notional stitches are being cast from the Tapestry of Time?

It will be seen that a lot of trouble has been taken over possible interpretations of this poem — both serious and facetious. But the fundamental problem still remains: What the hell is Going On? It seems that it is probably the Reader who is enveloped in these shadows — not Mrs. Eudy, nor Life, nor the corner of the street. Columbia ought to have done better by Mrs. Eudy.

Nevertheless, before we remain giggling too long in this jungle of poetic imagery, let us consider how like the poem is to the entanglement into which our prevailing ideas on the behaviour of the Universe are leading us. Is the inanimate World putting on some sort of a performance for our benefit — or indeed, at our peril? Or is it we, ourselves, who are on the move? In this case, any apparent liveliness in sight could be better attributed to the changing position of our point of view, as is the case with the vista outside the window of a railway carriage. There the apparent speed of an object that we know to be static, is dictated by its distance. The further away it is, the more slowly it appears to move — an effect, of course, that we explain as being one of perspective.

But it should be noticed that we are not consistent in the ways in which we think about the various items in this field of vision. The explanation that what we are looking at is simply a setpiece of scenery governed by perspective is abandoned when we come to consider some of its individual features. What about a road or a river that meanders along beside the track for a time, but then takes a turn, and goes careering up the window into the distant hills where it disappears from sight? These we consider to be static, too, yet lateral velocity changes as they fly away towards a destination where they finally cease to exist so far as we are concerned. We do not regard them as actually being on the move, any more than the background. It is our train that is travelling, and what we have now observed is not strictly one of perspective, but is a Derrynane Effect brought about by a change of angle or direction.

But when we turn to consider the water tumbling and bubbling in the bed of the river with an apparent vigour of its own — or more startling still, when another train dashes by in the opposite direction on the neighbouring track — we change our way of thinking altogether and assume an objective attitude. Here is a real velocity, we insist, that can be calculated. Not an absolute velocity, of course, because we have to relate it to something — probably to the ground. But why to the ground in preference to anything else, including the best scientific reference, namely ourselves? The selection of what we relate it to is quite an arbitrary decision, meaning no more and no less than any other that we might make. Furthermore, what justification is there for our switch to objectivity, on the assumption that the stream of water and the other train have got an actual speed that is in some way different from the condition of the so-called static scenery?

This doubt should grow even deeper when we turn our gaze upwards towards the heavens, where we find that the distances are so great that the stars do not appear to move at all, no matter how fast the train accelerates in a straight line. Yet we have other information to the effect that they are very much on the move in spite of the evidence of our eyes. Indeed, in the case of the Galaxies we are informed that, with the aid of the Spectrum, we may deduce enormous velocities away up there, which actually increase with the distance, rather than the reverse.

This cannot have anything to do with perspective, or with angle, or indeed with anything at all that we can perceive as visual motion. So we thereupon conclude from the Spectrum that the entire panorama is in the process of blowing up. The Universe, as represented locally by the scenery, is far from being static, after all.

So here we have it. In the first case we are quite happy to attribute the appearance of motion to perspective: in the second case to angle: while in the third case we decide to become objective, and insist that the water and the other train have got a unique dynamic quality that makes it necessary to distinguish them from the rest of the landscape. Meanwhile, in the case of the Galaxies, we admit that we have got no safe observable data at all, apart from the Spectrum, so we leave the whole problem to be fought out by the Abbé Lemâitre and Cambridge. In each case we are applying a different framework of thought to the same three dimensional field that is outside the window. This must surely be as nonsensical as the poem.

What is it that endows the flowing stream with the sense of having an observable velocity of its own within a general picture that we otherwise regard as motionless — or alternatively as an explosion? (We are not sure which.) It is simply the fact that its world line has a four dimensional difference of direction that is changing in relation to that of the landscape, as we ourselves proceed. What is it that we actually mean when we say that the Galaxies are receding at greater and greater speeds, the further off they are? It is simply an expression of the spherical curvature of the Universe, which in 4D grows larger as the Observer proceeds into a field where his co-ordinates are further apart.

To make consistent sense of the entire picture it is essential to consider it four dimensionally, rather than in the three dimensional manner that has been causing the confusion heretofore. The only constant on which to base any meaningful calculations is the speed and direction of our own Procession, as reflected in the behaviour of our train. On any other basis we will inevitably find ourselves quarrying crystals in company with Mrs. Eudy.

To put the fallacy in what, it is hoped, is a simple way, let us turn back briefly to the circling Satellites of Jupiter, the orbits and velocities of which are commonly plotted and estimated geometrically in relation to a 3D Fixed Point — namely Jupiter itself. But See p. 26 Jupiter is not a fixed point, even visually in 3D, from anywhere in the sky apart from itself. As we actually see them, these Satellites are neither following circular orbits, nor are they moving in a constant direction, nor at an unchanging speed. So whatever we may read in the books about their behaviour is entirely notional, since it is based neither upon their appearance nor upon meaningful calculations, but upon what they would seem to be doing if we were somewhere else — at some fixed point that is neither fixed nor a point — a conclusion that can only be classified as genuine Eudy.

The great question once was: does the Sun go round the Earth, or does the Earth go round the Sun? The answer of the more informed Astronomy of the day is that this is a question that cannot really be answered at all, because, in a sense, both answers are true, while in another sense, both are incorrect. All that should be said about these Systems is that the world lines of both extend in relation to a common centre of Gravity.

This is a 4D interpretation, and is in conformity with the Golden Rule expressed on page 88. The only consistent way of looking upon Velocity is as a dimensional Effect caused by our own Procession. From the angle of each individual Observer, there is no activity at all in the 4D physical

Universe. What moves is our own subjective observation in 5D. If we accept this as fundamental to our ways of scientific thought we will no longer lay ourselves open to the accusation of confusing Esse with Percipi, or of being unable to distinguish between 3D Appearance, 4D objective Reality, and the 5D behaviour of the Elan, which alone Proceeds.

APPENDIX J

HOLY SEPULCHRE AND HOLY SCRIPTURE
(See p. 156)

Before we resume the popular practice of denying everything within sight, let us pause for a moment to consider the curious case of Christ's supposed place of burial.

The first impression that many people get from a visit to the Church of the Holy Sepulchre is usually disappointing. One feels that the congested confines of this supreme goal of Christian pilgrimage could not possibly encompass a Hill of Calvary together with a garden that might have contained a tomb hollowed out of a cliff face. Apart from a short flight of steps leading to a sort of platform, there is no visible evidence of any hill at all. Nor is there any indication in the adjacent Basilica of an eminence in which there could have been a cave, housing the site of the tomb. The whole building is in one of the most crowded sections of the old walled City of Jerusalem, and it requires considerable sophistry to explain how such a site could ever have been hilly, or even outside the natural ambit of the walls. A great deal of willing credulity is needed to accept all the tortuous explanations that are offered on each of these difficult points.

This is an invention — one says to oneself — created three hundred years after the Event for the obvious purposes of a tourist attraction. From which conclusion it is only a short step to a sceptical disbelief in the entire story of the death and burial.

Yet not far outside the Damascus Gate there appears to be a quite credible site for Golgotha, in a garden that still contains a number of cave-tombs. The general location in relation to the City matches up perfectly well with the impression that one gets from the Scriptures. It has apparently never been built on, probably for the very reason that its reputation was uninviting to those who knew it to be both a graveyard and an ancient place of execution.

This is the spot known as Gordon's Calvary, in honour of its principal advocate, General Gordon of Khartoum. Yet, oddly enough, its unpretentious claim to provide a visible location for an event with an already doubtful history, is still dismissed by the clerical and archaeological establishment in language that smacks more of unexplained hysteria than that of any considered reason.

The Church of England, says Parrot, withdrew energetically and finally from the impossible position to which their inexperience had led them, hedged about as it was with fraud and misrepresentations.

Nothing whatever can be said in favour of the tomb.

(Macalister)

Why should we do the daydreams of Gordon and Conder the honour of taking them seriously?

(Clermont-Ganneau)

The rocky grave cannot seriously be considered as Jewish.

(Dalman)

Professor Macalister is the distinguished archaeologist who used to play the organ for us when we sang 'Gentle Jesus, meek and mild'. His generalisation, no less than the sentiments of the hymn, is untrue on its face. Dalman professes to be able to recognise the religious affiliations of a cave, while Parrot seems to attribute intentional 'fraud and misrepresentation' to General Gordon, whether or not this serious charge may be applied to some of his later supporters — as is probably the case. The whole dispute is only mentioned as an example of the manner in which controversies of this kind are carried on, particularly when matters of religion and of tourism are at stake.

At this point in the World's history it is clearly impossible to prove that any particular eminence is the actual site of an event, the very facts of which are open to some doubt. It may also be said that the same objection applies just as pertinently to the official selection as it does to Gordon's alternative.

Pilgrim's Guide

In a recent *Pilgrim's Guide to Jerusalem and Bethlehem* by Mr. Stewart Perowne, this well-known authority on the Middle East, after trampling briskly on 'the strange, half-mystical fantasies of General Gordon', goes on to make an illuminating contribution to the problem, by disclosing the evidence upon which the accepted site is usually based.

About three centuries after the date of the Crucifixion — which period straddled two substantial demolitions and rebuildings of the City — a Bishop Makarios instructed the Empress Helena on where to build the Basilica that was subsequently to become the Church that we now know. According to this Bishop, the Emperor Hadrian erected a Temple of Venus in his new City of Aelia Capitolina, which pagan edifice was intended to obliterate all remaining traces and memories of the most holy shrine of Christianity. The Bishop, of course, was reporting a wanton act that supposedly had occurred roughly two centuries before the time of his statement. Here in the present City, said the Bishop, were the remains of such a Temple, from the position of which it was clear that the actual site of Calvary could be firmly identified.

The fact that it was inside the ambit of the City's walls was a matter of no importance. An uncharted earlier wall must have taken a concave course, leaving the holy hill outside a vanished gate. Mr. Perowne supports this surmise by pointing to some signs of massive stonework in the ruins beneath a Russian Convent to the east of the present Sepulchre. The absence of any apparent hills in the area can be explained by the fact that all differences in level have since been covered over to put a stop to the depredations of Pilgrims.

Actually a much better argument can be offered on behalf of the traditional site. Recent archaeological excavations carried out by a party including Kathleen Kenyon, later Principal of St. Hugh's College, Oxford, have disclosed the fact that part of the area at present covered by the Basilica was at one time at or near a quarry, filled with the debris of Hadrian's construction to the depth of about ten metres until bedrock is reached. Since a quarry is more likely to have been outside rather than inside the walls of the old Herodian City, Miss Kenyon quite reasonably argues that the area must have been a derelict, unbuilt-upon stretch beyond the walls until the building of Aelia Capitolina. Thus the site of the Holy Sepulchre *might* be the authentic one — a discovery that in no way proves that it *is*.

Who Wrote the Bible?

As for the current treatment of the Scriptures, we seem to have lost track of the fact that they were not originally composed by some friends of King James I (on whose behalf copyright is still claimed), or by Saint Jerome, or even by Christopher Fry, who is credited with having authored a *Pentateuch According to Holywood*. People are continually talking about new translations intended to 'get back as closely as possible to the Original'.

What original? There is nothing to be gained by referring to the Vulgate in order to settle any controversy over 'Charity' versus 'Love' in First Corinthians 13, or over the line, 'Good will towards Men.' The Vulgate itself is a translation from translations, and all that we can fairly say about the first of these disagreements is that the passage in question is unlikely to have been written by some Saul who is also called Paul.

The Roman Catholic view of the authenticity of the Biblical text was expressed in 1879 in a Bull of Pope Leo XIII, called *Aeterni Patris*. According to this pronouncement, the Holy Spirit, by supernatural power, impelled the various originators of the Canon — whoever they may have been — to write the Scriptures according to God's direction. 'He so assisted them while engaged on this task, to write down the words which he ordered, and only those. These from the first were correctly understood, and expressed in suitable verbiage, and with infallible truth.'

In the absence of this original text, the question remains unanswered as to whether the same assistance was accorded to the long series of copyists and translators whose work and glosses are inextricably welded into the only versions that we have before us today? Or if not, at what point may we assume that the divine afflatus was switched off?

There is no original version of the Bible any more than there can be said to be any ascertainable primary text for the stories of Robin Hood, or of Hamlet or of King Arthur (or indeed of this book, if one may plunge downwards from the sublime.) Many fingers have been fiddling with the Holy Scriptures over the centuries, which is precisely what gives them their special interest — and, if I may say so, a greater general significance than the Koran or the Book of Mormon, which have not been so easy to edit.

The Bible is not the work of a few single geniuses or psychopaths in touch with the Almighty by private wire. It is the fluctuating dream — the wish-fulfilment of the human race, written and rewritten, amended and forged, twisted and reinterpreted, glossed and interlined, by dozens of communicants, honest and dishonest, but each with some obsession in his mind. It may not be the word of God as we know it now, but it is certainly the word of Man — which is only another way of saying that it contains the word of God as heard by Man in particular ages.

If that version of the Word is not exactly what we would hope to have from such a source today, we will not improve it by trying to decorate it with any further sophism, or by rewriting it in the language of the hour. We do not make sense of the Bible by bringing it 'up to date'! We should either take it or leave it. But let us think twice before leaving it, until we are quite sure that we have got something to put in its place. Otherwise we may find ourselves hurrying back to it in moments of stress, with very red faces.

Nor should we allow our natural irritation over various pious frauds that have been perpetrated over the years to dim our eyes to the valuable qualities in those very things that we may be impelled to destroy. Whatever may be felt about the Virgin Birth, Christianity in many ways was more right than wrong, and on the whole more right than Bertrand Russell.

The same may be said as truly of Islam and of Jewry and indeed of most of the other established world religions that have managed for a time to give an answer of sorts to the needs of Man. This is not intended as an expression of vicarious admiration for any kind of nonsense that may have attracted a congregation, but as a sensible recognition of the fact that mankind has usually been right in the head in demanding some sort of religious framework and an interpretation of the Facts of Life as they have appeared to thinking men and women of the period. Any religion that has managed to satisfy this need over a reasonable period merits our regard, though not necessarily our allegiance.

However, the complaint that we hear at present from most parts of the Globe is that there is no longer any religion that is in line with a common-sense view of the Data that we have today, except the religion of Politics which is the biggest liar of them all. They have all ceased to perform their proper function through an honourable old age. After all, what have we had in Theology since the reign of Honorius that is really new?

So the issue is not whether Jesus ever lived or not. Although a lot of very sound remarks have accumulated around his name, so much questionable decor has also become attached to the picture that it is doubtful whether he can be of much help today as an image of the workings of the Kerygma.

I once coined the phrase that every man is his own Jesus, with a sardonic rider to the effect that every other man's Jesus is a bore — and, Jesus, what a bore!

Christ, not Jesus!

Let me put it this way. In his private heart, many a person of ordinary good will and intelligence harbours a suspicion that he, too, might turn out to be Jesus. There is nothing outrageous about this, if we give it a moment's thought. All that it signifies is that we usually begin with the knowledge that, fundamentally, we mean well, that we are sure that we are good at our jobs, and that if Others would only *listen*, and pay some attention to what we are saying, everybody would be very much happier.

This is the expression of a rather loveable quality of immaturity that

248 THE BRAZEN HORN

usually lasts into early middle age when, with the onrush of some growing cynicism, and in the absence of election to public office, we change our position into a quiet readiness to accept a *draft* as Jesus, should the world grow sensible enough to insist. But in the end we usually arrive at the depressing conclusion that — No, we are definitely not Jesus after all. We will never be important enough to be crucified, and will only be given the sack, or be shunted in the course of time into Social Security.

But, oddly enough, this is often the start of our lives as tolerable people; for, having at last acquired and cast out the knowledge of Good and Evil, and made our peace with Heaven, we may then graduate to a final conviction that, after all, playing Jesus is only Sunday School stuff. In common with the rest of humanity of a like experience, we find that we can become something of much greater significance, once we have appreciated the universal sonship of the Elan with the causal source of its existence.

'The greasy denims of the Word' is an epithet that has been used to describe Man. To which the proper riposte is that of one whose wisdom was rooted, not in double-think, but in doubt.

'What we wonder at most of all,' he said, 'is that so great a treasure can make its home in such a slum.'

APPENDIX K

THE NATURE OF DREAMS

(See p. 65)

In an article in *The Sunday Times*, the psychologist, Christopher Evans, says that the function of sleep is not to give rest to the body, but to provide the physical brain with an interval resembling that required by an advanced Computer, when it goes into the condition known as 'off-line'.

In this phase the machine is undergoing what is termed a 'housekeeping' of waste material and out of date Data that must be cleared away before the apparatus is again available for use. Without such an occasional switch into a recessive condition there is liable to be trouble if the process is interfered with by any feeding of further information during the 'off' period.

Dr. Evans suggests that, in this respect, the human mind can be compared to a Computer, in that it requires to sleep and to dream in order to avoid hysteria and the acute derangement that, in all the more sophisticated forms of life, is a natural consequence of too much undigested data without a break.

The nonsensical quality of our dreams is not significant in any mystical or dream-book sense, but merely indicates that this process of assimilation is taking place without the control of a conscious mind. Dreams are as essential to the physical brain as 'housekeeping' is to a Computer. But the purpose of this undirected period must be distinguished from that of the hours of sentient life, which correspond to the provision of selected material to an implement of conscious intelligence.

Both phases are necessary, and it is as fallacious to treat the fantasies of sleep as actual experiences, as it is to imagine that the machine can, of its own volition, perform any significant operation without the element that presses the buttons.

Since the appearance of the myth of Pygmalion, through Samuel Butler and the Capeks to the current horror plays about demonic machinery, weavers of fiction have dallied with a sort of Frankenstein Fixation about the apparatus that Man constructs, and have often speculated on the possibility that his Robots might eventually take over and supersede the human race. However, Dr. Evans's thesis not only gives the lie to any such melodramatic nonsense, but also underlines the purely mechanical nature of sleeping and of dreaming, so providing us with another illustration of the difference urged in these pages between (a) the physical implement — the flesh — the mortal Cortex, which is the legitimate subject of Professor Bildad's menacing experiments, and (b) the Elan — the Operator — the conscious mind that gives the initial instructions, about which the Psychologists are, so far, telling us practically nothing.

In an amusing play by Joseph Krausman, *The Ice Cream Parlour*, the central character, who obviously must be a product of the Bildad Box, becomes immovably fixed in a snackbar because there is no reason why he should ever select any particular one of the proprietor's twenty-eight flavours of ice cream. Such is the fate of the ideal Behaviourist when spurred only by conditioning.

So far as the data of sleep is concerned, Dr. Evans does not hold with Dunne's proposition that the material of our dreams is drawn from the future as well as from the past. But his diagnosis does not rule out the suggestion made here, that it may be affected by an awareness of an Open Past. In short, it is not limited to the experiences of one continuum only — a fact that contributes to its apparent fantasy.

APPENDIX L

THE LESSON OF THE BRENNER

(See p. 212)

The general remarks in the text that attempt to relate the events on Hafelekar to the myth of Eden, may perhaps be carried somewhat further.

I threw away my gun on that hilltop, when faced with a realisation of the indifference of 'God' to either revenge or resentment, notwithstanding my attitude of rage and wanton defiance. Having done so, I did not have it to give to Suder in Take Two, which in turn meant that he could not have used it on me, even if we had met in that Take — which was not the case.

Yet it will be noticed that, in spite of the fact that he got no gun from me, Suder reached the same end in both Takes. How this actually happened here in Take Two I do not know, since his death has only been reported to me, and the letter from the German Red Cross throws no further light on the matter, except to confirm that he is a 'missing person'. But it illustrates the fact that, although my exercise of choice had a profound effect on me and on my own future, it had apparently no effect on *his* ultimate fate. In other words, our personal decisions do not always cause such significant differences to other people's futures as we are inclined to imagine. Whether the floating leaf swims down this or that side of a rock in the river, it reaches the same sea in the end.

But there is an even more significant turn to the story. Next morning, being still amongst those present, I went back to Hafelekar with Laurie Heyhurst and recovered my weapon. So my throwing of it away was neither final nor absolute; and in spite of some tentative efforts to get rid of it since then, it somehow continued to remain in my possession for a considerable time. I cannot say where it is at the moment, but I have a feeling that circumstances might arise in which it could turn up again. Without labouring the matter any further, all of this does seem to bear out the contention that the knowledge of Good and Evil, once acquired, is something that we can never quite get rid of so long as we live — even if we manage to cast it away in moments of peril.

A further point might be raised, that I created this final situation myself by going back on the following morning to look for a liability that events had shown me to be better without. What possessed me to do this, in the circumstances?

Various reasons might be offered, beginning with the cheap answer that I did not fully realise what perils I had actually escaped. But this, too, would be a lie. At that stage I knew well what I had escaped. Nevertheless I went back for my gun, and got it, probably because of the fact that — whatever it represented — it was mine.

With which enigmatic explanation the question is declared closed.

TABLE OF SUB-HEADINGS

DOLMEN EDITIONS XXII

THE BRAZEN HORN by Denis Johnston was designed by Liam Miller and printed and published at the Dolmen Press, North Richmond Street, Dublin 1, in the Republic of Ireland. The text was set in Pilgrim type with Perpetua titling by Jim Hughes and machined by Garrett Doyle. The book was seen through the press by Liam Browne.

The two-colour zodiacal figures are reproduced from the *Poetica Astronomica* printed by Erhard Ratdolt at Venice in 1482, by courtesy of the King Library Press, University of Kentucky, and the Unicorn device is a detail from a woodcut in *Die Reise in Heilige Land* by Bernard von Breydenbach, printed by Peter Schöffer at Mainz in 1486. Marcel Duchamp's painting, *Nude Descending a Staircase*, is reproduced by kind permission of the Philadelphia Museum of Art. The diagrams in the text were drawn by Rory Johnston.

Acknowledgement is made to An Chomhairle Ealaíon (The Arts Council of Ireland) for assistance in the production of the book.

An earlier version of the text (Linaea 6) was privately printed for the author in Alderney, 1968. This edition consists of one thousand and fifty copies. Finished in February 1976.

Distributed in the U.S.A. and in Canada by Humanities Press Inc., 171 First Avenue, Atlantic Highlands, NJ 07716.